W9-BET-048

The Bible Speaks Today
Series editors: Alec Motyer (OT)
John Stott (NT)
Derek Tidball (Bible Themes)

The Message of
Joshua

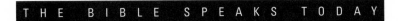

THE BIBLE SPEAKS TODAY

The Message of Joshua

Promise and People

DAVID G. FIRTH

IVP Academic

An imprint of InterVarsity Press
Downers Grove, Illinois

InterVarsity Press
P.O. Box 1400
Downers Grove, IL 60515-1426
ivpress.com
email@ivpress.com

©2015 by David G. Firth

Published in the United States of America by InterVarsity Press, Downers Grove, Illinois, with permission from Inter-Varsity Press, England.

All rights reserved. No part of this book may be reproduced in any form without written permission from InterVarsity Press.

InterVarsity Press® is the book-publishing division of InterVarsity Christian Fellowship/USA®, a movement of students and faculty active on campus at hundreds of universities, colleges and schools of nursing in the United States of America, and a member movement of the International Fellowship of Evangelical Students. For information about local and regional activities, visit intervarsity.org.

Unless otherwise indicated, Scripture quotations are taken from The Holy Bible, English Standard Version © 2001 by Crossway Bibles, a division of Good News Publishers. Used by permission.

Cover design: Cindy Kiple
Image: Marilee Whitehouse-Holm/Getty Images

ISBN 978-0-8308-2442-7 (print)
ISBN 978-0-8308-9977-7 (digital)

Printed in the United States of America ∞

g green
press
INITIATIVE

As a member of the Green Press Initiative, InterVarsity Press is committed to protecting the environment and to the responsible use of natural resources. To learn more, visit greenpressinitiative.org.

Library of Congress Cataloging-in-Publication Data

A catalog record for this book is available from the Library of Congress.

| **P** | 17 | 16 | 15 | 14 | 13 | 12 | 11 | 10 | 9 | 8 | 7 | 6 | 5 | 4 | 3 | 2 | 1 |
| **Y** | 29 | 28 | 27 | 26 | 25 | 24 | 23 | 22 | 21 | 20 | 19 | 18 | 17 | 16 | 15 |

For Stephen Ibbotson
A faithful pastor and teacher of the Word

Contents

BST The Bible Speaks Today

GENERAL PREFACE

THE BIBLE SPEAKS TODAY describes three series of expositions, based on the books of the Old and New Testaments, and on Bible themes that run through the whole of Scripture. Each series is characterized by a threefold ideal:

- to expound the biblical text with accuracy
- to relate it to contemporary life, and
- to be readable.

These books are, therefore, not 'commentaries', for the commentary seeks rather to elucidate the text than to apply it, and tends to be a work rather of reference than of literature. Nor, on the other hand, do they contain the kinds of 'sermons' that attempt to be contemporary and readable without taking Scripture seriously enough. The contributors to *The Bible Speaks Today* series are all united in their convictions that God still speaks through what he has spoken, and that nothing is more necessary for the life, health and growth of Christians than that they should hear what the Spirit is saying to them through his ancient – yet ever modern – Word.

ALEC MOTYER
JOHN STOTT
DEREK TIDBALL
Series editors

Author's preface

The book of Joshua has been a companion for some years now. I first began reflecting on it seriously while working in South Africa in 1993–96, when its themes of leadership and land were particularly important as the process of dismantling apartheid began – though it was always the unfashionable text in comparison with Exodus. It was in the chapel of the Baptist Theological College in Randburg that I first preached on a passage in it. On my return to Australia I preached through the whole book at St Ives Baptist Church when I took up the pastorate there; if anyone manages to trace tapes of those sermons they will probably find some echoes of them here, though my thinking on the book has moved on considerably since then. In particular, the challenges of New Atheism were not yet on the horizon, which meant I could take a far more innocent position on the issues of violence and warfare which have troubled so many than I can now. Perhaps I should have been more aware of them even then rather than waiting for others to point them out, but in the context in which I was working the issues of leadership seemed more pressing.

Since my move to the UK in 2003 I have continued to wrestle with this challenging text. The issue of violence within it has become much more important, and it is no exaggeration to say that Joshua has been the centre of a storm, becoming the text to which many point when wishing to dismiss the claims of biblical faith. God, it is claimed, emerges as a moral monster who practises genocide, and not the good and holy one that the gospel has claimed. This is not an issue of the book of Joshua in relation only to non-believers; it has also become a problem for many Christians, one that has been of evident importance in places where I have lectured and preached. I have had these people particularly in mind as I have written this book, though I hope it is not focused too narrowly so that we miss out on other important themes within Joshua.

As always, the writing of a book such as this is something that happens with the support of others. Although it is passing through enormous changes at the moment, St John's College, Nottingham, has been a congenial place to think, pray and write, and I want to record my thanks to the staff and students for making it so. As always, my wife Lynne has been a source of continued support and encouragement, and it has been a particular delight to have found the odd day to write in the library at Cliff College where she works. I can never thank her enough, but I hope that noting it here might at least be a start.

DAVID G. FIRTH

Abbreviations

Ant.	Josephus, *Antiquities*
ESV	English Standard Version
HCSB	Holman Christian Standard Bible
LXX	Septuagint
MT	Masoretic Text
NIV	New International Version
NRSV	New Revised Standard Version
REB	Revised English Bible

Select bibliography

Billings, Rachel M., *'Israel Served the Lord.' The Book of Joshua as a Paradoxical Portrait of Faithful Israel* (Notre Dame: University of Notre Dame Press, 2013).

Block, Daniel I., *The Gods of the Nations: Studies in Ancient Near Eastern National Theology* (2nd edn., Leicester: Apollos, 2000).

Boling, Robert G., *Joshua: A New Translation with Notes and Commentary* (Introduction by G. Ernest Wright) (Garden City: Doubleday, 1982).

Bonhoeffer, Dietrich, *The Cost of Discipleship* (Complete edn., London: SCM Press, 1959).

Brueggemann, Walter, *Divine Presence Amid Violence: Contextualizing the Book of Joshua* (Milton Keynes: Paternoster, 2009).

Butler, Trent C., *Joshua* (Waco: Word Books, 1983).

Coote, Robert B., 'Joshua', in Leander E. Keck (ed.), *The New Interpreter's Bible* (Nashville: Abingdon Press, 1998), pp. 553–720.

Craigie, Peter C., *The Book of Deuteronomy* (Grand Rapids: Eerdmans, 1976).

Creach, Jerome F. D., *Joshua* (Louisville: Westminster John Knox, 2003).

Davis, Dale Ralph, *No Falling Words: Expositions of the Book of Joshua* (Grand Rapids: Baker, 1988).

Dawkins, Richard, *The God Delusion* (London: Black Swan, 2006).

Earl, Douglas S., *Reading Joshua as Christian Scripture* (Winona Lake: Eisenbrauns, 2010).

———, *The Joshua Delusion? Rethinking Genocide in the Bible*, with a response by Christopher J. H. Wright (Cambridge: James Clarke & Co, 2010).

Faley, R. J., *Joshua, Judges* (Collegeville: Liturgical Press, 2011).

Firth, David G., 'The Spirit and Leadership: Testimony, Empowerment and Purpose', in David G. Firth and Paul D. Wegner (eds), *Presence, Power and Promise: The Role of the Spirit of God in the Old Testament* (Nottingham: Apollos, 2011), pp. 259–280.

————, 'Passing on the Faith in Deuteronomy', in David G. Firth and Philip S. Johnston (eds), *Interpreting Deuteronomy: Issues and Approaches* (Nottingham: Apollos, 2012), pp. 157–176.

Gangel, Kenneth O., *Joshua* (Nashville: Broadman & Holman, 2002).

Goldingay, John, *Joshua, Judges and Ruth for Everyone* (London: SPCK, 2011).

Gray, John, *Joshua, Judges, Ruth* (Grand Rapids: Eerdmans, 1986).

Gundry, Stanley N. (ed.), *Show Them No Mercy: Four Views on God and the Canaanite Genocide* (Grand Rapids: Zondervan, 2003).

Harris, J. Gordon, 'Joshua', in J. Gordon Harris, Cheryl A. Brown and Michael S. Moore, *Joshua, Judges, Ruth* (Peabody: Hendrickson, 2000), pp. 1–119.

Hawk, L. Daniel, *Every Promise Fulfilled: Contesting Plots in Joshua* (Louisville: Westminster John Knox, 1991).

————, *Joshua* (Collegeville: Liturgical Press, 2000).

————, *Joshua in 3-D: A Commentary on Biblical Conquest and Manifest Destiny* (Eugene: Cascade, 2010).

Hess, Richard S., *Joshua: An Introduction and Commentary* (Leicester: IVP, 1996).

————, *Israelite Religions: An Archaeological and Biblical Survey* (Nottingham: Apollos, 2007).

Hillers, Delbert R., *Covenant: The History of a Biblical Idea* (Baltimore: Johns Hopkins University Press, 1969).

Hofreiter, Christian, 'Genocide in Deuteronomy and Christian Interpretation', in David G. Firth and Philip S. Johnston (eds), *Interpreting Deuteronomy: Issues and Approaches* (Nottingham: Apollos, 2012), pp. 240–262.

Howard, David M. Jr., *Joshua* (Nashville: Broadman & Holman, 1998).

Hubbard, Robert L. Jr., *Joshua: The NIV Application Commentary* (Grand Rapids: Zondervan, 2009).

Johnston, Philip S., 'Civil Leadership in Deuteronomy', in David G. Firth and Philip S. Johnston (eds), *Interpreting Deuteronomy: Issues and Approaches* (Nottingham: Apollos, 2012), pp. 137–156.

Keil, C. F. and F. Delitzsch, *Joshua, Judges, Ruth, I & II Samuel* (Grand Rapids: Eerdmans, 1956).

Koorevaar, H. J., *De Opbouw van het Boek Jozua* (Heverlee: Centrum voor Bijbelse Vorming-Belgie, 1990).

Krause, Joachim J., *Exodus und Eisodus: Komposition und Theologie von Josua 1–5* (Leiden: Brill, 2014).

Lilley, J. P. U., 'Understanding the *ḤEREM*', *Tyndale Bulletin* 44 (1993), pp. 160–177.

Longman, Tremper III and Daniel G. Reid, *God Is a Warrior* (Grand Rapids: Zondervan, 1995).

Madvig, Donald H., 'Joshua', in Frank E. Gaebelein (ed.), *The Expositor's Bible Commentary* (Grand Rapids: Zondervan, 1992), pp. 239–374.

Magnusson, Sally, *The Flying Scotsman* (London: Quartet, 1981).

Mann, Thomas W., *The Book of the Former Prophets* (Eugene: Cascade, 2011).

McConville, J. Gordon and Stephen N. Williams, *Joshua* (Grand Rapids: Eerdmans, 2010).

McGrath, Alister, *Why God Won't Go Away: Engaging with the New Atheism* (London: SPCK, 2011).

Merling, David Sr., *The Book of Joshua: Its Theme and Role in Archaeological Discussions* (Berrien Springs: Andrews University Press, 1997).

Moberly, R. W. L., *Old Testament Theology: Reading the Hebrew Bible as Christian Scripture* (Grand Rapids: Baker Academic, 2013).

Motyer, Alec, *The Message of Exodus: The Days of Our Pilgrimage* (Leicester: IVP, 2005).

———, *Discovering the Old Testament* (Leicester: Crossway, 2006).

Nelson, Richard D., *Joshua: A Commentary* (Louisville: Westminster John Knox, 1997).

Pitkänen, Pekka M. A., *Joshua* (Nottingham: Apollos, 2010).

Polzin, Robert, *Moses and the Deuteronomist : A Literary Study of the Deuteronomic History. Part 1: Deuteronomy, Joshua, Judges* (New York: Seabury Press, 1980).

Prouser, O. Horn, 'The Truth about Women and Lying', *Journal for the Study of the Old Testament* 61 (1994), pp. 15–28.

Provan, Iain, V. Phillips Long and Tremper Longman III, *A Biblical History of Israel* (Louisville: Westminster John Knox, 2003).

Soggin, J. Alberto, *Joshua: A Commentary* (London: SCM Press, 1972).

Williams, Stephen N., 'Could God Have Commanded the Slaughter of the Canaanites?', *Tyndale Bulletin* 63 (2012), pp. 161–178.

Wood, Bryant G., 'The Search for Joshua's Ai', in Richard S. Hess, Gerald A. Klingbeil and Paul Ray Jr. (eds), *Critical Issues in Early Israelite History* (Winona Lake: Eisenbrauns, 2008), pp. 205–240.

Woods, Edward J., *Deuteronomy: An Introduction and Commentary* (Nottingham: IVP, 2011).

Woudstra, Marten H., *The Book of Joshua* (Grand Rapids: Eerdmans, 1981).

Wright, Christopher J. H., *The Mission of God: Unlocking the Bible's Grand Narrative* (Nottingham: IVP, 2006).

———, *The God I Don't Understand: Reflections on Tough Questions of Faith* (Grand Rapids: Zondervan, 2008).

Introduction

1. Joshua and the problem of violence

We should begin by noting the elephant in the room. Perhaps more than any other, Joshua is the book of the Old Testament that troubles modern readers. Writing from a perspective of outspoken atheism, Richard Dawkins describes Joshua as

> a text remarkable for the bloodthirsty massacres it records and the xenophobic relish with which it does so. As the charming old song exultantly has it, 'Joshua fit the battle of Jericho, and the walls came a-tumbling down . . . there's none like good old Joshuay at the battle of Jericho.' Good old Joshua didn't rest until 'they utterly destroyed all that was in the city, both man and woman, young and old, and ox, and sheep, and ass with the edge of the sword' (Joshua 6:21).[1]

Never one to go for understatement when hyperbole is possible, he goes on to say,

> . . . the Bible story of Joshua's destruction of Jericho, and the invasion of the Promised Land in general, is morally indistinguishable from Hitler's invasion of Poland, or Saddam Hussein's massacre of the Kurds and the Marsh Arabs. The Bible may be an arresting and poetic work of fiction, but it is not the sort of book you should give to your children to form their morals.[2]

The striking thing, however, is that Joshua – or at least a heavily edited version of it – has usually been given to children to read, often with the intention that it should indeed help them form their moral

---

[1] Richard Dawkins, *The God Delusion* (London: Black Swan, 2006), p. 280.
[2] Dawkins, *God Delusion*, p. 280.

values. That edited version usually contains something like God's initial charge to Joshua to meditate on his *torah*,[3] possibly something about the crossing of the Jordan,[4] and the capture of Jericho, or at least the part where the walls come down.[5] The last is a long-term Sunday School favourite, though it tends to avoid those parts of the story which Dawkins finds so troubling. Adults might later hear Joshua's charge to Israel at Shechem to 'choose this day whom you will serve',[6] though often in a rather decontextualized way. Actually, however, the extent to which most Christians today encounter the book is rather limited. Indeed, those in churches which use the lectionary to determine the readings on a Sunday will rarely even encounter it. Thus, although we do make some use of Joshua, many Christians today are remarkably ignorant of its contents.

As a result, when they do read it their reactions are surprisingly similar to those of Dawkins. Anecdotes cannot prove this, but they can illustrate the point. Precisely because Joshua poses difficulties for many today, I have sometimes taught a module for some of my final-year students on preaching Joshua. One student told me that she decided to take the module because she had come to appreciate the Old Testament more during her studies; however, she was concerned because a home fellowship her father attended had begun to study Joshua and had given up after only a couple of weeks, concluding that this was a book that did not represent the God made known to us in Jesus Christ. In effect, they read the text in the same way as Dawkins, and came to much the same conclusion. Only a little later I was attending the ordination of a student. At lunch afterwards I spoke to a couple who were there. Both were committed Christians who were active in their local church in teaching and evangelism. On discovering that I taught Old Testament, the issue they wanted to discuss with me was what to do with the book of Joshua. Was there not simply too much violence in the book, and was not this violence inconsistent with what we find elsewhere in Scripture? The issue is wider than this, as can be seen in the very diverse approaches to it evidenced in the book edited by Stanley Gundry;[7] but the simple reality is that the level of violence most find in the book of Joshua is something they struggle to reconcile with the gospel.

This is a very large and complex matter. However, it is appropriate to outline the main lines of how we might go about reading the book

[3] Josh. 1:8.
[4] Josh. 3 – 4.
[5] Josh. 6.
[6] 24:15.
[7] Stanley N. Gundry (ed.), *Show Them No Mercy: Four Views on God and the Canaanite Genocide* (Grand Rapids: Zondervan, 2003).

of Joshua, because it is my contention that both Dawkins and Christians who struggle with the book have misunderstood the ways in which it works because they read it in terms of the conventions of a modern text rather than an ancient one. The Bible is not, in general, a difficult book to read, provided one has some grounding in its context. Joshua, however, is one that poses a number of challenges to us. Two are particularly worth highlighting here, and they both represent significant barriers to be overcome if we are to understand this book. I do not suggest that, by doing so, we shall be able to put credits up at the end of the book declaring 'No Canaanites were harmed in the story this book recounts', because clearly that is not true.[8] Many were killed, though not as many as the popular imagination seems to believe, and their deaths occurred because they had chosen to place themselves under God's judgment. However, to appreciate why this was needed, and perhaps why it was not as extensive as often thought, we need to think about the questions of whose land this took place in and who exactly it was that made up Israel as those who received God's promises.

a. Whose land is it?

At one level, the answer to the question of who owned the land is simple. It was the Canaanites who lived there and it was their land. In a sense this is true. One of the great tragedies of colonialism was that it tended to assume that peoples already occupying a land did not have a right to it and that colonial powers could therefore claim it as *terra nullius*, a land not occupied by anyone. For example, Britain's Privy Council declared this to be true of Australia in 1889, though of course it was a legal fiction because the Aboriginal peoples were there for many thousands of years before European settlement began in 1788. It is probably impossible to unwind this now, and the reality is that over time the takeover of a land itself becomes the established norm (albeit with serious justice issues to resolve), but if a nation today was to make such a claim it would probably become an international pariah. We assume that whoever lives in a place, unless there is a clear and just reason in law to the contrary, may rightfully claim that place as their own. The Canaanites lived in Canaan, so, we reason, the land was theirs.

However, the Bible never thinks in those terms. One reason for this is that the idea of a sovereign nation state is a relatively modern invention; but even if we set aside this particular problem there is still the simple fact that the Canaanites were already living there.

---

[8] A number of Israelites were also killed.

There is, however, a more important reason why the Bible does not think in those terms, and that is simply because the whole world and all its peoples belong to Yahweh.[9] In the view of the Bible, and the Old Testament, no single people holds an inalienable right to a certain piece of land. Rather, they hold it as tenants responsible to Yahweh. This is why, according to the law of Jubilee, individuals within Israel could not sell land in perpetuity.[10] Although it is expressed within Israel's covenant relationship with Yahweh, this is also why Israel could lose the land if they lived in sin against Yahweh;[11] because the land was always Yahweh's, Israel could also lose it.

It was because the land belonged to Yahweh that he could give it to Israel. The land itself was initially promised to Abraham,[12] and entry to it was always the goal of the exodus since otherwise Israel would have remained in the wilderness. However, there was a significant delay between the initial promise and entry to the land; even in the earliest promises Abraham was told there would be a four hundred year period of waiting, because 'the iniquity of the Amorites is not yet complete'.[13] So Israel would receive the land only because the Canaanite population, for whom the Amorites are here a representative group, stood under Yahweh's judgment. From the perspective of the Old Testament, therefore, the land always belonged to Yahweh and he could give it to whomever he chose. He would only take it from the Canaanites and give it to Israel at a point where his judgment on the nation was appropriate. The framework for this is established in Abraham's intercession over the destruction of Sodom,[14] showing that Yahweh only acts in this way when it is indeed just to do so. It is not a case of Yahweh particularly favouring Israel above all others so much as the fact that in establishing Israel as a nation through whom his purposes would be established, a land was needed, and the land he gave was one where the local population stood under his judgment. Yahweh could therefore give the land to Israel, though the Old Testament is clear that Israel could equally forfeit the land if they lived in rebellion against him.

b. Who is Israel?

So in Yahweh's purposes the land was being given to Israel. But who is Israel? How is Israel defined?

[9] E.g. Ps. 24:1.
[10] Lev. 25:23–34.
[11] Lev. 26:27–33; Deut. 28:64–68.
[12] Gen. 12:7; 15:7–21.
[13] Gen. 15:16.
[14] Gen. 18:22–33.

This is actually a very important question in the book of Joshua, and understanding this is vital to understanding the nature of the gift of the land. There is an important hint of the answer in what we have already observed, which is that the land was given so that Israel could live out Yahweh's purposes, most notably that through them all peoples of the earth might find blessing.[15] Israel's right to the land depended on them living within those terms, and strange as it might seem, the same option existed for the Canaanite groups already within the land. Indeed, these groups could also become Israel.

Although this last point is not widely recognized, a brief survey of some key events within the book might explain it. Following the agreement of the tribes already settled east of the Jordan to join with those tribes not yet settled west of the Jordan, Joshua sent two (rather incompetent) spies to explore Jericho and its region. They stayed the night with the prostitute Rahab. Now, if God's purpose was simply to destroy all the Canaanites for their manifold wickedness, we might think Rahab was a primary candidate. A prostitute and presumably a worshipper of local deities, here was precisely the sort of person with whom Israel should have no contact, someone who should be devoted to destruction.[16] And yet she is not only the one who helped the spies and got them safely out of Jericho, but also the one who confessed faith in Yahweh[17] and who, along with her family, was saved at Jericho.[18] By contrast, the person who was then devoted to destruction was Achan, an Israelite who took goods placed under the ban (i.e. devoted to destruction in accordance with Deut. 7:1–5) and who therefore forfeited his right to be part of Israel. It is worth bearing in mind that roughly one-eighth of the whole book of Joshua is devoted to the stories of these two individuals, so that by the end of chapter 8 we have marvelled at how Yahweh has brought Israel into the land[19] and begun to wrestle with the question of who Israel is. Indeed, it is made more complex by the brief record of covenant renewal in 8:30–35, where 'all Israel' is described as 'sojourner as well as native born'. The question of the identity of the Israel who is receiving God's promise of the land is thus brought to the foreground for us. At this point, it looks as if Israel is functionally those who have committed themselves to Yahweh's purposes. Achan shows that an Israelite could be excluded, whereas Rahab shows that a Canaanite could be included. It is those who choose actively to oppose Yahweh's purposes who are excluded. Israel is a people

---

[15] Gen. 12:2–3.
[16] Deut. 7:1–5.
[17] 2:9–11.
[18] 6:22–25.
[19] Josh. 3 – 4.

with a missional role, not one with a genetic heritage. This is complicated by the story of the Gibeonites, a Canaanite group who join by deception,[20] though without changing the basic trajectory other than in confirming that the criterion for judgment is actually an active opposition to God's purposes for Israel.

In spite of this, we find Israel engaged in significant battles with various Canaanite groups in chapters 10–11 in which many are devoted to destruction. Is this perhaps the bloodbath of which many speak? If the answer to this is still 'yes', we find that we have to qualify it so heavily that it soon becomes clear that it is an answer that emerges only from asking the wrong question. In both chapters Israel defend themselves against groups that attack them, so in neither the south[21] nor the north[22] is Israel the aggressor. The trigger for these attacks against them appears to have been their inclusion of the Gibeonites within the nation. We are then repeatedly told that Israel moved through these regions and that they devoted to destruction whole towns and those living there.[23] On the face of it, this certainly looks like significant destruction.

However, we need to read these accounts carefully for what they actually claim. And the interesting thing is that when Joshua was finally allocating the land to the tribes, the towns concerned needed to be taken once again. For example, Hebron's destruction is recounted in Joshua 10:36–37; but it is also a town which is given to Caleb when the land is being allocated, and when this is done Caleb needs to expel the town's inhabitants.[24] If everyone had been killed before, who was left to expel? The answer is to understand the statements in chapters 10–11 within the pattern of ancient conquest accounts and recognize that they do not describe the wholesale destruction of the towns and their populace, but the destruction only of the local population who actively resisted. In fact, when an army was coming through most of the population would melt away into the hills to leave the battle to those involved and then come back later. Those killed at Hebron, and the other towns named, were therefore those who chose to resist. The option of Rahab, and even the Gibeonites, of joining Israel had always existed. Israel was thus not a closed community, and only those actively opposing Yahweh's purposes were killed. Let us be clear: this does not mean that there were not significant casualties, but they were considerably fewer

[20] Josh. 9.
[21] Josh. 10.
[22] Josh. 11.
[23] E.g. 10:34–35; 11:11.
[24] 14:6–15; 15:13–14.

than often thought and were only those who placed themselves under Yahweh's judgment by resisting his purposes.

As we read the account of the allocation of the land we continue to see this pattern. Caleb is held out as an example of faith for Israel,[25] but he is a Kenizzite and so most probably not an Israelite by descent. Rather, his most likely line of descent is through Kenaz, a grandson of Esau.[26] Since Othniel, who marries his daughter Achsah, is from the same clan, this pattern of faith in Yahweh's promises rather than biology continues to be important. Perhaps the most surprising element of this pattern occurs in the allocation to Ephraim of territory which includes that of the Archites,[27] a clan descended from Canaan.[28] This clan appears to have been included within Israel – note that David's trusted advisor Hushai was an Archite[29] – though the story of how that happened has not been passed down to us. It is therefore no surprise that when we have the list of the cities of refuge we are told that these were for both Israelite and sojourner.[30] Indeed, by the time we reach the end of the land allocation we are clear that Yahweh has indeed been faithful to his promise to Israel, but also that Israel is a far more diverse group than we might have imagined.

When we come to the last three chapters of the book it is not surprising that the question of Israelite identity is particularly important. In each we have a speech from Joshua in a context which explores the question of who is included in Israel. Chapter 22 makes clear that it is not a matter of geography, and that even though the eastern tribes lived outside the land actually promised, they were still included. Chapter 23 then addresses the whole nation, urging obedience to Yahweh, while in chapter 24 Joshua urges the nation to choose Yahweh. The nation by this stage clearly included native-born Israelites who had continued to worship other gods as well as Yahweh, native Canaanites who had joined Israel, and perhaps others, so the chapter functions to address the key question of Israelite identity. This is why the choice to be made there was so serious. Israel needed to be a people who lived out what it was to be Yahweh's people, and the reality by the end of the book is that all who had made this choice could continue to live within the blessing of Yahweh's promises, including that of remaining in the land.

[25] 14:6–15; 15:13–19.
[26] Gen. 36:11, 15, 42.
[27] 16:2.
[28] Gen. 10:15–17. The Japhletites (Josh. 16:3) may be another Canaanite clan, but their heritage is not outlined in the Old Testament.
[29] 2 Sam. 15:32–37.
[30] 20:9.

2. Reading Joshua today

How, then, do these considerations help Christians who read this book today? We can helpfully think of this in two areas: first, interacting with critics of the Bible and the Christian faith; and second, understanding Joshua within God's mission.

a. Joshua and critics of the Bible and Christian faith

From the outset, we should acknowledge that many critics of the Christian faith operate from a position of committed atheism which would deny that there is any validity to the idea of God judging anyone because of sin. In effect, this position is simply a flat denial of the claims of the Bible, and I am not sure that an extended conversation about the book of Joshua is the place to begin an apologetic with them.[31] However, those who are at least agnostic about the claims of the Bible in general or who operate from a position of openness to the reality of those claims often point to great difficulty with Joshua. Do these points help us address their concerns?

For many, the idea that God elected one nation is a troubling one because they then conclude that other nations are thereby excluded. Reading Joshua from this perspective tends to lead to the conclusion that Yahweh was in some way being vindictive towards the Canaanite population. They were being obliterated because Yahweh had decided that Israel should have their land. Now, the Old Testament's understanding of election is complex, and indeed one of the clearest statements of the importance of election is also the place where we read of the necessity of devoting the Canaanite peoples to destruction.[32] We cannot emphasize one theme (election) and simultaneously ignore the other (devotion to destruction). However, since we are told that Joshua did everything just as Yahweh had commanded through Moses,[33] and that Israel was faithful throughout the life of Joshua and his contemporaries,[34] we have to conclude that the fact that he did *not* devote many Canaanites to destruction was actually an expression of obedience. Conversely, those who were given to destruction were those who had set themselves against Yahweh's purposes, though like Pharaoh in the exodus, Yahweh was also said

[31] For a helpful exploration of how and why Christians can interact with the so-called New Atheism, see Alister McGrath, *Why God Won't Go Away: Engaging with the New Atheism* (London: SPCK, 2011).

[32] Deut. 7:1–5.

[33] 11:15.

[34] 24:31.

to have hardened their hearts so that they would die in battle.[35] Nevertheless, it is clear that many who we might otherwise have thought to be liable to destruction not only survived, but were also included within Israel.

There is, of course, always a degree of mystery in terms of God's purposes, but it seems clear that the book of Joshua is careful to lay out a pattern where there was always the possibility of people moving from a position where they stood under God's judgment to becoming part of his people and therefore living within his promises. In some sense, the judgment that is expressed within Joshua is probably to be understood as a foretaste of the final judgment, but just as the gospel today can be offered to those who currently stand under God's judgment and those people can find life in Jesus Christ, so also Joshua leaves open the possibility that those currently under judgment may choose life. The way in which it does so is quite distinct from any patterns of evangelism today, and from the perspective of the New Testament it is clear that no single people now stands under God's judgment in the same way as did the Canaanites then (and so *cannot* be devoted to destruction) – but the possibility is still held out.

Read in these terms, it seems that the book of Joshua is not the violent and wholesale exclusion of a people from God's purposes that it is often thought to be. There is still judgment here, but it is much more focused than most of the book's critics would claim. More particularly, emotive terms such as 'genocide' or 'ethnic cleansing', which are so easily bandied about when discussing the book, are inappropriate because only combatants are killed and an alternative was always available. Divine judgment will, perhaps, always make us uncomfortable. We would like God, as a loving Father, never to act in judgment – but that would be contrary to his nature. However, what emerges from the book of Joshua is that judgment remains his 'strange' work.[36] And, as Stephen Williams has suggested,[37] it is something he does with a heavy heart, which is perhaps why in the midst of judgment an alternative is always available. This, almost without fail, is what critics of the Christian faith, and of the book of Joshua as part of its canon, invariably miss.

b. Joshua in God's mission

Addressing problems that Joshua poses for us is important, but if this is God's word which speaks to us today, we also ought to be

[35] 11:20.

[36] Isa. 28:21.

[37] Stephen N. Williams, 'Could God Have Commanded the Slaughter of the Canaanites?', *Tyndale Bulletin* 63 (2012), pp. 161–178.

able to point to ways in which it continues to address us. Again, our comments can only be exploratory, but my basic contention is that we have to read Joshua as part of God's mission, one which for much of the Old Testament was centred on Israel but which finds its ultimate focus in Jesus Christ.

We can start by developing the points already made, showing how the story Joshua tells fits within the larger narrative of God's mission.[38] After God has called Abram and promised him land, descendants and a relationship with him centred on blessing for himself and all the clans of the earth,[39] we follow the story of the patriarchs through Genesis until the whole family has moved down to Egypt. Although this is initially positive because of Joseph's influence, Exodus tells us of a pharaoh who arose and set himself against Israel, enslaving them.[40] Israel's conditions became increasingly harsh, though all of this was consistent with what Yahweh had previously revealed to Abram.[41] Israel could not yet have a land of their own because the iniquity of the Amorites, a representative Canaanite group, was not yet complete. Thus God had promised Israel a land as part of their role in his mission, but there was also to be a delay because divine justice would not act against the Canaanites until it was merited – and as we have noted, even then an alternative was always available. The time in Egypt, for all its difficulties, was always part of Israel's role in God's mission; even these challenges would result in Pharaoh,[42] the rest of the world[43] and the people of Israel themselves[44] coming to know Yahweh.

Egypt was never an end in itself for Israel. Since land had been promised, the exodus was necessary, but it itself was never the goal because the exodus only made sense if there was also an 'eisodus', a point where Israel then entered the land.[45] However, the Israel which left Egypt was already a mixed group, since a 'mixed multitude' also went up from there with them,[46] and it was this group who were brought through the Reed Sea and who came to Sinai, where they entered into a covenant relationship with

[38] For which, see Christopher J. H. Wright, *The Mission of God: Unlocking the Bible's Grand Narrative* (Nottingham: IVP, 2006).
[39] Gen. 12:2–3.
[40] Exod. 1:8–14.
[41] Gen. 15:13–16.
[42] Exod. 7:17.
[43] Exod. 9:16.
[44] Exod. 10:2.
[45] The ways in which these themes are developed are explored in some depth in Joachim J. Krause, *Exodus und Eisodus: Komposition und Theologie von Josua 1–5* (Leiden: Brill, 2014), from which I also take the concept of an 'eisodus'.
[46] Exod. 12:38.

Yahweh.[47] So although incredibly important, Sinai was not an end in itself. Rather, the goal of the exodus was always that Israel should enter and come to live in the land that Yahweh had promised. A good deal of contemporary thought draws, quite rightly, on the exodus as a pattern which shows God's commitment to the poor, but we cannot thereby set the exodus against the entry to the land: the two are inseparable. Because they are inseparable we must note how Joshua and the exodus are linked; for example, in a number of repeated patterns for Israel (such as the crossing of the Jordan[48] and the crossing of the sea,[49] or the priority of Passover[50]), in the way that Joshua is gradually shown to be Yahweh's servant according to the pattern of Moses[51] and in the fact that the Canaanites follow the pattern of Pharaoh by having their hearts hardened.[52] However, the more important points are that Joshua shows that Yahweh had indeed fulfilled his promise to Israel that they would receive the land – though as we have seen, the Israel that receives the fulfilment of this promise is a more complex group than many have suggested. Since, though, this fits within the pattern of a mission that aims to bring blessing to all the clans of the earth, perhaps we should expect this, because even in judgment Yahweh extends his blessing to many.

Joshua is thus a book that encourages us today to recognize the faithfulness of God. We experience that faithfulness through Jesus, and this means that our experience of divine faithfulness is not tied to a particular place. But Joshua continues to address us today by reminding us that God's faithfulness to his promises is a central element within the Bible's story, a fundamental element within his mission. At the same time, Joshua challenges us to realize that God's purposes include far more people than we might imagine. That we begin the story by showing how Rahab is included among God's people[53] makes this clear from the outset, especially when we note how that story shows her in a much more positive light than any of the Israelites. It turns out that God is prepared to use people we might not expect, and that what matters is their willingness to work with him in his purposes. It is what they do, not their background, that matters.[54] So Joshua continues to challenge us to look at what

[47] Exod. 19:1–8.
[48] Josh. 3 – 4.
[49] Exod. 14:1 – 15:21.
[50] Exod. 12:43–50; Josh. 5:10–12.
[51] Compare Exod. 3:1–12 and Josh. 5:13–15, as well as the explicit statement of Josh. 24:29.
[52] Compare Exod. 9:12 and Josh. 11:20.
[53] Josh. 2.
[54] See also Jas 2:25.

people do in their response to God more than whether or not they conform to the patterns with which we are more comfortable.

Thus Joshua challenges us to think about who the people of God are today. This is an encouragement, but it is also a warning. That is why it is important that the book climaxes with chapters 22–24, though these have to be read in the context of the whole story that has gone before, and not just chapters 1–12. The book challenges those who have read it down through the ages to recognize that God not only includes those who join him in his mission, he also excludes those who choose to set themselves against it. This is most obviously seen in the story of Achan,[55] but it also underlies Joshua's appeal to choose Yahweh.[56] This choice, which involves serving him alone and in faithfulness to what he has revealed, is what will define those who live in God's blessing going forward. No doubt, for many who read it in Old Testament times, especially during the exile, this would have been a hard word; yet the call to decision was always a reminder that a better option, an option of living within God's desire to bless, was available. Those readers would appreciate that this was a call that meant they could once more choose Yahweh alone, even as we today are challenged to make that same choice in Jesus Christ.

[55] Josh. 7.
[56] 24:14–15.

Joshua 1:1–18
1. New leader, new land, same God

As the book of Joshua opens, the people of Israel are at a key transition point as they begin to consider life without their charismatic leader. Moses' death is narrated in Deuteronomy 34, and Joshua 1 follows immediately after this. Thus, when we read straight through from Deuteronomy to Joshua we begin to feel something of the challenge that was faced by Israel. They had not yet entered the Promised Land, and now they no longer had the one who had been their leader throughout the wilderness period. But they did have the promises of God, especially that he would give that land to them. And that was the crucial factor. Although there is a natural human temptation to assume that God's promises are fulfilled through a particular leader, Joshua stresses that the promises of God do not depend upon any human figure. What God had done in the past through his chosen leaders, he would continue to do through the next generation, though he might do so in different ways from before. What mattered were God's promises, and these were as sure as they had ever been. However, they still required the obedience of all his people. Joshua 1 makes clear that God's people could still go forward because God was the one who was leading them.

1. From Moses to Joshua (1:1–9)

a. Change of leadership (1:1)

Although Moses' death has just been recounted in Deuteronomy 34, we have known for some time that Joshua would succeed Moses. This first became clear when Moses was directed to commission Joshua as his successor in Numbers 27:12–23, a passage that particularly stresses the presence of Yahweh's Spirit in Joshua.[1] This in turn refers back to the anointing of the seventy elders,[2] when Yahweh had given his Spirit to the elders, including two whose activity had so troubled Joshua that he asked Moses to stop them 'prophesying' (probably understood as an ecstatic experience), only for Moses to express the wish that Yahweh would place his Spirit on all his people. Whatever lack of understanding that had shown in Joshua, he was at that time already known as Moses' 'assistant', the same term that is used for him here. The account of Moses' death also noted that Joshua was filled with 'the spirit of wisdom'[3] because of Moses' having laid hands on him. This is probably not another reference to God's Spirit, though the wisdom Joshua apparently displayed was perhaps evidence of God's Spirit. The book of Joshua never mentions God's Spirit, unlike Judges and Samuel, which have a number of significant passages referring to God's Spirit. One reason for this is that Joshua has previously been marked out by the Spirit as a leader among God's people, and the book of Joshua is recounting only a particular period of Joshua's leadership – albeit one in which he takes on a more significant role than before.[4]

That Joshua has already exercised significant leadership is clear also from the account of the spies in Numbers 13 – 14. There, he is initially introduced under the name 'Hoshea',[5] though we are also told that Moses renamed him 'Joshua'.[6] Although this is not particularly apparent in English, both names are related to the word meaning 'salvation', with 'Joshua' more specifically meaning 'Yahweh saves'.[7] His renaming by Moses makes clear a key theological theme that only Joshua and Caleb among the spies grasp when they point out to the people that, in spite of the apparent military advantages of the occupants of the land, Yahweh will indeed give the land to them.[8] Joshua thus exemplified his name. However, there is always

---

[1] Num. 27:18. Joshua is first introduced in Exod. 17:8–16, but although he is a military leader in the defeat of Amalek, there is no hint that he will become a major leader.

[2] Num. 11:16–30.

[3] Deut. 34:9.

[4] On the relationship between God's Spirit and the recognition of leaders in the Old Testament, see David G. Firth, 'The Spirit and Leadership: Testimony, Empowerment and Purpose', in David G. Firth and Paul D. Wegner (eds), *Presence, Power and Promise: The Role of the Spirit of God in the Old Testament* (Nottingham: Apollos, 2011), pp. 259–280.

[5] Num. 13:8.

[6] Num. 13:16.

[7] The name 'Jesus' comes from the Greek form of the name Joshua, so the statement to Joseph that 'he will save his people from their sins' (Matt. 1:21) is also playing with the meaning of the name.

[8] Num. 14:8–9.

a clear distinction between Joshua and Moses, a distinction that is maintained here in that Moses is consistently called Yahweh's *servant*, whereas Joshua is always Moses' *assistant* until his death, after which he too is called Yahweh's 'servant'.[9] By contrast, Moses is called Yahweh's servant sixteen times in Joshua, a title used elsewhere of David and of the enigmatic Servant of Yahweh in Isaiah.

There are some important themes about the nature of leadership which thus emerge from these opening verses. First, although the Old Testament has considerably less to say about God's Spirit than does the New Testament, it fully embraces the idea that empowerment by the Spirit is a crucial aspect of leadership. In saying this, we should note that although the Old Testament is consistent with the Trinitarian theology of the New Testament, it is not itself Trinitarian. Thus, some of the themes that the Old Testament applies to God's Spirit the New Testament in turn applies to Christ, though the most common development is indeed into the doctrine of the Holy Spirit. Put at its simplest, however, the Old Testament recognizes that those who are called to lead God's people will show evidence of the power of God at work in their lives. The means by which this evidence is seen will vary, though in Joshua's case it was notable in both his faithfulness to God's promises and his godly wisdom. However, it was also confirmed to the people of God through public affirmation and the presence of God's Spirit. It is clear, therefore, that leadership is something that is both initiated through God-given giftedness and recognized by God's people as they see evidence of it in practice. Second, we can also note that the nature of leadership roles will vary. Moses' leadership is clearly distinct from that of Joshua, so that even though Joshua becomes the principal leader after Moses' death he never takes on all the roles that Moses had fulfilled. Although finding appropriate leaders is important, we must also recognize that different phases in the life of God's people require different leadership structures. Moses would not be completely replaced because of his unique role, though neither would Joshua. God continues to raise up and empower leaders, but their giftings and roles are related to the particular needs that God's people then face.

Joshua is thus the leader designated for Israel as they prepare to enter the land that God had promised, but his leadership is dependent upon the promises that God has given. Joshua is not free to lead the people in any direction he wants, but only towards the fulfilment of what God has already promised. An important tension in the book of Joshua is that although Yahweh is giving the land to Israel, Israel must also claim it. To use a rather simple analogy, just as we know

---

[9] 24:29.

that a Christmas present addressed to us is ours while it sits under the tree, but it only truly becomes ours when we open the parcel, so also throughout Joshua the land is something that Yahweh is giving to Israel, but it is only fully theirs when they have taken it. This tension recognizes both that the land is a divine gift to Israel and that it requires faithfulness on Israel's part if the gift is to be realized. What is crucial is that the land belongs to Yahweh – it is always his to give. The same, of course, is true of the gospel message, where life and forgiveness in Jesus are both something that God is giving to us and something that we have to accept if the gift is to become real in our experience. So in Joshua, Yahweh is giving the land to Israel, but they have to go forward in faithfulness to him to receive it. There is both divine initiative and human response; but throughout, as Howard observes, 'God was the giver and guarantor of the process.'[10]

b. Moving to the land (1:2–5)

The importance of divine initiative and human response is apparent from the fact that the whole of verses 2–9 are presented as a speech from Yahweh to Joshua. Throughout, Yahweh is both directing and encouraging Joshua, doing so with words that are largely drawn from different parts of Deuteronomy.[11] The giving of the land, and of the Torah, comes from Yahweh's initiative, though Joshua can then appropriate the blessing of what Yahweh is giving through his own faithfulness. However, these gifts are then particularly understood through reading and reflecting on the Torah, a point that is reinforced through the allusions to Deuteronomy throughout this speech.

Yahweh's speech can be broken down into two basic sections. In verses 2–5 the focus is on preparing the people to enter the land with confidence in Yahweh's promises. This confidence starts with Yahweh's command, as the speech opens with two imperatives, *arise* and *go over* (2). Everything else in this speech is dependent upon these two commands. The blessings of which Yahweh speaks all begin with obedience to him, and though Joshua is called to be leader of God's people he is immediately reminded that all leadership is under God's authority. Nevertheless, although these two imperatives are addressed directly to Joshua, they also affect the people as they too must cross the Jordan.[12] They are to cross the Jordan in the

---

[10] David M. Howard Jr., *Joshua* (Nashville: Broadman & Holman, 1998), p. 81.

[11] Deut. 3:28; 7:24; 11:24–25; and 31:6–8, with slight modifications due to context. Cf. L. Daniel Hawk, *Joshua in 3-D. A Commentary on Biblical Conquest and Manifest Destiny* (Eugene: Cascade, 2010), p. 3.

[12] Although it is not mentioned until 3:15, the Jordan was apparently in flood at this time.

confident hope given by Yahweh's promise that he is indeed giving the land to them. But Israel is not free to take just any land. Although Yahweh assures them that he will give them *every place* they walk on (3), the boundaries of the land are carefully defined. Israel is not to walk just anywhere, but to the particular region bounded by the wilderness to the south and the Lebanon (roughly modern Lebanon) to the north, the Euphrates to the east and the Mediterranean to the west, defined here as the land of the Hittites,[13] though they stand here for all the peoples already in the land. As boundaries, these are only approximations, especially as the Euphrates is only really a north-eastern boundary; but they provide a general guide. It is into this territory, which roughly equates to the boundaries Yahweh had promised Abraham,[14] that Israel is to walk. In doing so they would effectively follow what appears to have been an ancient custom for marking a transfer of land, in which the land was walked by those who now owned it,[15] with a sandal exchanged to mark the transfer. In this case, Yahweh has already outlined the territory to be claimed, and it is here that Israel is to walk in the confidence that no-one will be able to resist them (though the rest of the book will show plenty who try). Just as Yahweh was with Moses, so now he will be with Joshua as he leads the people on this journey. Such promises are given by God when his people face challenges – such as when Yahweh had sent Moses to Pharaoh[16] – so that his promises themselves become a sign of grace. For Christians, this promise is shown to be of importance as we seek to live out the ethical demands of the gospel, as God's assured presence assists us in the challenges we face.[17]

It is important to remember that the promises given here to both Joshua and Israel were specific to the circumstances they were facing. The promise about claiming the land by walking it was specific to the land of Israel. It does not apply to any land that Christians today might want to claim for the gospel, especially as the church is not restricted to any one land. Rather, promises such as these must be appropriated by us today in terms of the things that Jesus has promised concerning his church. Most obviously, as we join Jesus

---

[13] The great Hittite empire in Turkey collapsed around this time, so it is possible that 'Hittites' here refers to people migrating south as a result of this. Alternatively, the label 'Hittite' might simply mean a Semitic group in Canaan, whose name by chance matches that of the empire to the north. Cf. Richard S. Hess, *Joshua: An Introduction and Commentary* (Leicester: IVP, 1996), pp. 70–71.

[14] Gen. 15:18–21.

[15] Though, as Robert L. Hubbard Jr., *Joshua: The NIV Application Commentary* (Grand Rapids: Zondervan, 2009), p. 78, notes, the land is so vast that Joshua will not walk out of it.

[16] Exod. 3:12.

[17] Heb. 13:5.

in God's mission we are assured of his presence with us no matter the circumstances we might face.[18] We must also note that the land was already occupied; Israel was not going to an empty land – something that they fully recognized, in contrast to the history of European colonialism which tended to operate on the principle that the lands they claimed were effectively empty. Such an approach denies the validity of the experience of native peoples, and can make reading a text like Joshua painful for them today when they identify with the Canaanites as people about to be displaced. Here we must openly acknowledge the problems caused by colonialism (even when well intentioned) in many parts of the world, but also recognize that using a text like Joshua to claim those lands misses the point of the text.[19] Much suffering has been caused by a misuse of the text, and it is right to acknowledge this, while also noting that all land ultimately belongs to God. Much of it has historically been taken by force, but that is not the pattern provided here. Rather, Israel is being given the land because the peoples already there stood under the judgment of God. Given that the church as a pan-national expression of God's people radicalizes all national claims, the same cannot be true of any nation since the time of Jesus.

c. Faithfulness first (1:6–9)

Yahweh's speech continues by addressing Joshua alone,[20] though still drawing on the language of Deuteronomy, especially from Joshua's commissioning in Deuteronomy 31. Joshua is told three times by Yahweh to *be strong and courageous*,[21] words of encouragement that are needed precisely because Israel is about to encounter a great challenge in claiming the land. Where the first part of Yahweh's speech had emphasized the divine initiative, Yahweh now emphasizes human response. Anyone faced with a threat is likely to retreat, so it is this danger that Yahweh addresses as he encourages Joshua to be strong and courageous, assuring him that he will cause the people to possess the land he promised to their ancestors. But courage here takes on a specific form; it is not a matter of Joshua screwing up his nerve to an act of daring in battle, even though that is the more typical use of such language. Rather, it means living a life that is

---

[18] Matt. 28:20.

[19] Thomas W. Mann, *The Book of the Former Prophets* (Eugene: Cascade, 2011), pp. 13–49, provides numerous examples of this in the context of his exposition of Joshua.

[20] In verses 3–4 the 'you' is plural, but elsewhere in this speech it is singular, addressing Joshua alone.

[21] 1:6–7, 9. In 1:7, he is to be 'very' courageous.

shaped by Yahweh's instruction. For Joshua, the act of daring is to live wholly by all that Yahweh has revealed in his Torah. Although the extent of allusion to Deuteronomy in this speech makes it almost certain that it is the Torah to which Yahweh refers, this is much more than the traditional translation of *law* might suggest. Deuteronomy is considerably more than just law – it is a pattern for the whole of life, giving shape to what it means to live for Yahweh. Of course, in the context of the conquest this can also mean a more specific concern with those passages particularly pertaining to taking the land and battle,[22] but the focus here is much broader. It is the whole of Yahweh's instruction that is required for success, not just those passages which are seemingly most appropriate for the coming battles. This is particularly important for the book of Joshua, which asserts both that Joshua did what Yahweh had commanded and also that he did not destroy all the peoples already in the land, even though Deuteronomy 7 would require this. It is not, as some have suggested, that there is a basic contradiction within the book which would seemingly claim complete obedience while showing the opposite,[23] but rather that through Deuteronomy there is a deep understanding of the missional impulse of Israel as the means by which Yahweh is reaching the nations.[24] Where Joshua would need courage was in the often challenging task of understanding exactly how it was that he was to apply the Torah, though this was vital to the fulfilment of his role as the one who would lead the nation to occupy the land Yahweh was giving them. Indeed, possession of the land would only continue to be legitimate when shaped by obedience to the Torah.[25]

The means by which Joshua was to understand and thus apply the whole of the Torah was through continued meditation upon it. The image used here is of the Torah as something that is always in his mouth, not as food but rather as something that is continually discussed, perhaps something that is to be read, though not only that. The importance of this becomes clear when we note that the word translated *meditate* (8) elsewhere means to 'murmur'. The implication would seem to be that meditation was not a fundamentally private action – rather like someone having a quiet time – but rather a corporate act. Joshua as leader was to ensure that

[22] Such as Deut. 7, 9 and 20.
[23] Cf. L. Daniel Hawk, *Every Promise Fulfilled: Contesting Plots in Joshua* (Louisville: Westminster John Knox, 1991), pp. 43–55.
[24] E.g. Deut. 4:6–8. See also Wright, *The Mission of God*, pp. 375–387.
[25] J. Gordon McConville and Stephen N. Williams, *Joshua* (Grand Rapids: Eerdmans, 2010), p. 14. That Joshua was successful in this is confirmed by the statement in 24:31 that Israel served Yahweh throughout Joshua's life.

Yahweh's Torah was at the centre of not only his own life, but also, by extension, that of the people. It was in this way that he would ensure success. The importance of this practice of meditation becomes greater when we note that exactly the same image occurs in Psalm 1, while Malachi 4 enjoins the people to remember Moses' Torah. In the Hebrew Bible, Joshua is the first book of the Prophets (the second division of the canon), while Malachi is the last, so the whole of the Prophets are marked by faithfulness to Torah. The Psalms then open the third division of the canon (the Writings) with this same theme. The Hebrew Bible is thus structured around this key theme, indicating that it was never something that was for Joshua alone, even though it was of particular importance for him. For Israel, success was dependent upon a deep understanding of the whole of Yahweh's Torah, a deep understanding from which they could not turn.

Given the canonical importance of such meditation, this ought to challenge Christians to consider our own practices. Certainly, a deep personal knowledge of the Bible ought to be a goal to which we all aspire, and for this there is no substitute for regular reading of it and reflection on what we read. However, the meditation spoken of here is ultimately communal, and this ought to mean that we work at creating practices that enable us to reflect on the Bible as a community. Small-group Bible studies are an excellent way of doing this, but a pattern of continued reflection should also mean that we develop larger networks of discipleship in which we challenge each other not only to understand what the Bible meant in its original setting, but also to consider how it speaks most effectively in our own setting. After all, it is as we consciously and prayerfully seek to shape our lives as a community by God's purposes for us in Christ that we too discover what it means to know that Jesus is with us wherever we go.

2. Leadership shared (1:10–11)

Having heard from Yahweh, Joshua's immediate response is to share this with the other leaders of the people. However important Joshua was, his leadership was shared with others who had more direct contact with other people. Joshua needed both the enabling of God's Torah and the leaders God had provided among the people. The presence of *officers* here seems to follow the pattern from Numbers 11, where the elders were appointed to share Moses' ministry, though the military overtones here draw on Deuteronomy 20:5–9.[26] Moses

---

[26] The term also occurs in Exod. 5:5–19, though the sense there may be different.

had found it impossible to lead the people on his own[27] and Joshua apparently continued that pattern. Nevertheless, it is clear that Joshua had greater authority since he was able to command these officers; leadership may have been shared, but it is clear that the levels of responsibility varied.

Joshua's directive to these officers is simple and direct: they are to pass through the camp and order the people to prepare their provisions because within three days they will be crossing the Jordan to enter the land Yahweh is giving them. Once again, we encounter the important tension that was already evident in Yahweh's speech to Joshua, whereby the land is both a gift that Yahweh is giving and something that the people need to take. There is a significant contrast with the exodus here. There, the people had to leave in haste and so could not organize provisions for themselves, whereas this crossing was an event for which they had to be prepared. Both the exodus and this crossing of the Jordan were journeys of faith. What was important was that the people were faithful to God's directives, so there was no greater faith involved in leaving without preparation – both could be expressions of trusting God. At this point, Joshua apparently anticipates that the departure will be fairly soon since the advice is to be ready to leave *within three days*, though the crossing would actually be later.[28] Perhaps this illustrates the fact that God's timetable for his promises is not necessarily the same as ours, but not knowing God's timetable is no reason for being unprepared when God has called for preparation. Israel were about to cross a flooded river and then encounter peoples who would resist them and their presence in the land, so proper preparation was essential. The same is true for Christians today as we seek to be faithful to the imperative of the gospel, especially in a world which is often resistant to our message. Depending on the Spirit does not mean ruling out all preparation!

3. Joshua and the eastern tribes (1:12–18)

Joshua is the leader of the people and he works through the officers of the people. Ultimately, however, it is the people as a whole who have to claim the land that Yahweh is giving. But there is an immediate problem that Joshua must face, which is that two and a half tribes (Reuben, Gad, Manasseh) have already settled in the trans-Jordan. Although this is technically outside the boundaries of the land (and this will be an important issue in Josh. 22), Yahweh had approved

---

[27] As well as Num. 11, see Exod. 18.
[28] Another three-day period is mentioned in 3:2, and we also have to allow time for the spies who went to Jericho, and who hid for a further three days after meeting Rahab (2:22).

this arrangement provided they joined their kinsfolk in claiming the land that was promised;[29] otherwise, they could not settle in this land. Joshua's task here is to remind them of their previous commitment and ensure that all are settled. That is why he needs to remind them of the previous arrangement made with Moses, by which they could build cities for their families and folds for their flocks,[30] but must leave them and cross the Jordan with those who would be occupying the Promised Land. The eastern tribes thus need to obey Yahweh's word through Moses, though in doing so they will also have to show great faith in Yahweh that he will keep their families and possessions while the men join the rest of Israel in battle. For Joshua, it is particularly important that all Israel participate in claiming the land that Yahweh is giving. There is no space here for one group to decide that they already have all that they need and thus to leave the others to fend for themselves. That Joshua has to speak this way to these tribes indicates that this is a risk he is already facing. Rather, the demands of faithfulness on those who already have their land are even greater because of the need to leave all behind while entering the land with their compatriots. Only when Yahweh has enabled those tribes settling across the Jordan to have rest in the land will they be able to return to the rest that he has already granted them. It is this that the eastern tribes accept as they in turn encourage Joshua to faithfulness, for they too know that they can only find rest if Yahweh is present.

The unity of the people in the purposes of God was thus vital to the full enjoyment of God's gifts. Joshua was well aware that such unity was difficult to maintain, as is particularly evident in chapter 22, though not only there. How Israel would move from the unity needed to claim the land to the unity needed to retain the land was a challenge that was never entirely resolved – but this does not remove the importance of this unity. As a parallel to this we might note that when Christians are working together in the work of the gospel, it is the gospel work itself that enables us to cooperate, especially in the early days of some work; but that cooperation becomes more difficult when the work is more settled. Certainly evangelical Christians seem to find it easier to separate from one another than to work together. However, as we face more resistance to our message, especially in the West, we need to be reminded of the importance of working together because, however much we have achieved in the past, the work continues to lie ahead of us. And for this we need to work with one another.

[29] Num. 32. Cf. Deut. 3:12–20.
[30] Num. 32:24.

So Israel here stood at a point of transition – a change from one leader to another, a change from one way of life to another. But one thing was consistent: they were still the people of God. They still had his promises and they still needed to live in obedience to him. Their hope did not depend upon their leader, no matter how effective Joshua was. Their hope, and ours, depended upon God alone as they were obedient and committed to him.

Joshua 2:1–24
2. New light from a lady of the night

Promises are important to us all. When we receive a promise it is often important to receive some evidence that the promise will be honoured. For example, when I order something online it is good to see the sale confirmation screen come up, but I never feel entirely sure of the order until I have the email confirming it. Somehow, this automated response reassures me that the company is processing my order, and of course with that email I can normally track the progress of the order. Promises which involve more significant financial transactions usually also require more evidence of good faith from those involved. For example, if we borrow money from a bank or building society to buy a home, the lender normally wants evidence that we really will repay the money we have borrowed, and this normally includes letters from our employer, payslips and the like. We may well promise to repay, but responsible lenders want to know that our promise is meaningful; so we need evidence that a promise can be trusted.

As we read this chapter of Joshua, we need to remember that Israel has received some astonishing promises from God. Abraham had been assured that Yahweh would give him descendants, a relationship with God, and land; and indeed Yahweh had even given Abraham evidence that his promise was meaningful.[1] The Pentateuch has shown how, among other things, the promises of descendants and a relationship with God had been fulfilled, but the promise of land has not yet been realized, though the land has in fact been a key theme throughout Deuteronomy, emphasizing it as the place that Yahweh is giving to them and thus towards which Israel is moving.[2]

[1] Gen. 12:1–9; 15:1–18.
[2] For a convenient summary, see Edward J. Woods, *Deuteronomy: An Introduction and Commentary* (Nottingham: IVP, 2011), pp. 65–67.

The preparations in Joshua 1 were directed towards the move into the land, and that theme continues in this chapter. However, where Joshua 1 largely prepared for the move into the land by looking back to previous events, this chapter is more about how Yahweh reassures Israel that his promise will be fulfilled going forward.

All of this comes about in a somewhat irregular way – who would have thought that a meeting with a Canaanite prostitute would lead to a report of the certainty of Yahweh's gift of the land? The narrative itself is full of double entendre,[3] and a sort of anti-James Bond tone is struck as the incompetence of the spies Joshua sends does not prevent Yahweh from delivering his word of encouragement through them. In this way the narrative also begins to open up questions about the identity of Israel. Rahab and her family can be saved, so what about the other Canaanites? Do they invariably stand under Yahweh's judgment so that they must be destroyed? Or is faith in the promises of Yahweh the more important point?

1. Sending the spies (2:1a)

Having arranged with the trans-Jordanian tribes that they will join their kinsmen in claiming Yahweh's gift of the land, Joshua here prepares to send two spies to scout the land, *especially Jericho*. At this point, Israel is camped at Shittim, and though we do not know exactly where this was, it was later remembered as the traditional starting point for their entry into the land[4] and so east of the Jordan. Israel at this stage has not been west of the Jordan, and though Joshua and Caleb survive from the spies whom Moses had sent previously[5] they can hardly be expected to remember the particulars of the land around Jericho, which will be the first obstacle they face across the Jordan. Since sending spies seems to have been a fairly standard practice for assaults on an area,[6] it is no surprise that Joshua decides to send two to scout out the land, in particular the region of Jericho.

---

[3] Cf. Richard D. Nelson, *Joshua: A Commentary* (Louisville: Westminster John Knox, 1997), pp. 43–44. It should be noted, though, that although the chapter uses the main euphemisms for sexual activity available in Hebrew, it is also careful not to suggest that anything inappropriate actually happened (cf. Hess, *Joshua*, pp. 83–84). But it seems clear that the dialogue between Rahab and the king of Jericho's messengers is intentionally saucy.

[4] Mic. 6:5. HCSB translates the name as 'Acacia Grove', reflecting the fact that 'Shittim', which means 'acacias', has the article (similarly, Robert G. Boling, *Joshua: A New Translation with Notes and Commentary* [Garden City: Doubleday, 1982], p. 144). In Num. 25:1–4 it is also the place where Israel engaged in sexual sin as an element of Baal worship that was instigated by Balaam.

[5] Num. 14:30.

[6] Joshua himself will later send spies to Ai (7:2), though the result of the battle there will be somewhat different. See also Num. 21:32; Judg. 18:2; 1 Sam. 26:4.

Some have criticized Joshua for a lack of faith at this point, arguing that he should have depended upon God to deliver up Jericho.[7] But there is nothing in the text to suggest any criticism of Joshua here, and there is an important distinction to be drawn between trusting God and presuming how God is going to act. At this point, Joshua has had no intimation that Yahweh will deliver Jericho by miraculous means. He merely knows that Jericho's capture is crucial to Israel's entry into the land. Thus Joshua is here employing a known approach to find out information about the region of Jericho as well as the particulars that Israel will face in Jericho. Put simply, Joshua could presume that God would go with him in the taking of the land, and he could do so with confidence; but he could not presume that the means by which God would act would be overtly miraculous. As such, it was right and proper that he take the appropriate steps. Likewise for believers today, we do not show less faith by assuming that God works mostly through more 'natural' means rather than through the miraculous. God may well do something miraculous, but it is presumption on our part to assume that God will act that way. So, when we are planning our work – whether it is the routine of weekly church life, a mission or anything else – we are right to trust the promises of God's presence with us in Jesus, but since miracles are, by definition, somewhat unusual we do not presume on them as the basis for our work, even though we recognize that God in his grace may well grant them. Like Joshua, we will contribute all we can to the task before us, asking that God might bless our contributions, but also knowing that God can indeed do 'far more abundantly than all that we ask or think'.[8]

2. The encounter with Rahab (2:1b–21)

a. Rahab and Jericho's officials (2:1b–7)

Although the chapter begins and ends with Joshua, its heart is the encounter the spies have with Rahab, a prostitute in Jericho. Now, it must be said at the outset that Joshua does not appear to have selected his spies on the basis of any particular skill set that they possessed, and they appear as bumbling incompetents who somehow end up with the right outcome. Although such characterization is quite a popular trope in contemporary comedy,[9] here it is understood as

---

[7] Hawk, *Every Promise Fulfilled*, p. 61, claims the narrator creates an 'ominous mood' by reporting Joshua as employing a method that had previously brought disastrous results.

[8] Eph. 3:20.

[9] In recent times, one might note the Johnny English films of Rowan Atkinson.

a sign of how Yahweh is at work, ensuring they do indeed take the right message back to Joshua. Perhaps the most obvious evidence of their lack of ability as spies is the simple fact that they are never reported as doing anything we might expect a spy to do; there is certainly no attempt to discover information about Jericho's defences. Instead, the first thing we are told is that they go to the house of a prostitute named Rahab and stay there. Although there is a long tradition, reaching back to at least Josephus, of treating Rahab[10] as an 'innkeeper',[11] the text is clear that she is a prostitute. Prostitution and taverns have long gone together, so it is not impossible that she is both; but the text here seems to delight in using verbs that were also employed as euphemisms for sexual activity. Thus we are told that the spies stayed at her house, but the verb used is also often translated 'laid with'. Other verbs which can be euphemisms are also employed throughout, and since some are redundant for the purposes of the narrative it seems likely that this is done deliberately as a device to sustain interest. However, when these verbs are used as euphemisms they normally require a preposition to indicate this, and these are absent. This seems to be a careful way of drawing readers into what is clearly a risky moment for the spies, while showing that nothing inappropriate actually happened. Nevertheless, the narrator is having fun in telling us that nothing happened.

Joshua may have sent the spies secretly, and although two visitors to the town heading straight for the brothel might not raise too many suspicions in the ordinary course of events, that is clearly not the case here. Rahab's confession will make clear that the residents of Jericho were well aware of Israel's presence, so even though the officials in Jericho do not finally look any more efficient than Israel's spies, it is hardly surprising that word comes to the city's king of the spies' arrival. It is not necessary to assume that the spies had somehow revealed their task since the presence of Israelite men in this context could only mean that they were spies. It is clear, however, that the spies attracted unnecessary attention to themselves. Accordingly, the king sends his officers to Rahab demanding that she send out the men who have come to her. Their message employs the verbs elsewhere used as euphemisms, and though nothing explicit is actually said it is clearly suggestive of what the officers believe has happened – though making clear that, whatever has happened in Rahab's house, the men have really come as spies. The start of verse

[10] Other Old Testament texts (e.g. Job 9:13) mention a mythical creature named Rahab, but in Hebrew the spelling is different. Rahab's name means 'broad', though unlike with US slang there is no association between her name and her occupation.

[11] *Ant.* I, 2.7. This interpretation is hinted at in ESV's translation, which indicates that the spies *lodged* in her house.

4 is then a flashback to what has happened earlier, making clear that Rahab had already decided to commit herself to the spies by hiding them, though at this stage we do not know why.[12] However, she clearly knew what their presence signified, so even before the king's officers arrive we see the faith for which she is commended.[13] Confronted by the king's officers, she continues by using the sort of language the officers have used, sounding rather coquettish, though again without actually claiming anything happened. But she knows what the officers expect of her, and she is apparently quite prepared to use this expectation in her response. However, even though we know the men are hiding on her roof – and verse 6 will offer another flashback to indicate that they are hiding under stalks of flax that she is drying on the roof – Rahab denies any knowledge of where they are or where they have gone, claiming instead that they left just before the gate closed. Thus, with the men hiding in her house she urges the officers to chase them, and they then head out on a fruitless pursuit to the fords of the Jordan. All might seem well for the spies at this point, especially with the officers heading off looking like the Keystone Cops – except for the ominous note that the gate is shut behind the officers, meaning that the spies are now trapped inside Jericho.

The epistle of James specifically commends Rahab for receiving the men and sending the officers off in another direction.[14] Yet that she does so by lying has troubled many, especially as the basic position of the Bible is to encourage truthfulness.[15] So how are we to reconcile Rahab's lie with her commendation in the New Testament?[16] One important element to note is that Rahab operates from a position of weakness, and the Old Testament as a whole is quite fond of 'underdog' stories.[17] Indeed, although the contexts are rather different, Rahab's approach is quite similar to that of Rachel in convincing her father that his household gods had not gone with

[12] Robert B. Coote, 'Joshua', in Leander E. Keck (ed.), *The New Interpreter's Bible* (Nashville: Abingdon Press, 1998), p. 595, emphasizes her poverty as a key factor. Sociologically, this is probably true, though it is not the theme developed by the text.

[13] Heb. 11:31. Donald H. Madvig, 'Joshua', in Frank E. Gaebelein (ed.), *The Expositor's Bible Commentary* (Grand Rapids: Zondervan, 1992), p. 260, points to an old Babylonian law that described a situation similar to this which required the death penalty.

[14] Jas 2:25.

[15] E.g. Prov. 24:26. For an overview of the ways Christians have generally sought to understand lying under circumstances such as these, see the helpful excursus in Howard, *Joshua*, p. 112.

[16] As well as the texts already mentioned, she is probably also included in Jesus' genealogy in Matt. 1:5.

[17] Cf. O. Horn Prouser, 'The Truth about Women and Lying', *Journal for the Study of the Old Testament* 61 (1994), p. 29.

Jacob even though she had them.[18] Neither deception could be considered as an absolute moral good, and yet in both cases human fallibility worked in the same direction as God's purposes for his people. In this chapter, Rahab's lie and the failings of the spies both show the reality of human weakness, and yet through this God's promise to Israel is confirmed. Of course, at another level Rahab shows absolute fidelity in how she deals with the spies, so perhaps it is not entirely appropriate to judge her on the basis of the Bible's wider morality of truth-telling. She operates as she believes enables her to show good faith to the spies, and because that means moving herself towards Yahweh and his purposes, this is acceptable. Her behaviour is therefore not presented as exemplary, but the direction in which her life was moving as demonstrated by her actions towards the spies can be commended. By way of analogy, we can note that we would not normally expect a new convert to Christianity, especially someone coming from another faith tradition, to behave perfectly and make complex moral decisions on the basis of an informed understanding of the faith. We look to encourage such people to have their lives shaped by the gospel, and as they grow we expect more of them. But we certainly must encourage them as they seek to move away from former patterns of life and to have their conduct shaped by the gospel message.

b. Rahab's confession (2:8–14)

We know that Rahab has acted for the spies, but so far we do not know why she has done so. Now that the officers have gone off to the fords, however, she is able to speak to the spies and explain why she has acted as she has. So before the men go to sleep she goes to the roof to speak with them. Although we might expect her to give some explanation for what she has done, we probably do not expect a Canaanite prostitute to speak as she does. Admittedly, what we have is probably a summary of what she said, written up as a classical Israelite confession of faith; but this does not mean that it somehow misrepresents her words. In short, Rahab confesses Yahweh as God, revealing a profound understanding of who God is through what he has done.

Two key themes run through her confession. First, she refers to what she has heard that Yahweh has done. She is not responding to claims about Yahweh that someone has randomly made; she speaks about specific things he has done for Israel. In doing so, she runs through Israel's story from the exodus in the crossing of the Reed

[18] Gen. 31:33–35.

Sea[19] at the start of their time in the wilderness, through to the defeat of Sihon and Og, two Amorite kings who had opposed Israel once they reached the limits of Moab.[20] It is not made clear how she knows about these events, but it is not unreasonable to imagine that word of them would have circulated in the region. What is also clear from these stories (and perhaps some from in between) is that she knows about Yahweh's power, and that forces that resist Yahweh are doomed to fail. It is because of this that she also emphasizes the dread that has fallen upon the inhabitants of the land – not just Jericho – so that they lack the will to resist. These two points thus substantiate her initial statement that she knows that Yahweh has given Israel the land. Yahweh is God, his purposes cannot be resisted, and Rahab now sides with him. Rahab's confession thus confirms in an unexpected way the point that Yahweh made earlier to Joshua: that no-one would be able to resist Israel.[21]

Beyond this, Rahab wants the spies also to favour her. Rahab has dealt kindly with the spies, and her request is that they deal kindly with her, and in particular that she and her family will be allowed to survive. But Rahab does not simply request this – she asks the spies to swear an oath to her that they will do so. By the end of the chapter Yahweh will have shown Israel how they can be sure he will keep his promises, and here Rahab wants an oath as similar proof for herself. This is a life and death matter, so she needs to be sure she will not be betrayed, and because of the seriousness with which oaths were viewed in that culture, making an oath is a means of ensuring this. That the oath is to be sworn by Yahweh means he is a party to it, thereby underlining its solemnity. Jesus would later discourage oaths[22] among believers because oaths would be used in circumstances where people could not be sure of the truthfulness of all parties involved, whereas Jesus' point is that we ought always to be transparently honest. Jesus was aware of abuses that were brought about through oaths, which is why he advocated simple honesty; but the value of this can only really be appreciated through a long-term relationship. Rahab lacked the benefit of this, so for her an oath was the crucial mechanism for ensuring the reliability of any promise the spies might make. Perhaps the point to make for Christian practice now is that among believers there should be no need for mechanisms to prove our trustworthiness, and in the longer term non-believers should also learn they can trust us. In the short term, however, it may be necessary for us to give

[19] Exod. 14:21–31.
[20] Num. 21:21–35.
[21] 1:5.
[22] Matt. 5:33–37.

evidence of our reliability to others. This certainly seems to be the attitude of the spies as they declare that their lives will be forfeit for hers and that, when Yahweh gives them the land, provided she has not reported them, they will deal kindly and faithfully with her.

But was this an oath they could legitimately swear? Taken at face value, Deuteronomy 7[23] would seem to require that all Canaanites should be devoted to destruction.[24] Was not the swearing of such an oath a breach of Yahweh's command, promising something that could not be given? Some have read it that way, so that Hawk can claim that the relationship established by this oath 'is a serious infraction of Moses' commandments'.[25] It would seem, however, that the reality is more complex than this, because although Rahab continually speaks of Yahweh as *your God*, she does so because she is speaking to the spies about their perspective. Her final confession of faith in verse 11, however, means she has now identified Yahweh as *her* God. Israel had always been more than just those who were biologically related to Abraham – note that the exodus community was a 'mixed multitude'[26] and not just ethnic Israelite – and that same pattern is evident here. By placing her faith in Yahweh, Rahab has effectively moved out of the people who stood under Yahweh's judgment in his giving the land and has joined Israel. As such, she is no longer one to be devoted to destruction, and as her family join her they too will be saved. It is important to note this, because the example of Rahab yet again shows that God's purposes have always been focused on those outside Israel, and that Israel's life (like that of the church) was meant to draw others to him.[27] The spies could thus legitimately swear this oath because Rahab no longer stood under Yahweh's judgment, and indeed through her Israel already had an initial presence in the land. More than anything else, this stresses the importance of reading Scripture carefully and in its full context. If we take only one passage in isolation (in this case Deut. 7) we miss God's missional purpose through his people. Rather, we need to encourage people to read the whole of the Bible to see how it builds to show what God is doing.

Apart from this, Rahab's own confession is again a reminder of the importance of us being clear about the great things God has done today in the death, resurrection and ascension of Jesus, in the gift of the Spirit and in the hope of Jesus' return. It is because she heard what God had done and was doing that she could declare her faith, and the same is true for many today.

[23] Cf. Deut. 20:16–18.
[24] On this concept, see the discussion on 6:17.
[25] Hawk, *Every Promise Fulfilled*, p. 68.
[26] Exod. 12:38.
[27] Deut. 4:6–8.

c. Negotiating with the spies (2:15–21)

One might think that the story could be quickly resolved at this point, but there is a further twist. The spies have been shut inside Jericho, but we now discover that Rahab's house was *built into the city wall*. Although more typically associated with later Israelite sites, this could represent what is known as a casemate wall, in which space existed between an inner and outer wall[28] with chambers in between. These could be filled with rubble for additional security, though at upper levels they might (as in this case) be occupied. However, it is perhaps more likely that the outer houses of the town, perhaps with small linking sections, formed the town's outer defence and thus its wall. Importantly, that meant the spies could be lowered with a rope.[29] And just as she has already done, Rahab takes the lead, directing the spies to go quickly to the hill country – that is, away from the Jordan, where the officers have gone – where they are to hide until the officers return to Jericho. As the narrative is presented it appears as if this conversation is taking place while Rahab is letting the spies down on the rope from her window. Certainly, one can imagine this as a final whispered injunction from Rahab. However, since this then leads to a lengthy conversation with the spies, many have felt that it must be another flashback.[30] This would mean that it happened before they were let down the wall, the argument being that this would be a more natural order of events, with it presented here so as to give prominence to the discussion. This is certainly plausible, but given the clear lack of competence demonstrated by the spies so far it may also be that they are indeed portrayed as having the conversation while hanging from the rope. If so, not only were they unable to arrive secretly, but also they appear to do their best to attract attention to themselves while leaving.

Whatever the actual order of events, the narrative does highlight the spies' insistence that they too need evidence of good faith from Rahab, though it seems it is intended as proof that the promise of verse 14 will be fulfilled. This means her tying a *scarlet cord*[31] into her window and guaranteeing that she will not report the matter. Moreover, any member of her family who leaves the house will not

[28] Note that there are two different words for *wall* in v. 15.

[29] Note the close parallel in Paul's experience reported in Acts 9:23–25 and 2 Cor. 11:32–33.

[30] Hence, NIV 1984 rendered v. 16 'Now she had said to them . . .'. (NIV 2011 translates this differently.)

[31] There is a long history of interpreting the cord typologically as a reference to Christ's blood because of its colour. However, although this works in English (and many other languages), 'scarlet' is not a colour ever used to describe blood in the Old Testament. Cf. Howard, *Joshua*, pp. 115–116.

be covered by the promise. The scarlet cord was apparently something already present in the house, perhaps near the sash, though it is not the rope on which they are being lowered since a different word is used. The presence of the cord could not really prove that Rahab had not reported the matter and so works more as a means of identifying her house, since at this stage the assumption is that Jericho will be attacked in a traditional manner. However, the evidence of her promise not to report the matter will be seen by the absence of anyone coming after them to the hill country. With this resolved, even these incompetent spies can go away safe in the knowledge that Yahweh is indeed fulfilling his promises.

3. The certainty of the promise (2:22–24)

With the spies now away from Jericho the rest of the story can be told quickly. As Rahab had directed, the spies go to the hill country for three days, waiting for the officers to return to Jericho. This hill country is an area with many caves, making it suitable as a hiding place.[32] The officers, by contrast, go all the way to the Jordan but do not find them. Then the spies can head back down to the Jordan valley, cross the river and come to Joshua, where they recount *all that had happened to them* (23). The terminology is probably deliberate – it is not what they have done but rather what has befallen them. Thus, when they report the certainty of Yahweh's promise of the land being fulfilled, it is not because of their successful espionage or even their careful gathering of information; rather, it is because God is at work in someone completely unexpected, and through her he has confirmed his promise to them. Indeed, their report is derived directly from Rahab's confession. Yahweh is known in the Bible as a God who promises, but promises are only meaningful when they are fulfilled or when evidence is given that they are being fulfilled. And God clearly delights in this story in providing such evidence through Rahab. Perhaps we too will discover evidence of the new life of the Spirit and encouragement to faithfulness as we also see the ways in which God shows us he is fulfilling his promises to us in Christ in those people and places where we least expect it, including those in his purposes we might otherwise exclude. But then, if God's power is made perfect in weakness, should we expect anything less?[33]

[32] C. F. Keil and F. Delitzsch, *Joshua, Judges, Ruth, I & II Samuel* (Grand Rapids: Eerdmans, 1956), p. 39.
[33] 2 Cor. 12:9.

Joshua 3:1 – 4:24
3. Crossing the Jordan and remembering

Memories are vital. Their importance is not only found in our ability to remember the events of our own lives – and as Western populations continue to age, the prevalence of Alzheimer's disease reminds us how damaging an inability to remember can be; but it is also seen in corporate memory, the ability of a people to remember those times and events which have been formative in their own identity. A community without memory is caught on a cultural and historical island, surrounded by various currents but lacking the ability to break out of the present and truly to approach its future. Memory shapes us, giving us a framework to interpret our present and thus also to move towards our future. Without memory we are doomed to repeat the mistakes of the past because we lack the ability to assess our present critically. In the modern world, remembrance is often associated with events in military history, as with the end of the two world wars commemorated on Remembrance Day. However, the commemoration of the tragic events at Gallipoli in 1915 on Anzac Day in Australia and New Zealand also indicates that such corporate memory does not have to be only of great victories. Sometimes there is more to be learnt from remembering times of great loss.

So whether it is about tragedy or triumph, remembering is important for any community – but it is especially true for the people of God. This, in part at least, is why remembering plays such a significant role in the Bible as a whole, and why it is so important in this account of Israel's entry into the land. Although the crossing of the Jordan is presented here as a miracle, it is notable that the emphasis is not so much on the event itself but rather on remembering the significance of the event, so that remembering becomes a proclamation to all the earth of the mighty acts (and thus character) of Yahweh.

Thus Israel can remember the miracle of the crossing, and in so doing be reminded of the nature of their place within the mission of God. Memory helps them understand their present, and reminds them of the future into which God has called them; it encourages them to remember the power and goodness of God which has brought them into the land, which then gives them hope for the future.

These two chapters need to be read together; the basic story of the crossing is told in chapter 3 and then reflections on it are provided in chapter 4. However, that it needs to bring so many key themes together into a relatively short space means that it is not always easy to follow what is happening, something complicated by the fact that this is a clearly dischronologized narrative – that is, for narrative purposes it does not recount everything in its actual sequence.[1] Instead, it uses constant flashbacks (especially) in chapter 4 which fill in the details of the crossing in order to bring out their significance. Although this might seem a counter-intuitive means of telling a story it is not uncommon in film, especially as it provides an opportunity to offer additional perspectives which enrich the initial telling. Perhaps we could think of this narrative as being like a layer cake, in which each additional layer builds texture and flavour, but does so by going over the same space rather than extending the basic structure. Of course, all analogies break down at some point, but we might in this case start by noting that the basic narrative occurs in chapter 3. However, the progress of the narrative is paused at 3:14–17, with the priests in the river with the ark. Chapter 4:1–10 then gives us a second pass at this event, exploring its significance beyond the event itself. The narrative then starts advancing again at 4:11. This approach still allows for geographical movement, with 3:1–13 in the trans-Jordan at Shittim, then 3:14 – 4:10 in the Jordan, and 4:11–24 looking back at events from the plains of Jericho. Israel has entered the land, and thus has entered a new stage of its life. This is why remembering is so important.

1. In the trans-Jordan (3:1–13)

a. Initial preparations (3:1–6)

Preparation for what Yahweh is about to do is important. As a first step, this involves the people leaving their camp at Shittim and coming to the Jordan itself in anticipation of the crossing. While there, however, it also involves the wider range of Israel's leadership that was mentioned in 1:10–11 because the level of work described

---

[1] Against Boling, *Joshua*, p. 159.

here cannot be carried out by Joshua on his own. This is important, because although demonstrating that Joshua is indeed Moses' legitimate successor is an important theme within this narrative, it does not ignore the contributions of others. Rather, it is understood that even though Joshua's role is primary, he acts as part of a team. All leadership is shared in different ways, and these officers fulfil their role, supplementing that of Joshua. As with many saints down through the ages we do not know their identity, but what matters here is that they are faithful in carrying out the tasks assigned to them. At the same time, there is a clear differentiation between the work of the officers in verses 2–4 and that of Joshua himself in verses 5–6, because even when leadership is shared there is still an appropriate differentiation of function and responsibility.

Here the officers' task after three days is to prepare the people for the process of the crossing, whereas in 1:11 they were to organize provisions in preparation for this move. Only now do we discover something about how the crossing is to happen, though in fact throughout this section we discover that there were things that Yahweh must have told Joshua before, but we discover them in the same order as the people. The narrative thus deliberately withholds information from us until it is necessary for us to interpret what is happening, so that our experience mirrors that of the people. And, of course, it also reflects the fact that God lets us know what is happening in our own discipleship when it is needed and not in advance. The way this narrative is told also reminds us that God knows considerably more than is revealed to us at any given point, though at least some of that is revealed to Joshua. Thus the command from the officers must be something passed on to them by Joshua but which is only revealed now.

In this case, the command from the officers focuses on the central role the *Levitical priests*[2] and the ark of the covenant will play in the crossing of the Jordan. Both are understood as signs of Yahweh's grace to his people. Different passages about the ark emphasize different aspects of its role, but it was a gold-covered box that was to be carried on poles and which primarily served to store the tablets of the Ten Commandments[3] and as a place where Yahweh's will could be revealed in the sanctuary.[4] As a symbol of Yahweh's presence

---

[2] Strictly, all priests are Levites since Aaron was of the tribe of Levi, but not all Levites are priests. But Deuteronomy typically speaks of 'Levitical priests', perhaps as a means of emphasizing their legitimacy as Yahweh's chosen priests, and Joshua uses this combined form here, though for the rest of the crossing narrative they are *the priests bearing the ark*.

[3] Exod. 25:16.

[4] Exod. 25:22.

it was also used in battle,[5] and there is a hint of that here as the ark shows Yahweh's power over the elements of nature in preparation for the battles ahead. And, of course, both the Levitical priests and the ark will play a significant role in the capture of Jericho.[6] At this stage, however, there is no hint of anything miraculous, only that the route of the ark will provide guidance for the people since they have not previously gone this way. However, that Israel must follow the ark indicates that Yahweh does know the way.[7] An element of this guidance is that there is to be a gap of two thousand cubits (about a thousand yards) between the people and the priests bearing the ark. This may be because of the jungle of the Jordan that grew in this area, and also because the Jordan has two banks, an upper bank and a true bank, and as the people stood on the upper bank they would then be able to see what was happening at the true bank.[8] How this would help the people know the way is not made clear here – its significance would only become apparent when they reached the upper bank; but it is typical of God that we only know why he leads us in certain ways when we reach the point where it becomes important.

The officers have not revealed that anything miraculous is to happen, but as Joshua speaks to the people and then the priests it is made clear that Yahweh is about to do something miraculous and that therefore the people need to prepare themselves for this. Indeed, consecration is required of the people precisely because Yahweh is about to do something miraculous among them, though at this stage we do not know what the miracle is going to be; that is, the holy God is about to act among them, so they too should make sure that they are holy. The exact means by which the people are to do this is not specified, though it probably included washing and possibly abstinence from sex,[9] but the principle was more important than the means. Something which belonged to God in the Old Testament was holy simply because it was his, and by consecrating themselves the people were marking themselves off as belonging to God. It is not necessarily the case that God will not work through an 'unclean vessel', since he seems to delight in working with people (such as David) who have made massive mistakes, but it is certainly true that in the Old Testament as a whole God summons his people to

---

[5] Num. 10:35–36, though as 1 Sam. 4:2–11 makes clear, the presence of the ark could not compel Yahweh to give victory.

[6] Josh. 6.

[7] Hubbard, *Joshua*, p. 151.

[8] Cf. Marten H. Woudstra, *The Book of Joshua* (Grand Rapids: Eerdmans, 1981), p. 81.

[9] Cf. Exod. 19:10–15.

consecration at points where he is about to act significantly among them.[10] This principle is then embedded more clearly in the call of Israel's Torah, which insists that Israel is to be holy because Yahweh is holy,[11] a theme which the New Testament also applies to the life of the church.[12] Rather than particular moments of consecration, the New Testament expects consecration to mark the entire life of the church. However, we should not make too sharp a distinction between the Testaments here, because the Torah also expects lifelong holiness from Israel. In addition, as here, there may well be times when some special moment of consecration is expected from God's people as they engage in his mission.

Joshua's directive to the priests is simpler: they are to take up the ark and set off before the people, though the meaning of this instruction will be worked out only when they reach the Jordan.

b. Ready for a miracle (3:7–13)

Leaving aside Joshua's speech to the people and priests, we now hear from Yahweh as he speaks to Joshua, preparing for the miracle of the crossing. The key point initially is that Yahweh will *begin to exalt* Joshua before all Israel, so that they will know that he is with Joshua just as he was with Moses. Yahweh had assured Joshua of this before,[13] but there may be a hint in the attitude of the trans-Jordan tribes that they wanted some evidence of this.[14] Yahweh has chosen Joshua as Israel's leader, so the point of exalting Joshua is not to boost Joshua's ego but rather that Israel might know Yahweh is present with him, demonstrating this to those who may be unsure. Joshua's status depends on Yahweh's initiative and his faithfulness to the pattern of Moses rather than on anything he has achieved himself.[15] This exaltation will occur through the miracle of the crossing, and it is only now that we learn what will happen; consistent with how information is held back until necessary, the full miracle is only explained when Joshua again speaks to the people, explaining that the priests are to carry the ark to the Jordan, and that once they stand in the Jordan with the ark the waters will be cut off upstream.

However, the announcement of the miracle is again delayed until the end of Joshua's speech, though it is clear that Joshua now knows

---

[10] E.g. Num. 11:18, when the Spirit is about to be shared among the elders.

[11] E.g. Lev. 19:1–2.

[12] 1 Pet. 1:13–25.

[13] 1:5.

[14] 1:17.

[15] Cf. Trent C. Butler, *Joshua* (Waco: Word Books, 1983), p. 46.

what is to happen. It is almost as if getting there too soon will distract the people. Instead, just as Yahweh's exaltation of Joshua was so the people would know that Yahweh was with him as he had been with Moses, so this miracle is to assure the people that Yahweh will grant the land to them, since it is his to grant, and that they will dispossess all the peoples known to be resident there.[16] So the two points of knowledge confirmed in this section draw together themes from the previous two chapters. The people who may have been uncertain about Joshua will know that Yahweh is with him, while the certainty of Israel taking the land that had been communicated to Joshua through the spies[17] is now to be revealed to the nation as a whole. Yahweh is indeed about to do a miracle, but it is important for Israel that they have a proper frame of reference to understand what Yahweh is communicating by it.

The principle here is an important one, because it is clear that miracles are not necessarily self-explanatory. For example, in John 9 there are radically different responses to the healing of the man born blind from the man's neighbours, the Pharisees and his family. None seem fully to grasp the significance of what Jesus has done, and even after Jesus meets the man a second time and summons him to faith, there is still opposition from the Pharisees.[18] What unites both these stories is that the interpretation given to the miracle is linked to God's missional purpose: for Israel, as they entered the land; for the man, that he comes to understand Jesus' identity. Although we have to be careful how we extrapolate from only a few texts, it seems that it is important to create a context in which miracles are able to be understood within God's missional purpose. Indeed, the close of chapter 4 will make it clear that all peoples of the earth needed to understand this miracle in those terms. We need, therefore, to guard ourselves against those who would claim the miraculous to increase their own stature and instead evaluate it through the framework of God's mission.

Only with this explanation in place is the nature of the miracle described, with its clear associations with the crossing of the Reed Sea[19] demonstrating the similarity between Joshua and Moses. However, where the crossing of the Sea marked the entry into the wilderness, this crossing will mark the end of the wilderness period as Israel finally reaches the land. Yahweh is shown to be present in

---

[16] For an accessible summary of what is known about the peoples, see J. Gordon Harris, 'Joshua', in J. Gordon Harris, Cheryl A. Brown and Michael S. Moore, *Joshua, Judges, Ruth* (Peabody: Hendrickson, 2000), pp. 35–36.

[17] 2:24.

[18] John 9:35–41.

[19] Exod. 14:21–31.

this crossing in both the miracle and the ark.[20] The instruction for each tribe to choose a man anticipates later events, again ensuring that at each stage the people of Israel, like us, know only enough of what is happening to progress, not more.

2. In the Jordan (3:14 – 4:10)

a. Recounting the miracle (3:14–17)

Although we have been waiting for the miracle for some time, it is now recounted quite briefly, again stressing that it is not the miracle itself so much as its significance that matters. The report is remarkably matter-of-fact, though an additional note about the Jordan being in flood is now introduced. This is important because most of the time the Jordan does not present a substantial barrier to crossing. Visitors today will see something that looks rather like a brook rather than a major river because modern dams have reduced its flow, but even in ancient times it was not difficult to cross except when there were floods.[21] So the note about the flood emphasizes the power of Yahweh in ensuring Israel crossed on dry land when they could not have done so themselves. In addition, along with the flax on Rahab's roof, it sets the narrative in spring, preparing for the celebration of Passover in chapter 5.[22] This note aside, the account states simply that as the priests entered the Jordan the water was cut off, and the people then crossed into the land while the priests remained in the river. The water, meanwhile, was effectively dammed in the area of Adam,[23] a town probably about nineteen miles upstream. The miracle can be told briefly because the important point is that it happened just as Yahweh had announced through Joshua. What matters is not so much that Yahweh performed a miracle, but rather how the significance of the miracle is to be understood. In this instance it demonstrates that Yahweh's miracle-working power is evident when the people do as he requires, preparing us for the more difficult demands Yahweh will make in the capture of Jericho. This highlights an important analogy with Christian discipleship. As we are faithful to God's call on our

[20] Although the ark is typically 'the ark of the covenant of the Lord of all the earth', ESV mg. more literally has 'the ark of the covenant, the Lord of all the earth', suggesting an identification between the ark and Yahweh.
[21] R. J. Faley, *Joshua, Judges* (Collegeville: Liturgical Press, 2011), p. 14, has a photo that clearly illustrates this.
[22] This is clearer in 4:19, which makes the Passover link more explicit.
[23] There is an internal variant in the Hebrew, with the water either blocked at Adam, or blocked up with the heap extending back to Adam. The most probable site for Adam is also where the Jordan was completely blocked as a result of an earthquake in 1927.

lives we discover how his power is at work in us, and this in turn prepares us for those times when he will make greater demands on us.

b. Memorial stones: a first reflection (4:1–10)

The importance of the miracle of the crossing is not just that Israel left the wilderness in much the same way as they entered it or that Yahweh begins to exalt Joshua. Rather, it is to be understood by using it as a memorial which shapes future generations. Yahweh has previously directed Joshua to select twelve men as representatives of all the tribes,[24] and we now focus on them. That directive is now expanded with instructions to Joshua about what is to happen, instructions that Joshua then passes on to those involved. As at 3:10, however, Joshua's speech provides additional information that helps us understand why these instructions are important. That there are twelve men involved is significant when we remember that the trans-Jordan tribes are included among those who have entered the land, even though their home is outside the boundaries Yahweh had promised. Thus the memorial is to be for all the people, not just those who will live in the land. The memorial itself is to be a simple one, with each man to take a stone from the place where the priests stood and to set it down at the point where Israel spend their first night in the land. The key expectation is that the presence of the memorial will trigger a conversation among subsequent generations as to the meaning of the stones. In this, Joshua follows the pattern of Deuteronomy, which also expects children to ask questions about Israel's life, providing opportunities to expound part of Israel's story so they in turn can pass it on.[25] Indeed, as most parents can attest, memorials often lead to children asking questions. I remember taking my children along the Kokoda Track Memorial Walkway in Sydney when they were younger; the presence of the memorial led to them asking a range of questions about the Kokoda Track and the experiences of those who served in the Second World War, providing a context to explore this important moment in their history. The memorial here is intended to have the same effect, and if the stones referred to in verse 9 are in fact those of the memorial,[26] it was still known when at least this chapter was written.

---

[24] 3:12.

[25] Cf. Deut. 6:20–25. On the significance of such passages in Deuteronomy, see David G. Firth, 'Passing on the Faith in Deuteronomy', in David G. Firth and Philip S. Johnston (eds), *Interpreting Deuteronomy: Issues and Approaches* (Nottingham: Apollos, 2012), pp. 167–175.

[26] ESV, with most other versions, treats these as a separate memorial left by Joshua in the river – something LXX makes explicit. But Howard, *Joshua*, p. 136, suggests that v. 9 is a parenthetical aside, indicating that these are the same stones brought across to form the memorial.

Christians have taken different views about the appropriateness of establishing memorials of various kinds in their churches, but in both the Lord's Supper and baptism we have powerful acts of memorial. In many congregations children are absent while the Lord's Supper is celebrated; in my experience it is more common for them to be present for baptisms. Although we have to be careful to ensure the proper solemnity of these events, there is no doubt that both trigger questions from children, and, properly celebrated, these two can lead to the sorts of discussions that Joshua anticipates here. What matters is not just that children are present as we celebrate them, but that we construct our worship so that there is a real opportunity for children to explore the meaning of these events in which we remember and celebrate what Christ has done for us.

3. In the land (4:11–24)

Although there are still points of flashback, from this point on the narrative is written from the perspective of being in the land. Once everyone has crossed, the priests leave the Jordan – though before recounting the return of the waters we again pause to remember the unity of the people as we are told of the leading role played by the trans-Jordan tribes: they crossed in the forefront of the people, just as had previously been agreed.[27] It is clear at this point that Israel enters the land anticipating military[28] action, so at this stage there is no sign that Jericho's fall will also be miraculous. More importantly, however, we also see the fulfilment of Yahweh's promise to exalt Joshua[29] so that he now receives the same level of respect as Moses. The clear parallels between the crossing of the Jordan and that of the Reed Sea obviously enable this, but this has happened because the people have faithfully carried out Joshua's instructions, recognizing that they have come from Yahweh. Joshua began the book as Moses' 'assistant'[30] but now he has become as well respected as Moses. Joshua has developed as a leader, and as the people realize that his faithfulness to Yahweh also works through to them, so their respect for him increases. In this respect he is similar to many other successful leaders whose people respect them more when they see how their leaders' own faithfulness to God leads them too to greater faithfulness and integrity. Like the best

[27] 1:14.
[28] Translating 4:13 is difficult, but there is much to commend in Boling's suggestion, *Joshua*, p. 176, that rather than *40,000* we have here 'forty contingents', which would be considerably fewer than a thousand, though probably more than he allows.
[29] 3:7.
[30] 1:1.

61

leaders, Joshua continues to grow through the book, even though he too will make mistakes.

With Joshua's authority confirmed, the narrative then returns to him directing the priests to leave the Jordan, resuming the action just before that described in verse 11, which mentions them leaving the Jordan. When the priests leave, the waters of the Jordan return, once more overflowing their banks. We now learn that the place where Israel camp on that first night in the land is called Gilgal.[31] It was to become an important shrine in Israel's history, though the significance of the name (or at least, one way it might be significant) is only revealed at 5:9. In spite of its importance in commemorating Israel's entry into the land, worship there would later be corrupted.[32] For Joshua, however, its significance is as a memorial which is intended to trigger intergenerational discussion, and it is with this theme that the chapter closes, returning once again to the questions that children will ask when they see the stones. In this closing speech Joshua makes explicit the links to the crossing of the Reed Sea that were implicit in the narrative. The key point is made in verse 24: these events have happened so that *all the peoples of the earth may know that the hand of the LORD is mighty, that you may fear the LORD your God for ever.*

In this we see that the crossing of the river and its memorial have a dual function. First, they are a continual reminder to Israel of the power of Yahweh, a reminder that it is important for them to recall whenever they face struggles in the future. Israel would go through many difficult times in the future, culminating in the exile, but this memorial was a spur to continued faith in Yahweh. Second, this memorial is also a summons to all peoples to know Yahweh's power. Joshua's words are thus very similar to those of David to Goliath,[33] and remind Israel that they do not exist simply for themselves. Rather, Yahweh has chosen to work through them so that all the clans of the earth might find blessing.[34] Memory strengthens Israel to face their own struggles and also proclaims the greatness of God to all peoples. The challenge for us today is to ensure that our own memorials (whether Lord's Supper, baptism or our own testimonies) do the same, inviting discussion about Jesus, strengthening us in our own pilgrimage, and ensuring that we also always look outwards to a needy world around us. Our worship must, in dependence on the Spirit, also be a testimony to the world of what God has done for us in Christ.

[31] Strictly, 'the Gilgal', so it may not be a proper noun. Meaning 'the circle', there may be several sites with this name.
[32] Hos. 4:15; Amos 4:4; 5:5.
[33] 1 Sam. 17:46–47.
[34] Gen. 12:3.

Joshua 5:1–12
4. Faithfulness first

An interesting historical game is to imagine what might have happened if alternative decisions had been taken at crucial points in the past. Obviously we cannot change the events of history by doing this, but this exercise does help us appreciate much more what was at stake at key times. For example, we might consider the events of late May and early June 1940 at Dunkirk. Here the German forces held the British and French Allied armies trapped with the Channel behind them. Having already lost a good many of their resources the Allies had no means of breaking back into the rest of France, and neither did they have the shipping they needed to rescue nearly 350,000 men. And yet the German forces held back, leading to the miracle of Dunkirk. The reasons for this are not particularly clear, though apparently the Germans had concerns about supplies and the vulnerability of their flanks. However, it is notable that on the day before the evacuation began, King George VI had called for a week of prayer, with this being led by Cosmo Lang, then Archbishop of Canterbury, and churches up and down Britain joined in. Because of wartime censorship few people knew of the challenge the Allied forces faced, but it did not change the commitment to prayer. Historians are not, on the whole, inclined to associate events in history with God's involvement, and as Christians we need to be careful about this too so as to ensure we do not have a theology that is subservient to nationalism; even so, I can't help but wonder what role those prayers played in the miracle of Dunkirk.

Whatever the reason, the Germans chose not to press their advantage, and although it would take time for its significance to be fully appreciated, this would ultimately prove decisive. Looking back from a purely military perspective, we have to ask whether the Germans missed their opportunity. It was a point where they lost the momentum that was theirs. Certainly, most historians believe that they made a major mistake in holding back at Dunkirk. The chance was there, and they did not take it.

The importance of taking a chance that presents itself was also a key theme in Peter Weir's film *Dead Poets Society*. An inspirational English teacher introduces his students to the wonders of poetry, particularly urging them to 'seize the day' (in Latin, *Carpe diem*, itself taken from a poem by Horace). In general terms I suppose we might consider that to be good advice. In the life of the people of God, however, that is not always the case. Indeed, there will be times when for us to seize the moment that is before us is the wrong option. Why? Because it will be us choosing our time for success, it will be our time for claiming the initiative. In addition, although we will often find these moments before us, we cannot seize them if we are aware that they are in conflict with what we know we are supposed to be. No matter how good the opportunity is, we cannot seize the moment when to do so means setting aside what God has already made clear we should do. Faithfulness to God is the priority, and only once we have established that can we know the moments that we truly are to seize.

Faithfulness first, in spite of the apparent opportunity, is the theme that runs through this passage, and though its message is in some ways counter-intuitive it shows us that, even if something that looks like a desirable opportunity lies before us, the priority must always be faithfulness to what it means to be God's people.

1. The opportunity (5:1)

For Israel, the counter-intuitive nature of what it might mean to put faithfulness first is evident from the description here of the terror of the peoples who live in the land when they hear about Israel crossing the Jordan. The assumption is that news of their crossing has travelled fast, but the message they have heard is not simply that the people of Israel have crossed the Jordan; it is that Yahweh *had dried up the waters . . . until they had crossed.* A statement such as this clearly reflects an Israelite perspective as it is unlikely that the Amorites and Canaanites (mentioned here as the representative peoples of the land) would necessarily have passed on word about what Yahweh had done. However, that a miracle had been wrought could certainly have formed part of the news they passed on to one another, and this meant that a god must have been involved. Had they had any spies close to the crossing point (though it would appear that Israel did not cross at a standard ford), they might have seen the ark being carried by the priests and then identified the ark with a deity of some sort. From Israel's perspective, however, what mattered was not the accuracy of their theology so much as knowing themselves that, whichever gods they may have mentioned, it was really Yahweh who had brought them across the Jordan.

The more obviously encouraging report for Israel is not just that the people of the land (or at least some of them) have heard about the miracle; it is that this has had a profound effect on them. The description of this effect matches exactly that used by Rahab to the spies apart from her confession of faith.[1] Since Rahab's words there are a summary written up in Israel's own terminology, it is no surprise to find the same language here, though the connection between the two is surely intentional. The crossing of the Jordan has generated the very response to Israel's presence that Rahab had suggested Yahweh's earlier mighty works had triggered. It was her words (along with the other experiences of the spies) that, when reported to Joshua, had reassured him that Yahweh was indeed giving Israel the land.[2] The implication is clearly that this report would have had the same effect, though the nation as a whole would clearly have been encouraged by the crossing of the Jordan. Thus, if Yahweh was giving Israel the land, the most obvious conclusion to draw was that the conditions Yahweh had promised[3] were being fulfilled. Surely, if the hearts of the land's inhabitants had melted so that *there was no longer any spirit in them*, now was the time to march on and take the land. Looked at objectively, one could well conclude that this was the time to seize the day and to enter into the promises that Yahweh had made. Although Israel had very little in the way of military experience, one can well imagine the officers urging Joshua to go forward and take the land. The argument would be simple: Yahweh has promised the land, he has brought us across the Jordan and he has created the context in which taking the land will be straightforward. It might almost seem a denial of faith *not* to go forward.

This might sound like a promising approach, especially as it draws on the promises of God. It would, however, be fundamentally flawed, and to appreciate this we need to recognize that the narrator of Joshua[4] has placed this verse at just this point for a reason. It is a hinge that joins the crossing of the Jordan with the initial period of Israel's life in the land. Reading this verse in isolation might encourage us only to look forward, but in fact it requires us to look

[1] 2:11.
[2] 2:24.
[3] 1:5.
[4] In this exposition, I have tried to use 'authors' to refer to those who compiled the book and 'narrator' to refer to the voice which is telling the story, though often enough these two blur into one another.

both forward and back. It is placed here so we do both those things before we read further. It sets us up with an expectation of a sudden and successful military campaign, only to stop us before that happens because in fact Israel's initial experiences of taking the land will not follow a classical military approach. However, just as the miraculous events involved in crossing the Jordan were not revealed before it was necessary, so also we do not yet know that Jericho will be captured by miraculous means. Our expectation at this point is, therefore, of a traditional military approach. With this good news, we expect Israel to advance and take Jericho immediately. Surely Israel will not make the sort of mistake the German forces later made at Dunkirk?

However, it was not the time for Israel to do that, and to appreciate the reasons for this we need to realize that this verse also points us back to what has been previously revealed. A key theme has been building through the last three chapters, even if its role is somewhat understated so that we only realize its importance now. It is that we have gradually been given information that enables us to place these events within the year. We were told that Rahab was drying flax on her roof.[5] Cultivated flax was probably not grown in Palestine at the time of Israel's entry into the land, so this was most likely the wild flax that could be collected in the early northern spring. This is confirmed by the narrative aside about the Jordan overflowing its banks throughout harvest,[6] which begins in spring. However, the decisive date reference is given only when it is said that Israel crossed the Jordan 'on the tenth day of the first month'.[7] This creates a further connection with the exodus, and in fact is the date on which the animal for the Passover was selected,[8] flagging up that Passover is only four days later. Looking back, we see that Israel was coming to a point where they had to stop and celebrate what Yahweh had done for them, and even though it might well seem that the opportunity to take the land was before them, 'faithfulness first' meant that they had to follow different priorities. In short, if Yahweh had promised the land to Israel, they had to trust him to provide it, and if the command of Yahweh was to celebrate Passover at this time, that was what was needed.

There are key moments in the lives of the people of God when we too need to recognize that, simply because an opportunity lies before us, it does not mean that it is God's timing for us to take that opportunity, even if what we are doing is consistent with God's purposes

[5] 2:6.
[6] 3:15.
[7] 4:19.
[8] Exod. 12:3. This falls within our March–April.

for us. The key test must always be the consistency of what is possible with the whole witness of Scripture and not only with those points which might seem most conducive to a particular opportunity. This is, admittedly, a difficult point to resolve in practice, and it calls us once again to recognize the importance of reading Scripture in fellowship with others so that we hear its whole counsel rather than just the passages that might be more familiar to us. To take one example, suppose in our particular congregation we have the opportunity to develop a new ministry, one that could make a significant difference to the community around us. Because the opportunity is there, should we take it? The usual answer is that we should; after all, does not the church exist for others, and does not Jesus mandate us to make disciples?[9] But what if we know that the funding that would enable this ministry would come with strings attached which might impede our ministry, so that a claim greater than the gospel itself on that ministry would be possible? Or suppose that establishing that ministry would harm the witness of others? These are complex issues which demand a whole-of-Scripture approach rather than a headlong rush into something simply because the opportunity is there. 'Faithfulness first' demands that we do not seize the opportunity simply because it is there but evaluate it within the framework of all that God requires of us.

2. Restoring the relationship (5:2–9)

'Faithfulness first' for Israel means giving priority to Passover before claiming the land, though doing so shows how closely entry to the land matches the exodus and so reminds them that the exodus was not just about leaving Egypt but also about coming into the land of promise. We now discover that there is an issue that must be addressed before they can celebrate Passover: the males born in the wilderness period have not been circumcised. Since Exodus 12:48 specifies that no uncircumcised male can eat the Passover, it now becomes apparent that Israel are in no condition to celebrate Passover. Not only must the taking of the land be put off until Passover is celebrated, but also Israel must act to restore their relationship with Yahweh so that Passover can be taken properly. It is not that Yahweh was inflexible on this. In 2 Chronicles 30 we read of Hezekiah celebrating Passover at the wrong time of year because so many had failed to consecrate themselves; it was held a month later, with Yahweh heeding Hezekiah's prayer to accept the people's willingness to celebrate it, even if they had not strictly followed the

[9] Matt. 28:16–20.

rules.[10] However, the fact that Israel had just entered the land did not provide special circumstances. On the contrary, in order to appreciate the link with the exodus it was vital that Passover be celebrated at the right time.

It is notable that the initiative does not come from Israel, but from Yahweh. Just as Israel have the land in their sights, Yahweh raises the issue that will prevent them from celebrating Passover. However, Yahweh's words to Joshua, which bookend this section, are not accusatory. Instead they simply direct Joshua to *make flint knives* and circumcise the Israelites *a second time* (2). This phrase might seem odd since one can only be circumcised once. So we then have a lengthy comment from the narrator in verses 4–8 explaining that, although all the men who had come out of Egypt had indeed been circumcised, those born in the wilderness had not. The first generation had died in the wilderness (save for Joshua and Caleb), just as Yahweh had indicated when they failed to accept his promise and enter the land from Kadesh-barnea,[11] but we now discover that their children had not been circumcised. Since male circumcision was meant to be the sign of the covenant that existed between Yahweh and Israel,[12] those who were not circumcised were effectively excluded from the divine promises, and that included the land.[13] So the *second time* in this instance is rather like rebooting the covenant relationship between Israel and Yahweh. The proper process had been followed before, and now must be started again.

So Joshua is to make *flint knives*[14] and circumcise every male. The text then simply records that he did this at Gibeath-haaraloth,[15] a hill somewhere near Gilgal. Now, in terms of military strategy this makes no sense at all, and is counter to the sort of thinking which is often expressed along the lines of 'when you've got them down, keep them down'.[16] Instead, it is effectively a means of crippling the army

---

[10] 2 Chr. 30:18–20.

[11] Num. 14:20–38.

[12] Gen. 17:9–14.

[13] Since circumcision was the mark of covenant commitment, it would be rather like a church today in which no one had been baptized. Cf. Col. 2:11–12.

[14] Possibly alluding to Exod. 4:24–26, where Zipporah also used a flint knife to perform a circumcision, though the details of that passage are notoriously difficult to resolve. See Alec Motyer, *The Message of Exodus: The Days of Our Pilgrimage* (Leicester: IVP, 2005), pp. 92–94. On the other hand, it may simply be that flint was chosen because it would be more hygienic and the knives could be produced more quickly.

[15] The name means 'Hill of foreskins', which is perhaps why most English versions opt for tact and leave the name untranslated in their main text, though some offer a marginal note. Since we do not know exactly where Gilgal is, it is no surprise that we cannot locate this place either.

[16] A somewhat less tasteful version of this was apparently on a poster in Charles Colson's office while he worked for Richard Nixon.

since they will not be able to walk,[17] which is no doubt at least one reason why Israel remain in their camp until all the men have been healed. Thus at one stroke it seems as if the advantage that was hinted at by verse 1 has been thrown away. The delay in progress that this implies means that the Canaanites have time to prepare for Israel's arrival, though their terror explains why they don't attack Israel at this time. And if this had been a traditional military campaign, perhaps Israel would have lost their advantage. However, Israel had to be reminded that their advance into the land was not, in the first instance, a military campaign; it was a journey into receiving the promises of God, and a journey like that needed to be shaped by faithfulness to what Yahweh demanded of them. And faithfulness to God means that we make God's priorities our priorities.[18]

The importance of this is then apparent from the fact that this section closes with another short speech of Yahweh's to Joshua, announcing that on that day the *reproach of Egypt* has been rolled away, which now explains the meaning of the name Gilgal for the location where all this has taken place. Although the name has been used in the previous chapter – and some scholars have concluded that since it means 'circle', the memorial stones there must have been placed in a stone circle – no explanation is given of the name there. Here the explanation is that the name *Gilgal* is similar to the Hebrew verb 'to roll'. Yet more important than the name is the removal of the *reproach of Egypt*. We are not told exactly what this is, though perhaps we are to understand it as the scorn that Egypt poured on Israel. Where Israel had formerly been an enslaved people, now they are free in their own land to serve Yahweh in the celebration of the Passover. The point is thus that Yahweh has summoned his people to faithfulness in spite of the apparent cost involved, and he has honoured their response.

That God honours those who put faithfulness to him above all else is well known, though we should perhaps be careful to express this truth in terms of the community of his people as a whole rather than in terms of every individual. Nevertheless, there are outstanding examples, such as that of Eric Liddell[19] at the 1924 Olympics, when he refused to run in his official event of the men's 100 metres on Sunday and yet went on to win the 400 metres. What happened was

[17] One need only consider what Levi and Simeon were able to do to the inhabitants of Shechem after persuading them to be circumcised in Gen. 34 to appreciate the danger posed to Israel.

[18] Butler, *Joshua*, p. 56, observes, 'Only a circumcised Israel could become a conquering Israel.'

[19] An excellent biography of Liddell is Sally Magnusson, *The Flying Scotsman* (London: Quartet, 1981).

not quite as dramatic as it is portrayed in the film *Chariots of Fire* since he had decided well before the games that he would not run the 100 metres and so began training for the longer event; arguably the greater memorial to Liddell's choice to put faithfulness first was in his decision to remain as a missionary in China even when the rest of his family was evacuated. Although he died there from a brain tumour shortly before the end of the Second World War he is remembered there as someone who embodied the call of Christ throughout his life, something of greater value even than an Olympic medal.

3. Celebrating the relationship (5:10–12)

Only now, with the males circumcised and thus able to celebrate the covenant relationship, do the people of Israel celebrate the Passover. Camped at Gilgal, they keep it on the designated day, the fourteenth day of the first month.[20] That this is a key moment in the narrative is clear from the fact that from this point on the chronological markers become much less specific. The whole of Israel's preparation for entering the land, the crossing of the Jordan and the circumcision of the men have all been building to this climactic moment. The Passover in Egypt had been celebrated in anticipation of the exodus as the point when Israel would head out towards the land Yahweh had promised to the patriarchs. This Passover is celebrated with the knowledge that Yahweh has indeed brought them to the land in fulfilment of his promise, and that therefore they can also anticipate moving beyond their toehold at Gilgal. In other words, it can simultaneously look back with thanksgiving to the things God has done while also looking forward to the additional things he will do. By way of analogy, our celebration of the Lord's Supper is simultaneously a memorial of what God has done for us in the death and resurrection of Jesus, and an anticipation of the day of Jesus' return. It is because we know what God has already done for us that we go forward with hope and confidence, sure because we have already experienced God's faithfulness. This is Israel's position as they celebrate this Passover, with its location on the plains of Jericho already pointing to the next step in their journey – even though the fact that they have paused to celebrate Passover means that they are still not taking advantage of the melted hearts of the inhabitants of Canaan.

The celebration of the Passover also marks a significant change in Israel's life. The day after it is celebrated they eat some of *the produce of the land* (11). This may have been from wild cereal grasses, though

---

[20] Exod. 12:1–28; Lev. 23:5–6.

their first point of claiming the land might have been to take some of the cultivated produce. Whatever the source of the land's produce, it is clear that these were the sorts of foods one ate in a hurry. Although the celebration of Passover is linked with unleavened bread,[21] in both the exodus and here its presence is more a marker of the haste involved in preparing the meals than anything else, though no doubt it is mentioned precisely because it is the sort of food that should be eaten at Passover. Unleavened bread is much quicker to prepare because there is no need to wait for the dough to rise. Likewise, *parched grain* is a very simple and quick meal, more or less the closest the ancient world came to a takeaway or at least a packed lunch; it was, for example, the food available for a meal when Boaz met Ruth.[22] These are effectively the first fruits of Israel's life in the land, though their means of acquiring them continues to remind them that it is Yahweh who provides for them.

They have, in faithfulness to the call of God, paused to prepare for and then celebrate Passover, and this first meal of the land's produce is effectively the means by which Yahweh acknowledges their faithfulness while also pointing them to what lies ahead. It is a simple provision, and it is important to note that although God chooses to lavish us richly with every spiritual blessing,[23] the form that these blessings can take is often quite simple. Indeed, the simplicity of this provision is in marked contrast to the manna which was Israel's staple throughout their time in the wilderness,[24] a miraculous provision for that time and one which ceased from the day after Israel first ate from the land's produce. Yet both the simple meal prepared from the local grains and the manna were divine provision; though one was obviously 'miraculous' while the other was more typical of the daily experience of most of us (even if various food producers and supermarkets have had a hand on the way), there is no hierarchy here in terms of the quality of God's provision. In both cases, God has provided for his people, granting them what they need not only to survive but also to flourish.

The absence of any hierarchy here is important, especially as we think about how God continues to provide for his people today. My wife and I spent a number of years working in theological colleges in Africa, and there were times when the mission budget dried up and we would genuinely wonder how we would eat for that month. Yet every time that happened, funds would come in that we had not

---

[21] It should be noted that no mention is made of the other foods associated with the Passover here, though no conclusions can be drawn from this.

[22] Ruth 2:14.

[23] Eph. 1:3.

[24] Exod. 16:35.

expected, funds that had often been raised some time earlier and yet for whatever reason only reached us at the point when we needed them, in amounts that were virtually identical to the shortfall. They were, for us, like manna from heaven. I continue to be thankful to God for his provision through his people at those times. But should I not be equally thankful that through the faithfulness of God's people we usually had enough anyway? A dramatic story of God's provision is naturally easier to tell, and people will join us in giving thanks, but most of the time God provided for us in more 'routine' ways. Likewise, for Israel from this point it was the more routine means by which God would provide, but that too was part of his gift of the land.

Are there, then, times when we as the people of God must seize the day? No doubt there are. This passage, however, helps to put that concept into its proper context. Opportunities may well arise, but when they do so we can only take them when that is consistent with what it means to be faithful to God in Christ. We cannot put aside the things that we are called to do and be, no matter how enticing the opportunity. For Israel, that here meant virtually crippling their army and pausing to celebrate Passover. Yet through this seemingly counter-intuitive approach they were now prepared to receive God's promise of land. The days we seize can only be those when in every way we glorify God – and we need a rich grounding in Scripture and the leading of the Spirit to discern when they are. However, it is vital for us to remember that it is in faithfulness that we most truly experience God's provision for us.

Joshua 5:13 – 6:27
5. Yahweh fought the battle of Jericho

It is remarkable how often things we learn as children can stay with us as adults, and perhaps even more remarkable how those things sometimes stay with us in the face of evidence to the contrary. For example, when I was younger I learnt the traditional song 'Joshua fought the battle of Jericho'. The words are well known (though with some variations):

> *Joshua fought the battle of Jericho,*
> *Jericho, Jericho,*
> *Joshua fought the battle of Jericho,*
> *And the walls came tumbling down.*

It has a catchy tune, as well as the benefit of pointing us to the biblical text, and some of the subsequent verses refer to other events while providing hope in the present. I have no particular qualms about those verses, but we ought to recognize a fundamental problem with this opening verse: simply that it is Yahweh, not Joshua, who fought the battle of Jericho.[1] Indeed, the battle itself is not really the focus of this narrative since its outcome is announced in advance,[2] and as we shall see the 'battle' is much more like an extended act of worship. Rather, the focus is on how Yahweh summons his people to obedience through Joshua and how he grants them his gifts in their obedience. Put simply, God's people advance in God's purposes for them when they follow God's directions for them.

---

[1] Hence Dale Ralph Davis, *No Falling Words: Expositions of the Book of Joshua* (Grand Rapids: Baker, 1988), p. 51, rather trenchantly heads his exposition of this passage 'Joshua Did *Not* Fight the Battle of Jericho'.
[2] 6:2.

1. Divine preparation (5:13 – 6:5)

In many ways, the act of circumcision and celebration of Passover[3] have acted as preparation for Israel's occupation of the land, representing the point where they are definitively in it with no going back. They cannot cross the flooded river on their own, and in any case the manna has ceased, so they need to live in the land if they are to sustain themselves since that is now the means by which Yahweh is providing for them. Equally, the circumcision and Passover are the points that bring the story of the entry into the land to a close as the first eating of food from the land decisively announces that the time in the wilderness has ended. Israel has to go forward and claim Yahweh's gift of the land, and it is this that will be the focus of the text until the end of chapter 12. However, Jericho has stood as the main barrier to this almost from the beginning. It was to Jericho that Joshua sent the spies,[4] while Jericho stood as the point of reference as Israel entered the land,[5] prepared for battle[6] and celebrated Passover.[7] Although the account of its capture has been delayed within the narrative, we have now reached the point that it must be taken if Israel is to claim the land.

a. Joshua and Yahweh's commander (5:13–15)

Before the narrative describes the means by which the city was taken, there is a strange, numinous encounter between Joshua and a mysterious figure. In the period while Joshua is by Jericho he is apparently alone one day when he sees an armed figure. This figure is called a *man*, perhaps because that is how Joshua initially interprets what he sees, though as the man speaks we discover that he is rather more than this. The man is clearly a warrior, and since Joshua sees him with his sword drawn he is on duty. Although this could be understood as a threatening stance,[8] Joshua still approaches the man to ask if he is with Israel or their adversaries. The question is perfectly reasonable, but the answer immediately makes clear that this is no ordinary man since he has come as the commander of Yahweh's army. As such, he is neither for Israel nor for their adversaries. Instead, he is there to do Yahweh's will. It is no wonder that Joshua falls to

---

[3] 5:1–12.
[4] Josh. 2.
[5] 3:16.
[6] 4:13, 19.
[7] 5:10.
[8] Cf. Num. 22:23; 1 Chr. 21:16.

the ground before him,[9] recognizing that as the commander[10] of Yahweh's army he must have a message for him. And indeed there is a message, though a curious one, as the man directs Joshua to remove his sandals because the place he is standing on is holy ground – something Joshua does.

We might expect more, but that is all we get. It seems that a story which could have been much longer is stopped abruptly because apparently that is all we need to know. But why? The most obvious reason is the clear parallel here with Moses' encounter with God at the burning bush, where he too was to remove his sandals because the ground was holy.[11] Parallels between Moses and Joshua have been prominent in the opening chapters of the book, and this one is particularly strong. The saying thus reaffirms Yahweh's promise to be with Joshua just as he was with Moses.[12] This will be particularly important as Israel face their first example of siege warfare. Although Jericho will fall in a highly remarkable way, Joshua does not yet know this, but he has now been encouraged to know not only of Yahweh's presence, but also of Yahweh's own forces. Indeed, that this is holy ground can only mean that Yahweh is present.[13] We therefore do not need to know more about this encounter (however much we might wish to!) because it is enough to know that God continues to encourage his servant by demonstrating that his presence is not simply a matter of words that are uttered. When God is present with his people, he is present with power. It is for this reason that the writer to the Hebrews, clearly reflecting on God's promise to be with Joshua, cites the reassurance of God's presence found in Psalm 118:6.[14] To a people who struggled with the cost of their faith, this same reassurance provided them with a reason to continue, even as it now offers hope to Joshua himself.

b. Joshua and Yahweh's instructions (6:1–5)

After the remarkable encounter with this heavenly being, the opening verse of chapter 6 might seem a little pedestrian, though it performs some important narrative functions. First, by noting that Jericho is

[9] *Worshipped* here probably has the sense of 'to prostrate oneself' rather than treating the man as God.

[10] As *my lord* is pointed in Hebrew, Joshua uses this as a polite form of address rather than the form used when it refers to God, suggesting that the common practice of capitalizing 'Lord' in most English versions might be misleading. Most likely, the text is kept intentionally ambiguous.

[11] Exod. 3:1–6.

[12] Josh. 1:5.

[13] Cf. Hubbard, *Joshua*, p. 186.

[14] Heb. 13:6.

completely *shut up* it points back to 2:7, reminding us that Rahab's story is not yet resolved. Second, it indicates that Israel now faces a new challenge – siege warfare. Clearly prepared for a difficult siege, Jericho allows no-one out or in, so there are not even foraging parties bringing in grains to sustain the residents. However, as somewhere completely closed up there is no easy access for Israel, and as a people who have previously been in the wilderness they have no military experience in dealing with this. They need Yahweh's aid to take the town, and since the town controls the region, they need to take the town.

The form that aid takes is initiated in verses 2–5. Since verse 1 is clearly an aside, it is not impossible that Yahweh is here speaking through the commander, though this is not necessary. The crucial point is that even before the battle has begun Yahweh announces the result. Military strategy does not matter. What counts is that before battle has commenced, Yahweh has already won. Just as he has already given the land to Israel – though they must still claim it – so also he has given Jericho, its king and its fighting forces into Israel's power. Once again, we see the balance that is retained throughout the book between the certainty of God's promises to his people and their need to claim them. To take an analogy from the New Testament for Christians today (since we are not bound to any one land), we are simultaneously a people who are already holy because of what Jesus has done for us, and a people who are called to holiness. Objectively, the reality is already ours, but the experience is still something that we are to claim as we walk with God in dependence on his Spirit. This is why Paul's wonderful prayer in Ephesians 3:14–19 both looks to what God has already given us and asks that we would experience it fully. In Jesus, the victory is already won, but its fruits are to be claimed.

Israel too are to claim God's promise to them, though it quickly becomes apparent that this is not to happen in any routine way. Instead, they are to capture Jericho in what is effectively an extended act of worship. Jericho will not fall to military strategy but rather to a people who are submitted to doing God's will, because no matter how inexperienced Israel were in the conduct of siege warfare, we can be reasonably confident that this was *not* a plan they would have come up with themselves.[15] It was an exercise in trusting God, believing that if he had promised and was present, they would indeed receive the promise. The plan itself is simple – Israel's forces are to march around the city once with seven priests in the middle blowing

[15] Though when the Crusaders attempted to replicate it at Jerusalem in 1099 it was notably less successful.

their ram's-horn trumpets in front of the ark, symbolizing Yahweh's presence. They are to do this for six days, and then on the seventh march around the city seven times. When there is a long blast on the horn, the people are to give a great shout and the walls will come down. Then everyone can go straight ahead into the city. Militarily it makes no sense, unless one remembers the presence of Yahweh's army – and then it becomes a reminder that it is Yahweh, and not Joshua, who is fighting the battle of Jericho.

Although it is an odd plan, it is not an impossible one. Marching around the city on a single day, even seven times, would be far from challenging. Although the archaeology of Jericho at this time[16] is much disputed, it seems clear that Jericho was not a large site. It is important to note that the text never claims that it was,[17] and portrayals of it as a large, fortified town (long a standard element of children's Bibles) emerge from the history of interpretation instead. We do face the problem that extensive erosion of the site (which is not disputed) means that there is little evidence of settlement in the Late Bronze Age (LBA),[18] though in fact a largish central house was found which can be dated to LBA. There is also evidence of a successful attack, possibly in this period, as there is a burn layer which can be dated to the spring because of the grains found in it. All of this is consistent with the biblical material. Instead of Jericho having separate walls, however, Joshua most likely presents a town whose outer houses are joined in a sort of terrace to form a defensive wall that blocks off the inner town from the outer world rather than major fortifications. This is consistent with Rahab being able to lower the spies from her window and also to hide the spies on her roof, since if the walls were primarily defensive fortifications she would have hidden them in full view of the defending troops. It may well be, therefore, that the frequently made claim that the absence of evidence at Jericho disproves the biblical material is misplaced, as it rejects a history of interpretation rather than the text itself. That Jericho was a relatively small LBA city (occupying an area the size

[16] Among those who accept that there was a conquest, it is normally dated to either c.1400 or c.1250 BC. For our purposes it is not necessary to choose, though my preference would be for 1250 BC. In either case, we are dealing with the Late Bronze Age, though with the later date we are verging on the Early Iron Age. See further, Iain Provan, V. Phillips Long and Tremper Longman III, *A Biblical History of Israel* (Louisville: Westminster John Knox, 2003), pp. 138–192. For a helpful summary of the archaeological material, see Pekka M. A. Pitkänen, *Joshua* (Nottingham: Apollos, 2010), pp. 162–169.

[17] Unlike Hazor in Josh. 11.

[18] Earlier archaeologists believed that a collapsed wall was to be dated to the time of Joshua, but most now date it a millennium earlier. Some recent studies have challenged this, so we may be in for a new debate about the archaeology of Jericho.

of a couple of football pitches at most, now mostly eroded) does not reduce the importance of its capture since it could still be locked up and did have armed forces, and it was these that Yahweh overcame. God may well have asked Israel to do something odd to capture the city, but what Israel was commanded to do within that plan was far from impossible.

2. Divine warfare (6:6–21)

Israel are to capture Jericho by their faithfulness to Yahweh's command, and the goal of this section is to show that this is exactly what happens. Joshua initially summons the priests, directing them to take up the ark, with seven of them to take their ram's-horn trumpets to blow before it. He then directs the people to *Go forward*[19] and march round the city with the armed men ahead of the ark. Joshua has done as Yahweh commanded, and we are then told that the people do as Yahweh commanded – though verse 10 notes an additional point: that Joshua commands the people to be silent until they are summoned to shout. There was clearly to be no confusion as to the shout, perhaps as Joshua was aware that the war cry was an important element of ancient warfare and knew that there would be a natural inclination to shout at the defenders, much as opposing football fans seek to provoke one another through their chants today. Even without anything being said by the people, however, it would have been a fairly noisy procession going around the city each day, with the trumpets offering blasts of sound rather than anything tuneful. One could imagine that this was some sort of psychological warfare. Indeed, a children's video I have of the story[20] imagines Jericho's king complaining about the noise of the trumpets and the absence of any visible representation of a god, but in fact the narrative steadfastly refuses to enter into any such speculation. Rather, by its emphasis on the role of the priests and the ark we are reminded that the war that was being fought was Yahweh's war, and that Israel's strategy was thus one of engaging in a ritual procession that acknowledged this. It might not be recognizable to many today as an act of worship – and as a one-off moment in Israel's history it is rather difficult to reproduce in our own context

---

[19] The verb used here is the same as that for when Israel was to cross the Jordan (1:2; 3:6; 4:5), which along with the role of the priests and the ark shows the close link between these events.

[20] A somewhat expurgated version of the story – clearly the producers liked the idea of the walls coming down but, like many since then, rather balked at what happened to the inhabitants of the town when telling the story for children. Madvig, 'Joshua', p. 278, offers a similar interpretation.

– but that is effectively what it was. Crossing the Jordan and celebrating Passover have both had a strong focus on worship, and that
carries over into the capture of Jericho. A people who obey God and
receive his promises are thus a people who are committed to the
worship of God, though it is always worship that is rooted in
the concrete reality of life. In other words, as Israel enter the land
and prepare to take the first city,[21] their life is shaped by worship
that draws on what they have already experienced, and it is this that
prepares them for what follows. Obviously, Israel's worship could
not always reflect their circumstances as immediately as this, though
later there were perhaps moments when these events were remembered;[22] but if these times generated structures for worship that could
later be used it shows that they, like the stones at Gilgal, were not
simply events that happened in the past. Rather, they were a continual
source of nourishment for God's people. However, Joshua insists
that this was not simply a ritual that could be enacted. Rather,
worship patterns emerge from the discovery of what God has done
in actual experience, and it is this that shapes our worship in future,
worship that is sustaining and hopeful.

From verse 12 we go from a general summary back to the first day
of Israel circling Jericho, though the statement *Joshua rose early*
deliberately echoes 3:1, reminding readers that just as Israel crossed
the Jordan by Yahweh's miraculous intervention, so also they will
take Jericho. Again, the concern is to show that Israel have done
exactly as Yahweh commanded, and this is carried on to record their
obedience on the second day. However, from this point we then pass
straight to the seventh day since the opening days have established
the pattern to be followed. Even for a relatively small site, an earlier
start is needed to get around the city seven times, so the people of
Israel rise at dawn. That Israel are obedient is stressed by the narrator
noting that this was the only day on which they marched seven times
around the city. Their obedience is then shown as Joshua directs the
people at the appropriate point to shout, *for the LORD has given you
the city* (16). Again, what is stressed is that it is Yahweh who is giving
the city. Israel simply need to obey.

Nevertheless, before the shout itself is recorded Joshua offers some
further explanations. First, everything in the city is to be devoted to
destruction. However, Rahab and everyone in her house are to be
left alive because of the oath sworn by the spies to her. There is no
attempt to find a way out of this oath, but the importance of devoting

[21] Gilgal would appear to have been an unoccupied site.
[22] For example, Ps. 149 might draw on the experiences of the conquest, while
Ps. 114 reflects on the crossing of the Jordan, though the conquest does not play a
major role in Psalms.

everything else to destruction is emphasized when Joshua then instructs the people to be sure to keep themselves from everything devoted to destruction, lest they *bring trouble*[23] upon Israel. Indeed, should they take anything that is devoted to destruction, they will make themselves liable for devotion to destruction. Instead, everything is to go into Yahweh's treasury. Only after these additional instructions does Israel shout, with the walls collapsing as Yahweh had said and the people able to enter the city directly. And everyone in the city, with all the livestock, is devoted to destruction. God's people have obeyed him, and he has fulfilled his promise to them.

In spite of this, this passage has troubled many readers, seeming to fuel the sorts of attacks that some, including Richard Dawkins,[24] regularly make against Christian faith. Certainly the idea of devoting people and objects to destruction sounds suspiciously like what is known today as the war crime of genocide. Is there a way that we can understand and appropriate this for Christian faith, or should we be like those who suggest that it is something we must reject as a barbarous remnant from the past?[25] In many ways it would be easier to take the latter approach, one that seemingly sets the New Testament against the Old – but in fact many images in the book of Revelation look suspiciously like this, as do other texts which discuss God's final judgment.[26] Similarly, attempts to treat this concept as a myth which really stands for the importance of shaping community identity seem inadequate because, even as a myth with a different function from the text's surface meaning, the text still says these things;[27] that is, reading the text *ahistorically* does not

[23] Joshua's verb here particularly prepares readers for the events of chapter 7 where Achan's sin leads to the valley being called 'Achor', which has the same root as the verb *bring trouble*.

[24] See, for example, *The God Delusion*, p. 31.

[25] So Mann, *Former Prophets*, p. 22, insisting this is a necessary theological judgment.

[26] See Christopher J. H. Wright, *The God I Don't Understand: Reflections on Tough Questions of Faith* (Grand Rapids: Zondervan, 2008), pp. 80–81. For an overview of the concept, see J. P. U. Lilley, 'Understanding the *ḤEREM*', *Tyndale Bulletin* 44 (1993), pp. 160–177; different responses to it are admirably summarized in Christian Hofreiter, 'Genocide in Deuteronomy and Christian Interpretation', in David G. Firth and Philip S. Johnston (eds), *Interpreting Deuteronomy: Issues and Approaches* (Nottingham: Apollos, 2012), pp. 240–262.

[27] See Douglas S. Earl, *Reading Joshua as Christian Scripture* (Winona Lake: Eisenbrauns, 2010). A briefer summation of his views can be found in his *The Joshua Delusion? Rethinking Genocide in the Bible*, with a response by Christopher J. H. Wright (Cambridge: James Clarke & Co., 2010). Earl's approach is profoundly theological and with strong convictions about the importance of Scripture, and thus well worth reading. Although it merits a longer response than can be offered here, it seems to make assumptions about the New Testament in relation to the Old that need to be challenged.

resolve the fact that it still uses this sort of imagery. However, if Joshua reflects the entry of Israel into the land, these issues become more acute. Likewise, suggesting that we transfer such language to the realm only of spiritual warfare must be judged insufficient because, although the Canaanites were understood as a potential snare to the Israelites within God's mission, they were not just a spiritual problem.[28]

A key principle in all such Old Testament examples that are associated with warfare is that Yahweh is engaging with his enemies through Israel. It is not something that Israel may initiate. Thus Israel are not attacking Jericho simply because they want to occupy some land; they are attacking a people who are Yahweh's enemies, with the warning that, should Israel transgress the devoted things and claim them for themselves, they too will become Yahweh's enemies. To understand this we have to go back to Genesis 15:16, when Yahweh promised the land to Abram. There it is stated that Abram's heirs could not yet claim the land because 'the iniquity of the Amorites is not yet complete'. So Israel's entry into the land and receipt of it was to be Yahweh's judgment on the occupants of the land. In this case, then, the judgment on those inhabitants was a portent of the final judgment, something the New Testament describes in language not dissimilar to that used here.[29] This is God's justice, and it was because the people of Israel were not to become ensnared by them that they were not to enter into relationships with them.[30]

Yet in spite of this, Rahab and her family are spared, something Deuteronomy does not seem to countenance. Is this in breach of the commandment?[31] The question becomes more acute when we consider the Gibeonites in chapter 9. However, since Joshua 11:12–15 affirms Joshua's absolute obedience, this seems unlikely. Rather, we need to read the devotion of humans, livestock and objects to destruction on a graded scale. Total devotion of everything was possible, but not something Yahweh always demanded; indeed, Jericho is the only example in Joshua.[32] In other instances the demand could be less severe. However, when people gave their allegiance to Yahweh and thus became holy by belonging to him (rather than by being devoted to destruction, which had the same effect), they

[28] Tremper Longman III and Daniel G. Reid, *God Is A Warrior* (Grand Rapids: Zondervan, 1995), esp. pp. 136–164, note how one dimension of Paul's thought moves in this direction, but recognize that this is not the whole story.

[29] E.g. Rev. 20:7–10.

[30] Deut. 7:1–5; 20:16–18.

[31] So Hawk, *Every Promise Fulfilled*, pp. 59–71.

[32] Though note Saul's responsibility towards Amalek in 1 Sam. 15.

were no longer liable to such destruction. The issue, then, turns on
whether or not a people had set themselves as Yahweh's enemy. Israel
could not initiate such a war; and even here it seems that grace
remained a possibility. God's holiness ultimately brooks no opposition, but it always contains at least an implicit invitation to change,
'illustrating the priority of mercy over judgment'.[33]

3. Divine outcome (6:22–27)

When Israel obey, the outcome is God's outcome. And it is an
outcome of both judgment and salvation – judgment on the sinful
people of Jericho, and salvation for Rahab and her family – and
further evidence of Yahweh's presence with Joshua.

The city was destroyed as an act of obedience. However, Rahab
was saved as another act of obedience because she had already
committed herself to Yahweh. Even in the Old Testament there
is a very real sense that the people of God are those who commit
themselves to Yahweh, and that his salvation is more important
than anything else – a salvation that is apparent in the fact that the
family of Rahab could still be identified generations later when
the book of Joshua was written. And, of course, her line probably
continued into the genealogy of Jesus.

There is a final act of obedience on the part of Joshua. Since
Yahweh has decreed the destruction of the city, Joshua announces a
curse on whoever rebuilds what Yahweh has destroyed. This is not
an act of cruelty but obedience, an act that wants what Yahweh
wants. Sadly, this curse had its outcome four hundred years later
when Hiel of Bethel rebuilt the city (1 Kgs 16:34).

This, then, is a powerful story. It offers us a battle plan that is so
bizarre that no-one in his or her right mind would follow it – unless,
of course, it was an opportunity to obey Yahweh. Then , however,
it does make sense, since the foolishness of God is wiser than the
wisdom of this world.[34] Here, then, is the central issue for us today:
are we prepared to go with the foolishness of God, or do we fear
that our obedience will make us seem less than we would like? After
all, it is easy to hold back from obedience! And so this story is a
powerful proclamation of the truth to us: if we want to achieve God's
purposes, the only option is to do so in God's way.

This does not mean us walking around things, as some exponents
of 'spiritual warfare' would have it. It does, however, mean that our
weapons are those of prayer, care and sharing. They may not seem

[33] Hawk, *Joshua in 3-D*, p. 73.
[34] 1 Cor. 1:25.

powerful on their own, but used in obedience to our Lord they are the weapons that will see us advance towards the purposes that God has for us. Indeed, we will not win the battle any more than Joshua did. God will win it for us.

Joshua 7:1 – 8:29
6. Yahweh at war against sin

The story of the capture of Jericho ended on a triumphant note, with the comment that Yahweh was with Joshua and 'his fame was in all the land'.[1] Israel had obeyed Yahweh's somewhat unorthodox instructions for the capture of the city so that only Rahab and her family had survived. On the basis of those events one might expect Israel now to sweep triumphantly across the land, claiming all that Yahweh had promised. After all, he had promised to be with Joshua so that no-one could resist him,[2] and Jericho was obvious evidence for this. What Rahab had confessed was indeed happening: Yahweh was giving Israel the land.[3] Certainly Israel's actions here suggest that they believe this is the case – but there are also clues that things are not quite as simple as that. When Joshua encountered the commander of Yahweh's army and asked if he was for Israel or their enemies, the commander had responded that he was there only to do Yahweh's bidding.[4] Israel could not presume that Yahweh would fight for them; that depended on them continuing to practise Yahweh's will. Likewise, when giving instructions about what was to be done to Jericho Joshua had warned Israel not to take any of the devoted items because to do so would make them liable for destruction and bring trouble on them.[5] Because the victory at Jericho was so complete we might read over these notes, but they have been carefully woven into the narrative so that at the point where it seems Israel must triumph, we are able to realize why things go spectacularly wrong at Ai. Indeed, Joshua's warning at 6:18 might

[1] 6:27.
[2] 1:5.
[3] 2:9.
[4] 5:13–14.
[5] 6:18.

almost be the text around which the events recorded in this much longer narrative have been built.[6]

Before exploring this story in detail we should therefore pause and take our bearings, because although not as well known as the story of Jericho, this one is intentionally paired with it to provide contrast. Jericho represents the possibility for Israel when they obey Yahweh. By contrast, Ai shows how sin within Israel makes them Yahweh's enemies, though sin will not have the last word. Nevertheless, this is a story that shows that a little sin goes a long way, and just as a small piece of yeast affects a whole lump of dough,[7] so also the sin of one affects the whole community. In spite of claims that certain activities 'do not hurt anyone else' and should therefore be accepted, this passage is clear that sin does not work that way. Sin is never isolated because that sin will affect other aspects of our life and, even if only indirectly, the community of which we are a part. So here, because of the sin of one man, Israel was unable to take the small town of Ai. Indeed, because of Achan's sin, Israel now found itself in the position of being Yahweh's enemy, meaning that until the people had dealt with their own sin they were in the same position as the Canaanites. There is thus a great irony in that the previous chapter had concluded with the rescue of Rahab and her family – the Canaanites who had confessed Yahweh and were thus included with Israel – while here Achan's sin means he and his family become (effectively) Canaanites, thereby taking Israel to the brink of the same position. Thus it becomes clear that Yahweh's giving the land to Israel is not a reward for their righteousness, but rather is because of Yahweh's war against sin.[8] An Israel that steps outside of the covenant is no better off than a Canaanite,[9] whereas a Canaanite who accepts the covenant enjoys its blessings. It is this fundamental point which distinguishes the events in Canaan from genocide, even though the charge is routinely made. Yahweh is not some petty national deity who demonizes the 'other'; he is the God of all the earth whose purpose is to bring all back into relationship with himself, and who therefore also works with a restored Israel so they can finally take Ai.

---

[6] In the same way that ch. 6 prepares for ch. 7, so also ch. 7 prepares for ch. 22, again pointing to the care with which Joshua has been written.

[7] 1 Cor. 5:6; Gal. 5:9.

[8] Deut. 9:4–5.

[9] Indeed, Achan's name contains the same consonants as the word 'Canaan'. Since it is difficult to associate his name with a known Hebrew root, it may be that his name is given as an anagram of Canaan, so that his actual name is unknown. Similarly, Hawk, *Joshua in 3-D*, p. 87.

1. The sin of Achan (7:1–26)

a. Defeat at Ai (7:1–9)

After success, therefore, comes failure – and sin is at the heart of that failure. Indeed, in this case the importance of sin is highlighted at the very beginning as we are told that the people of Israel *broke faith* (1) in respect of the things devoted to destruction at Jericho. Although the text then immediately goes on to identify Achan as the individual responsible for this because he took some of the devoted items, he is not isolated from the community as a whole; it is still *Israel* that has broken faith with Yahweh. That Achan is part of a wider community is immediately established by his lengthy genealogy, though this also prepares us for the process by which he will be revealed as the culprit. Yahweh has given Jericho to Israel but not permitted them to take any spoil, and Israel have broken faith. The verb used here can refer to marital unfaithfulness,[10] and though it is more commonly used to describe unfaithfulness to God, this background points to the pain that Yahweh experiences in his people's sin. This corporate approach to sin stands in marked contrast to the individualism that typifies much of Western society, and which tends to assume that something is acceptable if it does not overtly hurt anyone else. This, however, is to fail to recognize that no sin, whether of commission or omission, stands in isolation. We are embedded within communities, and no sin is ever purely personal; rather, all sin is interpersonal. Although in some cases it is easier to see how it affects others, we should not imagine that our sin has no wider impacts.

Only when Israel's sin has been made clear do we begin what might look like a repeat of Jericho. As before, Joshua sends out spies, this time heading to Ai, a town roughly ten miles west of Jericho. Although the general area can be identified, the exact location of this city is much debated. For many years it was assumed to be et-Tell,[11] a site that shows signs of only very limited settlement in the time of Joshua and which was therefore a parade example for those who wished to claim that the book of Joshua does not reflect historical reality. However, there were always those who disputed this location, and there is now growing evidence that Ai might be identified with Khirbet el-Maqatir. These sites are quite close to one another, though

[10] Num. 5:27.

[11] Identifying Ai as et-Tell has led to the widespread claim that Ai (which in the Hebrew text is always '*the* Ai') means 'the ruin', though this suggestion comes from the fact that the Arabic means 'the mound (of a ruin)'. But as Howard, *Joshua*, p. 179, makes clear, there is no clear linguistic case for linking these terms.

identifying the latter as Ai means identifying a different site for Bethel. However, the traditional identifications make it difficult to find a site for Beth-aven, which is also supposed to be in the area.[12] This is a matter of considerable debate, but it is worth noting that the archaeologist excavating the site claimed to have found Bronze Age fortifications in the 2012 excavation season, though at the time of writing this claim is only found on his website,[13] not in a full report that can be assessed by other archaeologists. There is not yet conclusive evidence to support this identification, and we must always be careful of trying to make the archaeology fit our interpretation of the Bible; nevertheless, it does at least point to a strong possibility that the site of Ai is Khirbet el-Maqatir.

The sending of the spies is deliberately reminiscent of the events at Jericho, except that this time the spies seem to be fairly efficient and actually return with information that could be militarily significant. Joshua does not mention a particular town they are to spy out, presumably because he does not know what the next fortified town will be, but the spies find their way to Ai, following a road into the central highlands, one that will take them to a strategic point that meets the main north–south road. What they find is a small town, somewhere that does not require the effort of taking all Israel into the hills,[14] needing only two or three large units.[15] What is notably lacking in all this is any reference to Yahweh, perhaps suggesting that Israel are overconfident and have lost sight of the fact that their reason for being in the land is to glorify God, though the text never makes this explicit. Joshua follows their advice, but this force is routed by the men of Ai, fleeing before them with thirty-six dying on the way to Shebarim.[16] The number of casualties is not large overall, but it is thirty-six more than died at Jericho. More worrying, though, is that it is now the hearts of the Israelites that melt and become like water. Melting hearts have previously been the domain

---

[12] On the case for making these identifications, see Bryant G. Wood, 'The Search for Joshua's Ai', in Richard S. Hess, Gerald A. Klingbeil and Paul Ray Jr. (eds), *Critical Issues in Early Israelite History* (Winona Lake: Eisenbrauns, 2008), pp. 205–240.

[13] Bryant G. Wood, 'Outstanding Finds Made at Khirbet el-Maqatir: May 28–June 8, 2012', Associates for Biblical Research, 17 July 2012, http://www. biblearchaeology.org / post / 2012 / 07 / 17 / Outstanding-Finds-Made-at-Khirbet-el-Maqatir-May-28e28093June-8-2012.aspx.

[14] Ai is well over 3,000 feet higher than Jericho, and so a substantial journey for Israel's forces over a relatively short distance.

[15] Or *thousand*. But with Hess, *Joshua*, p. 146, it is better to understand this as describing large companies rather than a specific number.

[16] This location is unknown, and indeed it is not clear that it is a proper noun – HCSB, for example, translates the word as 'Quarries', reflecting the fact that the root on which it is based means 'to break'.

of the Canaanites[17] but this condition now affects Israel. Because of sin the people of Israel have become indistinguishable from the Canaanites. Indeed, whenever God's people become mired in sin, we become indistinguishable from those around us.

If there were hints of overconfidence when Israel first set out against Ai, the same is not true when Joshua, along with the elders, responds on behalf of the nation, with him tearing his clothes in a typical attitude of mourning[18] and them all putting dust on their heads as they fall before the ark. The ark here clearly represents Yahweh's presence among his people, though its involvement in both the crossing of the Jordan[19] and the capture of Jericho[20] is a reminder that this is a powerful presence. However, although Joshua at least knows he has to ask Yahweh what has gone wrong, his prayer shows that he is not looking in the right direction. Joshua is, perhaps, typical of many in not seeing that the problem lies within. Instead, his prayer is not unlike many of the complaint psalms[21] in believing that Yahweh himself has caused the problem – a type of prayer that the Old Testament as a whole deems acceptable even if such a prayer has to be open to God showing an alternative way of seeing things. Joshua's prayer also echoes the earlier prayers of Moses in Numbers 14:13–19 (following the initial spying out of the land) in its concern for Yahweh's renown, though it is flawed in that it assumes that this one defeat will initiate a run of Canaanite victories that will lead to Israel being destroyed. However, where Moses' prayer had been a response to Yahweh's announcing punishment on Israel, Joshua's prayer assumes that Yahweh has for some reason decided to give Israel over to their enemies. So, although Joshua is right to pray and to draw on the model of other biblical prayers in his concern for Yahweh's renown, his prayer shows that he is operating from a flawed perception.

In spite of its flaws, or perhaps even because of them, this prayer still has much to teach us about a theology of prayer. In my experience, many regard prayer as a means by which we bring our requests – perhaps with 'if you will' or some such phrase attached – to God in the expectation (or hope) that he will answer them. There is nothing intrinsically wrong with this provided our prayer is, like Joshua's, shaped by a concern for God's glory and is not simply the divine equivalent of a spot of online shopping, where we then sit back and await the delivery of the request. Yet prayer is much more

[17] 2:9–10; 5:1.
[18] Compare e.g. Job 1:20.
[19] 3:8–13.
[20] 6:4–14.
[21] E.g. Ps. 44.

than asking, or even interceding. Prayer is, more fundamentally, a means by which we consciously place ourselves in the presence of God in Christ and seek to bring our own lives and practices into line with the purposes of God. This will involve intercession and bringing requests to God, but it will also mean times when we discover that, however well intentioned were our requests in prayer, they are contrary to God's purposes. Prayer is not when we reshape God's purposes to get what we want; it is an act whereby God reshapes us so we can recognize what he is actually doing and asking of us. As that happens, we will discover that the things we ask of God will themselves change.

b. Achan's sin revealed (7:10–26)

Yahweh's response to Joshua shows that he has indeed heard Joshua's prayer, but that he is not prepared to accept its fundamental premise. Israel has not failed to capture Ai because of a failure on Yahweh's part; the failure is because of Israel's sin. Joshua does not receive the response to his prayer that he wants, but he does receive the response that he needs. Indeed, Yahweh's reply is terse and direct; commanding Joshua to stand up and then asking why he has fallen on his face is effectively telling him that his approach is wrong. The nature of Joshua's error is then made immediately clear as Yahweh points to the reality of sin. The vocabulary for sin here is well developed, with two more general comments (*Israel has sinned; they have transgressed my covenant*) followed by the more specific allegations of their having *taken some of the devoted things*, which can then be described as theft and lying through hiding the things taken – in this case, lying not only to one another but also to God in claiming faithfulness to his commands. As becomes clear, Yahweh already knows that Achan is the individual responsible, but his speech reinforces the narrator's comment in verse 1 that, although the sin was the act of an individual, it is still something that affects all the people. It is this sin that means Israel flee before their enemies rather than claiming the land Yahweh has promised. Indeed, rather than the Canaanites being liable for destruction, it is the people of Israel that now stand in that position.

From verse 13 Yahweh initiates a new set of commands for Joshua in light of what he has just disclosed, again telling him to *Get up*. However, where Yahweh's initial response was to show Joshua where his approach was flawed, it is now through Joshua that Yahweh will reveal the truth to the people as a whole. Joshua is therefore to consecrate himself and also arrange for the people to consecrate themselves. The means by which this was to be done is not stated, though it may well have involved some ritual activity. Hess is probably right to suggest that it would have included an act of reflection by which the people would consider how they might have transgressed Yahweh's commands.[22] The importance of this reflection is highlighted by the message Joshua is to bring concerning the presence of the devoted things among them. This message emphasizes that Israel cannot succeed as long as the devoted items are present. So, where the initial promise to Joshua was that no-one could resist them,[23] now Israel cannot stand before their enemies. Put simply, until Israel have dealt with their sin, not only can they not receive God's promise, but also they are in the same position as those whom Yahweh is judging.

So everyone knows the devoted items are present. The question is, how is the guilty party to be exposed? The answer is that each tribe is to be presented, then the relevant clan, household and individual, until the person responsible is identified. The structure thus works through the various levels of 'family' within Israel, though it also provides a link to Achan's lengthy genealogy in verse 1. The means by which Yahweh will make his choice is not indicated, but it seems likely that either lots[24] or the Urim and Thummin would have been involved. The text is not particularly concerned with the mechanism by which Yahweh's will is made known; what matters is its outcome. What is striking in this regard is that the verb usually translated as *take* in this process is one that is actually more commonly used in contexts of something being captured, especially in war,[25] though it is also used in situations parallel to this one.[26] It is the same verb as will be used when Joshua does capture Ai,[27] and in this context is thus another reminder that this is a story of Yahweh at war against sin among his people. However, as the people consecrate themselves they also know the penalty that awaits the guilty: to be burned along with all that belongs to them – which is the way the devoted things were to be treated (apart from those placed in Yahweh's treasury). In other words, since the person who transgressed the covenant has made himself something devoted to destruction, so the punishment must be that which applies to the devoted things.

Accordingly, Joshua rises early[28] and follows Yahweh's command, so that Achan is eventually revealed as the guilty party. As Yahweh

[22] Hess, *Joshua*, p. 150.
[23] 1:5.
[24] Lots were used in the case of Saul's selection as king in 1 Sam. 10:20–24, a passage that has clear echoes of this one.
[25] E.g. 1 Kgs 16:18; 2 Kgs 18:10.
[26] See also 1 Sam. 14:41–42.
[27] 8:21.
[28] Creating a parallel with 3:1 – in effect this is a new beginning for the nation.

announced, the various levels of his family are successively 'captured', gradually rewinding the genealogy given in verse 1. Once Achan is exposed, Joshua charges him to *give glory* to God and to *praise* him (19). These two statements are functionally equivalent to his next two directives, to reveal what he has done and not hide it. In other words, in this instance Achan glorifies God by admitting his sin.[29] This demonstrates something important about the Bible's theology of praise which is easily overlooked. We might think that praise is the declaration of the greatness of God and his works for us – and it certainly includes this. In this instance, however, we also see that praise is truthful confession of failure and sin. Although the public confession of sin might not seem much like praise, the reality is that it is because it reminds us that the essence of praise is authenticity before God. To declare God's greatness while consciously living contrary to what this means cannot be praise. Instead, it is a form of blasphemy that takes the great truths about God as something to announce in words while denying them through our quality of life. Real praise which glorifies God brings these two things together, something we find throughout the book of Psalms.

Challenged by Joshua, the hitherto silent Achan confesses that he has indeed sinned, with the particular form of his sin being that he saw *a beautiful cloak from Shinar*,[30] *200 shekels of silver* (between five and six pounds) and *a bar of gold weighing 50 shekels* (about one and a half pounds) (21). His pattern of looking, coveting and taking is reminiscent of Eve's response to the fruit in Eden,[31] and indeed this is the classic pattern of temptation. After all, no-one is tempted by anything that does not lead to a second look, but from there the desire to have can be overwhelming, which is why James reminds us that we are tempted when we are lured by our own desire, and that desire then leads to sin and death.[32] As with Eve, Achan has claimed what belongs to Yahweh alone and he will suffer the consequences. There may be a hint in his description of the goods he took as *spoil* that he felt he had a right to at least a share of them, rather than seeing them as devoted to Yahweh alone.[33] After he has revealed where they are hidden in his tent the narrative swiftly recounts the confirmation of his confession as the goods are indeed where he has said. As a result, the punishment Yahweh has already

[29] The Pharisees address the man born blind in the same way in John 9:24. Although their assumption that the man has collaborated with a sinner is fundamentally flawed, they understand the concept of giving glory to God in the same way.
[30] An alternative name for Babylon – see Gen. 11:2.
[31] Gen. 3:6. Note that in Hebrew 'desirable' and 'coveted' are related words.
[32] Jas 1:14–15.
[33] Madvig, 'Joshua', p. 288.

decreed is carried out, as Achan and all that is his – including his children – are taken to the Valley of Achor. The name of the valley apparently comes from this story since it means 'trouble', and Achan has brought trouble to Israel. Joshua asks him why he has brought this *trouble* on Israel (25), but this is a rhetorical question to which there is no answer. Yet just as Achan has troubled Israel, so Yahweh will trouble him, which in this case means Israel stoning him and then burning him and all that is his.[34] This severe punishment shows how sin infects God's people as a whole and how seriously God views sin,[35] though part of the tragedy of Achan is that Jericho was the only city where the ban prevented Israel from taking any spoil for themselves. Had he waited, he could have had some spoil.[36] The cairn that Israel raise to mark this spot was apparently still known when this text was written and served as a continuing reminder of Yahweh's war against sin, while also standing in contrast to the cairn in 8:29, which would point to all that could be achieved by a repentant people. This first cairn, however, is a perpetual reminder to all that sin is something that God takes seriously and that the occupation of the land is above all else an assault on sin. From this point, the people of Israel know that Yahweh's burning anger has turned away and that they can again know his presence, since it is Yahweh's presence that fundamentally distinguishes them,[37] even as it is Jesus' presence among us that fundamentally distinguishes the church.

2. The capture of Ai (8:1–29)

a. Preparations (8:1–13)
Israel has dealt with its sin, but because this is Yahweh's war against sin there is still the issue of Ai to be resolved. What is notably different now is that where Yahweh was not mentioned in the initial planning to take Ai, this time the plan is again his. Where the capture of Jericho was militarily unusual, the capture of Ai will be more orthodox – but the important point is that it is Yahweh's plan. First, however, Yahweh addresses Joshua's own misgivings. In his prayer[38]

---

[34] There are some textual difficulties here since the Hebrew appears to have Achan stoned twice – once before he is burnt and once after, though there are two different words used for 'stoning'. Perhaps we are to think of the second reference as related to the process by which the cairn that marked the grave came about (similarly, Hess, *Joshua*, p. 155).

[35] Boling, *Joshua*, p. 228, sees this as dealing with the contagion of Achan's sin, effectively an ancient form of quarantine since the presence of the banned goods in the tent meant all had come into contact with them.

[36] Howard, *Joshua*, p. 198.

[37] L. Daniel Hawk, *Joshua* (Collegeville: Liturgical Press, 2000), p. 124.

[38] 7:7–9.

Joshua had expressed a concern that the initial defeat would trigger a run of defeats, and even though this prayer had been based on a flawed interpretation, Yahweh now graciously speaks in terms of Joshua's concerns, reassuring him that not only is there no need for concern, but also that Joshua is to take the people with him to Ai because Yahweh has already given it and its king over to Joshua's control. In effect, Yahweh reveals to Joshua that because the people of Israel have addressed the issue of sin in their midst, the promises of victory with which they had entered the land have been reinstated. This in itself highlights something of the grace of prayer, because although Joshua's prayer had misconstrued events, Yahweh still addresses its concerns, even if he has also shown Joshua that the issues he raised were the wrong ones. In addressing Joshua's concerns, however, these directives also show Joshua the appropriate way forward, which is again to advance only in terms of Yahweh's plan. An obedient Israel is the one which can succeed, with the people this time taking the city through an ambush and then treating it as they had treated Jericho. Since the treatment of Jericho had included the saving of Rahab's family, presumably any such converts in Ai would also be delivered, though otherwise the town and its king were to be destroyed. Nevertheless, an important distinction with Jericho is also noted: this time the spoil and livestock can be kept as plunder. Jericho was unique in being the only town where everything would be reserved for Yahweh. This distinction served as a reminder that everything in the first instance was Yahweh's, since the whole land was his, but at the same time he could graciously grant the spoil to Israel.

The arrangements by which Israel was to take Ai can be difficult to understand as there are repetitions and points that seem confusing. However, it makes most sense to see verses 3–9 as describing Israel's preparations, with verse 10 describing the commencement of the battle and verses 11–13 as a flashback to the preparations which show Joshua's faithfulness in fulfilling them;[39] otherwise the ambush force spends two nights camped out, which is highly improbable since the men needed darkness to remain hidden. The probable arrangement, therefore, is that Joshua selected thirty large units[40] and sent them out, but of these, five units would constitute the ambush force that would hide west of Ai. Joshua spent the night with the main group, with the plan being to approach the city but then fall back in a feigned retreat in order to draw out the Aiites. Once they had come out of

[39] So also Howard, *Joshua*, p. 200. Woudstra, *Joshua*, p. 137, treats vv. 3–9 as proleptic.

[40] Again, seeing the word commonly translated *thousand* as describing the largest of Israel's military divisions rather than an exact count.

the town the ambush would respond to a signal from Joshua and attack from the side and seize the city.

The crucial point, however, was not so much the detail of the plan but the fact that Israel was to do what Yahweh said. Moreover, there is an interesting contrast between Yahweh's declaration to Joshua that the city had been given into his hand (1) and the statement in verse 7 that Yahweh would give the city into Israel's hand. The two statements do not contradict one another but rather show that what Yahweh had already declared still needed to be made a reality, and that reality would be achieved through an obedient Israel. This is a truth that runs through the book of Joshua and which remains true today. God's promises are sure and can be relied upon, but God's people are still to act in faithfulness upon them if we are to see them realized. For the church today the analogy might be in the area of evangelism: we are assured that God's Spirit is with us and leads us to witness to Jesus,[41] but we only truly discover this power when we in fact consciously engage in acts of witness to Jesus. The promise is always there, but its reality is only experienced when we act upon it. That said, we are also wise to be like Joshua here and make full preparations for all work, preparations that are themselves expressions of our commitment to what God has revealed in Christ.

b. Capturing the city (8:14–29)

Following the flashback in verses 10–13, the main narrative resumes here, demonstrating immediately that Yahweh's plan for Israel will succeed. So, when the Aiite king sees the approach of the main body of Israelites, the Aiites hurry to confront Israel at a location that looks back towards the Rift Valley. Crucially, the king does not know about the ambush behind the city. So as Joshua and his forces feign defeat by fleeing towards the wilderness, the Aiites come out in pursuit, letting themselves be drawn away from the city. Indeed, so completely are they taken in by the Israelite ruse that all their forces come out in pursuit,[42] leaving the city completely undefended. It is at this point that Yahweh directs Joshua to give the signal to the

---

[41] Acts 1:8.

[42] Bethel, a much larger city than Ai, is also mentioned in v. 17. Although Boling, *Joshua*, p. 240, suggests that this refers to the Aiite sanctuary (Bethel means 'house of God' and can refer to a sanctuary), we would expect a suffix to indicate it was Ai's sanctuary. More likely, then, Bethel was supporting Ai, and although the narrative concentrates on Ai because of its association with Achan's sin, this is also the point where Bethel is captured. However, because the primary concern is Yahweh's war against sin rather than a complete record of the conquest, the focus is on Ai. This may also explain the fact that separate kings are listed for Ai and Bethel in the summary of the cities captured (12:9, 16).

ambush force, stretching out a weapon[43] in his hand. The crucial point within this narrative is that this happens only at Yahweh's command because Ai, like Jericho, must ultimately be captured by Yahweh. Unlike with the first assault on Ai, Israel is not determining its own strategy. This is Yahweh's war, and Israel must follow Yahweh's directive. As was the case at Jericho, Israel could succeed only through obedience to Yahweh's command. Although in a different manner, this is something that continues to form the pattern for Christians today. Obedience to Christ is both a duty and a delight, something that demonstrates the reality of our discipleship.[44]

It is unlikely that the men in the ambush could clearly see Joshua's signal, so we have to assume that it was relayed to them. Once they see it, however, they immediately rise and capture the city. Where previously the Aiites had hurried after Israel, now it is Israel that hurries to capture the city. And just as Yahweh had earlier captured Achan in his war against sin, so now he captures Ai through his people. Meanwhile, Joshua continues to hold up his weapon, a symbol that is reminiscent of Moses holding up his staff in the battle against Amalek,[45] except that there Joshua led the army while Moses gave the signal. Moses had kept his arms raised until the victory was achieved, and Joshua does the same here as the Israelites set the city on fire. The burning of the city attracts the attention of the Aiites, and as they are discouraged by this evidence that the ambush has captured the city, they suddenly find the Israelites who had been fleeing coming back at them, so that Joshua can strike the Aiites down as they are trapped between the main force and the ambush force.[46] As a result all the Aiites are killed except the king, who is captured alive and then brought to Joshua.

The king's fate is left to one side so the narrator can tell us of the destruction of the city and all still in it. As a result of this battle the equivalent of twelve large units, men and women, are killed. That this happens at Yahweh's directive is made clear by the fact that Joshua does not withdraw the signal until all has been devoted to destruction, though this time Israel is permitted to take the livestock and spoil of the city. Had Achan waited he could have had what he wanted. Of course, the destruction of so many is inevitably troubling to many today, though we will read of more in subsequent chapters.

[43] Exactly what this weapon was is unclear. ESV translates this as *javelin*, whereas HCSB renders it 'sword'. It is most likely some form of curved sword, perhaps a scimitar.
[44] John 14:15; 1 John 3:19–24.
[45] Exod. 17:8–13.
[46] We have to assume that as the Israelites were on two sides only, there was no additional route allowing flight.

There is no simple answer to the various problems this poses, though see the discussion of 'Joshua and the Problem of Violence' in the Introduction. However, we do need to consider each case in terms of the evidence provided. At Jericho we saw that Rahab and her family were saved because she confessed Yahweh. That Joshua was to treat Ai as he treated Jericho indicates that this same option existed here. In Yahweh's war against sin it is those who resist his purposes who are destroyed, just as will happen in the final judgment. And, as the story of Achan makes clear, this was not just Canaanites – it was all who stood against Yahweh's purpose of bringing blessing to all the clans of the earth.[47] It is because of this that Joshua burned Ai so that it remained as a ruin until the time the book was written. In addition, the king of Ai was initially impaled on a tree until Joshua ordered his corpse to be brought down at sunset, when he was buried under a cairn at the city's gates, something that also could be recognized at the time of writing. Although this may seem a gruesome footnote to a bloody story, it demonstrates Joshua's commitment to Yahweh's purposes, faithfully following the requirements of the law.[48] The people of Israel were not to triumphantly abuse the bodies of those defeated, but rather were still to show proper respect because this showed that they stood with Yahweh in his war against sin. Likewise, Christians today may not act abusively towards others, not least because for us it was Jesus who was hung on the tree and became a curse for us, enabling us to stand on God's side in the war against sin – doing so as those who know we are there solely by grace and thus experiencing the blessing of God through Abraham.[49]

So at Ai there remained two cairns. Achan was buried under one, the king of Ai under the other. Each pointed to the outcome for those who set themselves against God's purposes, and for each it seems the outcome could have been different. This therefore is a terrifying story. It reminds us of the extent of sin, and how what may seem almost trivial expressions of sin stand in the way of us achieving the purposes that God has for us. More than that, it reminds us that just as radical surgery is necessary if we are to remove a cancer, so the same is true of sin. Yet it also points to the fact that sin does not have the last word, and that a people who renew their relationship with God can progress with him.

Lest we think of this as some vestige from the Old Testament, we should not forget the equally uncomfortable story of Ananias and Sapphira[50] in the New Testament. The basic pattern remains. An

[47] Gen. 12:1–3.
[48] Deut. 21:22–23.
[49] Gal. 3:13–14.
[50] Acts 5:1–11.

THE MESSAGE OF JOSHUA

obedient people *will* still go forward because God's purposes will be achieved. If we are not doing so, we have a responsibility to ask God to show us what our sin might be and how it prevents us from doing so, because as we too remove the sin from our midst we too will go forward as God desires.

Joshua 8:30–35
7. As Moses commanded: law and blessing in renewal

A student leading a chapel service I attended announced that the psalm for the morning was Psalm 119. After pausing for a moment while there was a sharp intake of breath, she went on to say, 'But I'm sure you'll be glad to know it's not all of it.' Actually, I was not particularly glad, but I have a sneaking suspicion that I was the only one present of whom that was true. After all, for many of us that lengthy paean to the Torah sums up all that is wrong with the Old Testament, and 176 verses that endlessly extol the Torah is a bit much. Unlike the psalmist, most Christians I know would find it very difficult to exclaim, 'Oh how I love your law!'[1] This is not the place to extol the virtues of Christians having a deeper understanding of the Old Testament's laws;[2] however, we will never appreciate the importance of a passage such as this unless we recognize that faithfulness to the Torah is regarded as essential by the book of Joshua. Indeed, this passage is all about obedience to Torah as a marker of blessing.

Of course, readers reaching this passage might also feel a sense of surprise. After all, we have just had the fall of Jericho, Achan's sin and then the ultimate capture of Ai. Suddenly, all that stops and we are transported nearly twenty miles to the north to recount a worship service at Mount Ebal, near Shechem. Given that we return to the conflict in Canaan immediately after, it feels almost like an ad break in a film we are watching on television, something that breaks into an interesting story to tell us information we don't really want to know. This is therefore a curious passage for many because of its focus on the law and also because it seems to break the story line

---

[1] Ps. 119:97.
[2] Though those who are interested in thinking about the law and Christians could do worse than start with Alec Motyer, *Discovering the Old Testament* (Leicester: Crossway, 2006), pp. 25–31.

that we have been following. Indeed, it breaks the story line quite
sharply, because the story that follows shows that Joshua and the
main Israelite forces were still in the region of Gilgal[3] and so a
considerable distance from Mount Ebal. Perhaps because of this, the
location of this passage varies somewhat in the textual tradition. At
Qumran it is between 5:1 and 5:2,[4] while LXX puts it after 9:2.[5]
These textual variants recognize that it is highly unlikely that Joshua
would have made a dangerous journey north through Canaanite
territory, especially going so near the major centre of Shechem,[6]
immediately after the capture of Ai. Actually, however, none of the
variants really solve the problem so much as highlight its presence
and show that ancient readers were aware of it too.

What are we to make of this? Perhaps the key point to note is that
although Joshua tells the story of Israel's entry into the land in a
broadly chronological way, it does not follow that everything is told
in sequence. Indeed, a writer can break the chronological sequence
precisely because it is a good way of emphasizing a key point. In all
likelihood, this is a time of worship that happened late in the
conquest, but it is told here because doing so emphasizes and applies
the central theme the passage develops.[7] Before Israel entered the
land, Yahweh had told Joshua that he was not to depart from
the Torah that Moses had commanded.[8] Faithfulness to Yahweh's
commands through Moses was intended to shape Israel's life. At Ai,
trouble had come because Israel had not been faithful to Yahweh's
command. The city was captured when Israel recognized this and
followed Yahweh's command, but they had not dedicated themselves
to such faithfulness. This time of worship at Mount Ebal is a time
when the people of Israel do this, because after the sin-induced
failure at Ai, what is needed is a people who once more are committed
to knowing and doing Yahweh's will. It is this that must always mark

[3] 9:6.

[4] The Qumran text (4QJosh[a]) places the event at the beginning of Israel's time in
the land, which is most consistent with Deut. 27:2, a key text in the background here.
However, it is an obvious correction that a scribe might make and so unlikely to
represent the original position of the text.

[5] Placing the event here means that the worship at Ebal is a response to the threat
of the Canaanite kings, but again, this looks like the sort of correction a scribe might
make. Though more probable than the Qumran reading, it is still less likely than MT.

[6] Shechem lies between Mount Ebal and Mount Gerizim. One of the great curiosities
of this passage is that Shechem is never mentioned, perhaps because its significance as
a site for covenant renewal is being held back to ch. 24, where it is explicitly identified
as the place of Joshua's ceremony.

[7] Recognizing this does not, however, require us to follow J. Alberto Soggin, *Joshua:
A Commentary* (London: SCM Press, 1972), pp. 222, 241–244, and simply move the
whole passage to ch. 24.

[8] 1:7.

out God's people, and it is this that comes to the fore here as we are repeatedly told that what was done was just as Moses had commanded. Indeed, this phrase is a refrain that shapes the passage. The Torah as the living word of God was to shape God's people, and worship was the appropriate way to respond to it. Indeed, it is still obedience to God's Word that gives hope to God's people as they live out their relationship with him.

1. Building the altar (8:30-31)

Worship was to be at the heart of Israel's life, but even more than that, Deuteronomy 27 specified that when Israel entered the land they were to go to Mount Ebal and conduct what was in effect a covenant renewal ceremony when the Levites would announce the blessings and curses of the covenant. Given Mount Ebal's location in Israel's central highlands, it cannot have been expected that this would be the first thing done on entering the land, but at the same time it is clearly meant to have happened promptly. It is this command of Yahweh through Moses that Joshua fulfils here as he builds an altar made of *uncut stones* (31). This type of structure is mandated by Deuteronomy 27:5-6, though it in turn derives from the earlier altar law in Exodus 20:25. The central point is found in the twice-made affirmation that what is done is in accordance with what was required by Moses.[9]

As the highest mountain in northern Israel, Mount Ebal was important because of its control of the major trade routes through that region and also because it was a point from which most of the land could be seen. It was thus a strategic and symbolic site. The emphasis here, however, is on neither of these things. What matters is that the altar and the sacrifices are in accordance with what Yahweh had revealed through Moses. Hence both burnt offerings and fellowship offerings[10] are offered, just as Deuteronomy required. The burnt offerings were intended to atone for sin, whereas the fellowship offerings were to reaffirm the relationship with both God and the community. Placed immediately after the events at Ai this account reminds readers that the failure there was not final and that there

---

[9] An Iron Age altar, or what is most likely one since the interpretation of the archaeological evidence is disputed, has been found on Mount Ebal. It is possible that this is indeed Joshua's altar since it was only used for a limited period, and the evidence of the site is consistent with it being Israelite. Nevertheless, as with much archaeological evidence, an exact identification is difficult to make. See Richard S. Hess, *Israelite Religions: An Archaeological and Biblical Survey* (Nottingham: Apollos, 2007), pp. 216-221.

[10] Or *peace offerings*.

was a way forward, with forgiveness possible for God's people, and that that forgiveness ultimately leads also to fellowship with God and with his people. These, in fact, are God's gift to his people, a gift that is found already in obedience to his revealed word.

It is perhaps notable that although Joshua's actions here are based on Deuteronomy 27, the order in which they are recounted is not the same. The reason for this is found in the position of this passage immediately after the events at Ai. The sacrifices point to forgiveness and renewed fellowship, and these are what was needed in light of Israel's failures there. In the same way, Christians celebrating the Lord's Supper are reminded both of the forgiveness we have in Christ and also the fellowship we share with him and with one another.[11] At the same time, we are reminded that this too comes from our obedience to what God has already revealed through Jesus. The form in which we discover forgiveness and fellowship differs, but the message is the same. We serve a God who forgives, renews and provides hope, and indeed a God who has already revealed to us the means by which we discover these things.

2. Copying the Torah (8:32–33)

Before mentioning the sacrifices, the instructions in Deuteronomy 27 had stipulated that Israel was to set up large stones and cover them with plaster[12] so that the Torah (perhaps Deuteronomy itself) could be transcribed on them. It appears that these stones were separate from the altar, perhaps something like the tablets on which the Decalogue was inscribed or standing stones which could serve as a public display. A superficial reading of this passage might suggest that the Torah was inscribed on the altar stones, but it is more probable that we are to assume from the background found in Deuteronomy that separate stones were used[13] and were covered with plaster so that the Torah could be written on them. Levels of literacy in ancient Israel were probably not particularly high, but the presence of a site like this was still a powerful proclamation of the importance of God's word for his people, effectively publishing it for all and thus providing a spur to literacy even if most would continue to access this material orally.

However, the word of God does not exist separately from the people of God and worship. Thus the record of the transcribing of at least a portion of God's word is linked to the worship of all God's people – and here they include both foreigners and native born. The

[11] Matt. 26:26–30; 1 Cor. 11:22–34.
[12] It is notable that there is evidence of the use of plaster on the site of Mount Ebal.
[13] Similarly Howard, *Joshua*, p. 216.

inclusion of these peoples comes as something of a shock if we have been reading Joshua as the destruction of the peoples already in the land, as if Israel was engaged in the process of ethnic cleansing. Actually, however, even at this point Israel is a mixed people. This was true of the people who came out in the exodus as a 'mixed multitude',[14] though the inclusion of Rahab's family (and exclusion of Achan's) has already pointed to the fact that Israel was made up of those who aligned themselves with Yahweh's purposes. If we ask how these people, from their diverse backgrounds, were to align themselves with Yahweh's will, the answer given here is that they would know it through his word, both as it was acted out and also as it was written. Both of these are means by which it was taught and so could be obeyed. That is why as well as the writing of the Torah, all these people gathered around the ark, with half on Mount Ebal and half on Mount Gerizim. Again, this was in accordance with Yahweh's command through Moses. Although Deuteronomy 27 records both the blessing and the curse of covenant (since there are implications for both obedience and disobedience), the emphasis here is only on the blessing, though as with the stones we can assume that the curse was also announced. However, a community reflecting on the events of Ai would already know the curse from their experience. What they needed now was the blessing, and this was something already present in Yahweh's Torah.

Again, we need to reflect on what such obedience might look like today. Many churches place great emphasis on the reading and exposition of Scripture, and this is certainly consistent with the pattern of this text. Some form of regular public reading enables people to hear God's word, and perhaps also to encounter texts that they would not have chosen to read given the choice, which is no bad thing. But we should also note that the worship at Mount Ebal was structured in order that the people as a whole, an inclusive people, should also experience the significance of this word through their participation in the service. This would suggest that the process by which God's word comes to the centre of our communal life is not one way, in which some (usually, but not necessarily, clergy) proclaim it to the people. Rather, we need to discover means of structuring our worship so that it becomes part of the lived experience of the people. This, of course, is especially possible in highly structured worship events such as baptism or the Lord's Supper, but need not be restricted to them. We might, for example, dramatize readings so that the congregation as a whole participates in them, or perhaps take more seriously the range of voices found in many passages so that each is heard

[14] Exod. 12:38.

through a separate reader. Whatever means we find, however, we must ensure it enables the whole people of God to discover the blessing of obedience.

3. Reading the Torah (8:34–35)

Finally, we are told that Joshua read out the whole of the Torah to those assembled. The assembly that is present is again an inclusive one, including women, children and *the sojourners who lived among them*. The point of this listing is again to make clear that the people who hear and respond to God's word are more than just those who can claim genealogical descent from Abraham. It is in worship that the whole people of God come together, and they do so in hearing the whole Torah, both blessing and curse, read to them by Joshua.

The pattern modelled here is again one that bears reflection. Although the Torah was written, not everyone present could read, so it was necessary to ensure that this word was presented in a way that all could understand and which also included all. This is why Joshua read it out to all those gathered. I don't imagine that the children present would necessarily have found the reading of the whole Torah particularly exciting, though the instruction they received was not only in the reading of the word but also in the various acts of worship, especially the sacrifices. Indeed, it is in the bringing together of more formal worship acts and the reading of God's word that an opportunity is provided for all God's people to grow. Obviously, different members of any particular congregation will find different parts of a service more instructive than others, but the integration of different aspects of worship has the potential to be more inclusive. Paul could say that in Christ there is 'neither Jew nor Greek, there is neither slave nor free, there is no male and female, for you are all one in Christ Jesus' while reflecting on baptism in the context of his discussion of God's promises.[15] Although Joshua is clearly not thinking of baptism, the concept of worship as a means of bringing all of God's people together through worship that also wrestles with God's word is one that joins both these passages.

Worship that is inclusive of all God's people is here also inclusive of all God's word – including blessing and curse. So, where the blessing alone was mentioned in verse 33, here we are told that the people heard *all* the word. No doubt many then, as now, would have preferred to hear only the blessing. After all, it is immeasurably more pleasant to hear this alone. Nevertheless, faithfulness to the whole of God's word also means wrestling with those passages that

[15] Gal. 3:15–29 – the quoted passage is 3:28.

we find more difficult, especially those which speak of God's anger or judgment. It is notable that when the lectionary leaves out portions of passages it is usually those speaking of God's judgment that are omitted, but we have no right to leave out those texts which we find less congenial. Worship that includes all God's people must also include all of God's word. We especially understand this when we read this passage in light of Achan's earlier failure, because then we see that God's judgment does not have to be the last word – but we must also understand that it can be his word to us at a particular point of time.

So is this just one of those moments in the Old Testament where we get too much law and not enough action? A distraction from an exciting if sometimes difficult narrative? Well, only if we fail to attend to the reasons why it is placed here, because it is intended to make us focus on the Torah as God's instruction for his people, and to remind us that endless action isn't everything. Instead, a people who wish to live in the promises of God must first be a people who know those promises and are shaped by them. This people also need worship that genuinely allows them to encounter that instruction and to be shaped by it. The surprise might be that we discover that the law is actually more interesting and relevant than we thought, though we might also be surprised to notice just how inclusive the worship that is associated with this word turns out to be. A pause in the endless cycle of activity that drives many churches to rediscover these things might be no bad thing. After all, this effectively means that the people as a whole do what Joshua was told to do in 1:8, and both leaders and people need to have a sound knowledge of God's Word.

Joshua 9:1–27
8. Who's in, who's out?
Gibeon's deception and covenant

Although the opening chapters of Joshua focus on the story of how Israel came to occupy the land promised by Yahweh, we have also noticed another theme running parallel with it: the question of who exactly the people of God are. At one level, this might seem to be a curious issue to raise. After all, weren't Israel God's people in the Old Testament? And weren't they the descendants of Abraham whom Yahweh had brought out of Egypt in the exodus and then through the wilderness to this point? Well, yes. However – and this is an important point – although it is easy to reduce Israel's story to these terms, it is rather like reading a newspaper only in terms of the headlines. If all we see is the headline, we might know the main lines of the story (at least, if it is a more reputable paper!), but we will not pick up the subtler issues that sit on the fringes of the story.

In Joshua those fringes are important. Already we have seen Rahab and her family incorporated into the life of Israel so that she and her descendants continue to live among Israel.[1] By her confession of faith and her commitment to Israel's spies[2] she had shown a commitment to Yahweh's purposes, and that commitment was why she was included in God's people even though she was a Canaanite. In addition, Achan's story has shown that Israelites who rejected Yahweh's purposes could place themselves in the position of Canaanites,[3] and his cairn was a continual reminder to Israel of this possibility.[4] So far, though, the equation seems fairly simple. Those who consciously chose to commit themselves to God's purposes, even though from a condemned people, could become part of God's

[1] 6:25.
[2] 2:8–21.
[3] Josh. 7.
[4] 7:26.

people and thus share the blessings God had for his people. By contrast, Israelites who rejected God's purposes were excluded and now shared the position of those condemned.

The inclusion of a Canaanite and exclusion of an Israelite might initially surprise us, but once we recognize that the logic of this relates to commitment to Yahweh, it is much less surprising. God's people have always been made up of those committed to him. In addition to this, however, we have also observed that the people who worshipped at Mount Ebal defined all Israel as 'sojourner as well as native born',[5] although to this point Rahab and her family were the only foreigners explicitly included. Already, then, Joshua hints at a larger group within God's people who were not ethnically Israelite. Yet so far the distinction has been clear cut, even if it is at some levels surprising. Nevertheless, as two of Jesus' statements also make clear, recognizing who is included in God's purposes is challenging. Jesus could affirm both that 'whoever is not with me is against me'[6] and that 'the one who is not against us is for us'.[7] Although these statements are clearly related, they are not saying the same thing. In the first instance, Jesus excludes those who do not join themselves to his purposes, while in the second he includes those who do not oppose him. Obviously, the full meaning of both these statements depends on the contexts in which Jesus spoke at the time, but their difference is striking. So far, the position of both Rahab and Achan could be assessed in terms of the first statement: Rahab had clearly committed herself to God's purposes while Achan had rejected them. But what of those who simply were not *opposed* to God's purposes? It is this weaker sense of God's people that is now considered through the account of Gibeon and its deception of Israel. The story is assuredly not presented as a model of how to become part of God's people, nor indeed of how God's people should make decisions, though we do see something about these matters along the way. However, it does show that those who do not oppose God's purposes can become part of those purposes, and yet at the same time not enjoy all the benefits of full commitment.

1. The kings respond (9:1–2)

Before we are introduced to the Gibeonites[8] we need to know that there is a new response to Israel. In the closely parallel 5:1 we are

[5] 8:33.
[6] Luke 11:23.
[7] Mark 9:40.
[8] The Gibeonites are pivotal to the whole of chs. 9–11. They are introduced here, the reaction to their covenant with Israel drives ch. 10, and they are then mentioned as part of the summary statement of 11:19–20.

told that when the Canaanite kings heard about Israel crossing the Jordan 'their hearts melted'. Here, however, we are told that when they *heard of this*, they instead gathered with the specific purpose of fighting Israel. We are not told exactly what it was that they heard, but it is unlikely to have been the ceremony of 8:30–35. Instead, the reference is probably to the events at Ai,[9] where Israel's initial failure to take a relatively small site has now encouraged the local kings. This represents a dramatic change, and one that will continue to determine Canaanite response in chapters 10–11, where their kings again respond to news about Israel and the battles that verse 2 suggests are about to happen are recorded.

Although the bulk of this chapter will record the story of one group who choose a different path, it is clear that the book wants to highlight this more bellicose response first. Achan's sin at Jericho and its implications at Ai were not uniquely his, which is why chapter 7 had stressed Israel's corporate responsibility. Now we see a further result of that sin, evidence that sin's results go further than we normally imagine, as the various Canaanite kings no longer melt in fear but instead gather with the united resolve to attack Israel. Where previously hearts melted in fear because of what Yahweh had done,[10] they are now encouraged to attack because of what Israel has done. Moreover, where they previously appear to be divided, they are now united. Sin has opened a door for Israel's enemies – just as it opens a door for those who would attack the church today – and emboldened them to go on the offensive. Today's enemies of the gospel might not join in a military attack – at least, not in the West – preferring to use ridicule through the press, but the result is the same. Once people respond to our failings rather than to the greatness of God, we are always liable to attack. Likewise, as recent scandals about child abuse within churches and church institutions has demonstrated, the less vigorous we are in dealing with sin, the more we open ourselves to such attack. Israel had been called to be a people committed to Yahweh and his ways, and the practice of circumcision and celebration of Passover after crossing the Jordan was meant to demonstrate this[11] – and the same is true for the church today. This means committing ourselves to God's purposes and also addressing the sin that so easily arises among us, both because doing so reflects the holiness of God and because it does not give enemies of the gospel an easy target.

[9] 7:1 – 8:29.
[10] 2:9–11; 5:1.
[11] 5:1–12.

2. The Gibeonite deception (9:3–15)

Although most of the Canaanite kings are prepared for war, there is one group that takes a different approach and seeks to make peace with Israel, albeit through deception. In the case of the Gibeonites it is not only the events at Ai that shape their decision; it is also those at Jericho. Israel's failings at Ai have not led all to oppose them as the Gibeonites take into account the wider picture. As a people who live in the land, however, and who are apparently well aware that the events of Jericho and Ai could be replicated with them, they face a problem. There is no reason to suppose that they know about Rahab and her family and their deliverance from the destruction at Jericho, since the information that would have reached them would have focused on the city's destruction. They might perhaps not be aware that an open and genuine confession of faith in Yahweh is an option, and so instead they opt for deception.

Gibeon itself is generally identified as el-Jib, about eight miles north-west of Jerusalem and a similar distance south-west of Ai. The Bronze Age material at the site itself has not been excavated to a significant degree, but some important tombs there indicate that there was considerable wealth in the area, and wine jar handles bearing the name have also been discovered there, though the town itself has not been found.[12] Its location means that its people would have quickly heard about events at Jericho and Ai and thus needed to decide how to respond to Israel, though given Israel's general lack of knowledge about the land they might not yet have known about Gibeon. Although the Gibeonites will later speak about having heard what Yahweh has done to Sihon and Og, the narrator here tells us that they are responding to what they have heard that Joshua has done, which might be a hint that they are responding solely to the military reality of Israel's presence; on the whole, though, people in the ancient world did not separate their theology from general life, especially military situations.[13]

The challenge for the Gibeonites is to convince Israel to make peace with them and to ensure that peace remains. Their plan is to disguise themselves in old and worn-out clothes and footwear and to take with them provisions that are old and equipment that is equally worn out. The aim is to provide evidence for the claim they will make: that they have travelled a great distance and thus are not inhabitants of the land. The listing of items to support this is lengthy,

[12] On the archaeology of the site, see Pitkänen, *Joshua*, pp. 214–216. He concludes that Gibeon does not pose significant problems for the historicity of Joshua.
[13] See Daniel I. Block, *The Gods of the Nations: Studies in Ancient Near Eastern National Theology* (2nd ed., Leicester: Apollos, 2000), pp. 75–92.

but is given because it will be presented as evidence that they have come a long way. Accordingly, they travel to the Israelite camp at Gilgal to put their plan into action. Gilgal is a common place name in Israel with at least three known sites, including the site where Israel first entered the land,[14] though it is unlikely that Israel has returned there at this point, so this is probably a now unknown site with that name,[15] though the Gilgal a little to the north of Bethel[16] is just possible. However, even if it is not the Gilgal in the Jordan valley, the place name should at least evoke memories of the crossing and remind Israel of what it means to obey Yahweh.

It soon becomes clear that it is not Israel (in obedience to Yahweh) that is setting the agenda here, but rather the Gibeonites. Accordingly, this section of the story is a textbook example of how the people of God should *not* make decisions. The Gibeonites arrive and make their opening gambit, addressing both Joshua and the people more generally, claiming to have travelled a great distance and asking for a covenant with Israel. The nature of the covenant is not defined, but the context they establish demonstrates that their cunning goes further than just their disguised appearance. Deuteronomy 7:2 expressly forbids Israel from making a covenant with any of the inhabitants of the land – though Deuteronomy 20:10 does permit Israel to offer terms of peace to cities outside the land, and though the word 'covenant' does not occur there, what is described would certainly be understood as such. Thus the Gibeonites' approach is to give the appearance of being those with whom Israel might make a covenant, though initially leaving it open to Israel to define the terms that covenant might take. The initial response from the people of Israel shows that they are aware of the possibility of being duped, noting that the Gibeonites might indeed be from nearby, and so they ask why they should make a covenant with them.

In response the Gibeonites adopt a more subservient position, describing themselves to Joshua as Israel's servants. This makes clear that they are seeking a covenant arrangement in which Israel is the main power, rather than a meeting of equals, which is how their initial request might be understood. In response, Joshua questions them more closely, asking directly who they are and where they have come from, though the narrator has already indicated that they are Hivites and thus people of the land. Again, however, the Gibeonites are careful in their response not to offer direct information about themselves other than reasserting their claim that they are Israel's servants, saying merely that they have come from a very distant land

---

[14] 4:19.
[15] So Howard, *Joshua*, p. 224.
[16] 2 Kgs 2:1. The other Gilgal is in Judah's allocated territory, Josh. 15:7.

111

and that they have come because of the fame of Yahweh, claiming like Rahab to have heard what Yahweh did in the exodus and also to Sihon and Og.[17] Thus, although we know they have heard about the events of Jericho and Ai, they claim knowledge only of events *before* Israel entered the land, since to admit to knowledge of more recent events would give the lie to their claims. In addition, they claim that their elders and inhabitants of their land (implicitly not *this* land) had urged them to take their provisions and go and make a covenant with Israel as their servants. At this point they bring forth their provisions and equipment as evidence of their claim, emphasizing that it has all deteriorated because of the length of their journey. In a telling irony, the Gibeonites' self-presentation is precisely what Moses had declared was *not* Israel's situation,[18] so that the Gibeonites claim to be what Israel would have been without Yahweh.

Israel's response to this is telling. They sample their provisions but do not inquire of Yahweh. This simple comment from the narrator makes clear the fundamental problem while highlighting a key issue in discernment. The implication is that, had they inquired of Yahweh, they would have known that they were being duped – not least because they would have realized that provisions could have been purchased on the way. But they do not inquire and so are taken in by a simple ruse, one that perhaps had they just taken some time out for reflection alone would have been shown up for what it was. After all, simply being presented with old food and equipment does not demonstrate that it has deteriorated on the current journey. It is simply old. However, when we are caught up in the moment of something being presented to us it is difficult to find the space to understand what we are really being shown, something every door-to-door salesperson knows only too well. Precisely because they do not take the time to ask God, Joshua and the leaders of the congregation not only make peace with the Gibeonites, but they also make a covenant with them that is sworn by an oath. In short, a failure simply to ask God means that a wrong decision is made, and one that will be binding. The danger of prayerlessness could not be more clearly illustrated.

This part of the story thus raises an important issue for the life of the church today as we are faced with many key decisions about what it means to be God's people and how we should continue to join God in his mission. Whether overtly or covertly, we are frequently challenged to make quick decisions. What is emphasized

---

[17] 2:9–13. For details on Sihon and Og, see comments there.
[18] Deut. 29:5. Cf. Hawk, *Joshua in 3-D*, p. 104.

here, however, is that these decisions have to be made through a genuine seeking of the mind of Christ. There are many areas of practice where Christians have real freedom but still manage to find ways of debating – styles of worship, for example – and in reflection on Scripture we should recognize that freedom as something God gives us in his mission. There are other matters, however, where we do not have freedom because such things are contrary to God's purposes for us. We do not, for example, have the freedom to proclaim a gospel without repentance – but some packaged evangelism tools do not seem to include this, and we are often encouraged to adopt them because they seem to be 'effective'. This does not mean that everyone who enters a church building has to understand the gospel fully, but it does mean that we need to exercise discernment in determining which of these tools, however well meant, will actually lead people to a living faith in Jesus Christ. Serious prayer and seeking the mind of Christ through studying the Scriptures (perhaps with disciplines such as fasting) are vital if we are to engage in witness that truly brings people to life in Christ. Here the people of Israel have not sought Yahweh, and so they have made a decision with which they will have to live.

3. Living with the deception (9:16–27)

All decisions have consequences, even those that are right. Here, however, Israel have seemingly created a problem for themselves by entering into a covenant with a people who stood under Yahweh's condemnation. Compounding this is the fact that, shortly after making the covenant, they discover that the Gibeonites are in fact a people who live in the land. Accordingly they set off to their cities, which we now find are the four towns of Gibeon, Chephirah, Beeroth and Kiriath-jearim, all within a few miles of each other. However, instead of attacking these towns the people of Israel can only grumble against their leaders because the oath they have sworn permits these people to live. This grumbling has overtones of Israel's time in the wilderness, such as their complaints about the lack of water[19] or food.[20] Yet here there may be some validity in their complaint in that this time it is the oath of their leaders that has caused their frustration. Nevertheless, since such grumbling in the Old Testament is never a positive thing, we are probably intended to see that the desire of the congregation to kill the Gibeonites is fundamentally flawed. The response of the leaders to this is instructive, for while they do not

[19] Exod. 15:24.
[20] Exod. 16:2–3.

113

deny that they have caused the current situation, they also believe that to go against the oath they have sworn by Yahweh would trigger wrath. In other words, they take the view that there is no point in compounding their previous mistake by breaking their oath. Put simply, one does not resolve one error by committing another. Accordingly, they now explain to the Gibeonites what the covenant will mean – that they will be *cutters of wood and drawers of water for all the congregation* (21).

The decision is that they can live – Israel cannot go against an oath sworn in Yahweh's name – but given that the Gibeonites entered the covenant under false pretences they cannot simply live as they were before. If Israel are to put things as right as possible it needs to be in a way that Yahweh will recognize. Accordingly, they seem here to bring together two texts from Deuteronomy. First, Deuteronomy 20:10–11 permits Israel to put peoples from outside the land who are captured in warfare to forced labour, and that is certainly what is intended by the phrase *cutters of wood and drawers of water*. However, this latter phrase also occurs in Deuteronomy 29:11 to describe the foreigners who dwell within Israel and fulfil this role. Thus in seeking to resolve the problem they have created the solution is to go back to what God has already revealed. The initial problem was caused by a failure to seek Yahweh, so the solution needs to have seeking Yahweh at its heart. No doubt there will be many times when God's people make faulty decisions, especially when we have failed to seek God faithfully. But this account does not stay with the mistake; it goes on to model a response that can make the best of the situation. It might be objected that Israel here reverts to a legal fiction, treating the Gibeonites as if they are a people from outside the land when they are clearly a people from within the land. However, the option of treating them as a people from within the land has been removed from them by the oath sworn by the congregation's leaders. The people of Israel are thus working with the problem by making the best of what they have, exploring scripture to discern an approach that will address an ethical issue that the Bible does not deal with directly.

Clearly, no scripture is going to address this particular problem for them, and as a result the approach they take is to look to principles already found there to resolve their problem as effectively as possible. Such a situation is not dissimilar to the many ethical problems Christians face today. How, for example, should we respond to the possibilities and the challenges of social media? We will not find a passage in the Bible that provides us with clear guidance on this issue because it was simply not on the horizon for any of the Bible's writers. However, we can surely examine the Bible for principles that allow us to decide the most effective way to respond to and make use of social media so that our response is shaped by a concern to replicate God's concern for community that is genuinely transformative. It was this approach that shaped the concern of the leaders of the congregation here.

A transformative society is one that is most effectively built on truth, and it is this issue that Joshua himself addresses as he now speaks with the Gibeonites, asking why they deceived Israel by claiming to live far away when in fact they are from the land. For Israel, the deception was always at the heart of the problem, though the deception was also a problem for the Gibeonites since, although they now had a covenant relationship with Israel, they were also cursed so that they could not escape their status as servants. What is striking is that this question will actually usher in a small but significant change in status for the Gibeonites, one perhaps hinted at already as Joshua associates their service with the central sanctuary. They, like Israel, cannot escape their past, but as truth comes into the discussion new possibilities open up. So, although the Gibeonites now present themselves as Israel's servants, they admit that they had indeed heard what Yahweh had commanded Moses, which is that the people of the land were to be destroyed as the land was to be given to Israel. Although the technical vocabulary of Yahweh war is missing, it is clear that they know at least the main themes of Deuteronomy 7 and 20. It was because of this that they were greatly afraid of Israel – as indeed anyone who knew these commands would be. Yet, as we have seen in the case of Rahab, these commands did not prevent someone from confessing faith and thus no longer standing under God's condemnation. The Gibeonites' response here is not as articulate as Rahab's was, but it makes clear that they were not opposed to what Yahweh was doing, so long as they themselves were not on the receiving end of it, though they knew that they were in Israel's power. Although this is not a confession of faith as Rahab's was, it is sufficient for Joshua to deliver them from the power of the rest of the Israelites so that, rather than being slaves to Israel as a whole, they are instead to serve at the central altar at the place Yahweh will choose, which perhaps leads to Gibeon becoming a Levitical city.[21] So, rather than being servants to Israel, the Gibeonites have now become servants to Yahweh. Israel's initial solution was their attempt to resolve the problem as best they could, but in the sharing of truth an improved solution became possible, one that recognized that the reason for the destruction of the peoples of Canaan was to prevent idolatry. The Gibeonites, by their (partial)

21 21:17.

confession, have shown that that is not a threat they pose, and so they can more effectively live out their covenant at a place where they serve Israel because they serve Yahweh. As truth is finally spoken we get a clearer picture of the Gibeonites as a people who are not opposed to Yahweh's purposes for Israel and as a result discover that they too can have a role that contributes to them.[22] We might well wonder, then, what might have happened had they spoken truly in the first place! However, although we can never know that with certainty, it is at this point that we clearly see that those who stand under Yahweh's condemnation are those who oppose his purposes, those who resist his gift of the land to Israel and those who lead his people into idolatry.

Reflection on this chapter thus leads us in at least two directions. First, we have to ponder the ways in which we make decisions as the church today, as the first half of the chapter reminds us of the importance of seeking Yahweh in all decision making. Second, though, the inclusion of the Gibeonites in God's mission through Israel, in spite of their flawed approach, makes us pause to consider the fundamental nature of God's people. We might observe that the Gibeonite approach means that they did not live in the blessing that God offered – their status as servants certainly points to this. Yet they were still there, and subsequent attempts to remove them would only cause more grief for Israel.[23] It seems, then, that the people of God might be defined more widely than just those who confess faith openly, and there may be some for whom such a confession is seen more in their willingness to accommodate themselves to what God is doing in Christ. The challenge for us, then, is surely that we do not leave them in that state, but rather bring them into the full life of blessing, and encouraging them in truth is surely a starting point for this. However, perhaps the great surprise for many people is that here in a book which is mostly seen as being about the destruction of the native peoples of Canaan we see an example of inclusion, and it is this pattern of the inclusion of both Jew and Gentile that is also at the heart of so much of the New Testament.[24] How we live out what it means to be the inclusive people of God while also remaining truly faithful to the gospel and its demands will always be a challenge, but a story like this one reminds us that it is the sort of challenge that reaches back even into texts which many might think of as primarily exclusive. Within the book of Joshua, exclusion is always

---

[22] 11:19–20 raises some wider questions for us about the reasons for the Gibeonites' actions, but we consider that text in the treatment of chs. 11–12.

[23] 2 Sam. 21:1–14.

[24] See, for example, Paul's great statements about the gospel in Rom. 1:16–17 and the inclusion of Gentiles in Eph. 2:13–20.

seen in terms of those who oppose God's purposes – as will be evident in the next two chapters – but the quality to which inclusion is enjoyed will depend on the extent to which faith is actively confessed.

Joshua 10:1–43
9. Faithful to the promises: the southern campaign

The events of the previous chapter have raised important questions. Fundamentally, these coalesce around the issue of faithfulness to the promises of God. This issue runs in two directions, both of which are important for understanding this chapter.

First, there is the matter of how Israel will remain faithful to their promise to Gibeon. It was a promise made and solemnized by a covenant that assured the Gibeonites of life. However, there are numerous times in the Bible – quite apart from our own experience – when people find ways of somehow honouring the words of a promise without keeping to their spirit. Judges 21, for example, shows Israel looking for ways to get around a promise they had made to Yahweh – and also the damage that it caused – as one more example of what happened in Israel in those days. So will Israel keep their promise to the Gibeonite cities? Or might they see an attack from other Canaanites as a convenient way of not technically breaking their promise – 'We haven't destroyed the Gibeonites, it's just that the Canaanites did'? In short, will pressure from within the land lead to Israel looking for a way to abandon their promise?

Second, however, there is the matter of how God will be faithful to his promises to Israel. Will he see the covenant with the Gibeonites as an act of unfaithfulness on Israel's part, making peace with one of the peoples they were meant to destroy? Will he see this as equivalent to Achan's sin at Jericho that caused so much pain at Ai? Or will God honour Israel as they in turn honour their commitment to the Gibeonites? We must remember that there was no point at which God spoke in the previous chapter, so although we might infer certain things about his attitude to the events there, we have no clear statement on this point. That is why it is these questions that lie at the heart of this chapter. And it is through wrestling with these questions that we see the book of Joshua affirming that God is indeed faithful to his promises – and, more specifically, that he is faithful to them in remarkable ways as Israel in turn are faithful to their promises to the Gibeonites. Israel's failures, like ours, will continue to impact them on their journey into the promises of God, but God remains faithful to his promises. It is this hope, rooted in the faithful character of God, which should continue to encourage us as the people of God in our journey today.

1. Southern kings unite (10:1–5)

There is an immediate parallel here with the opening verses of chapter 9. There, we were told that all the kings of Canaan gathered against Israel when they heard about something, presumably the events at Ai. That aspect of the story was not taken up as we focused instead on the Gibeonites and their efforts at securing a covenant with Israel. In this chapter and the next, however, we see how this union of Canaanite kings works itself out, first in the south of the land (ch. 10) and then in the north (ch. 11). All the kings may have gathered at 9:1, but it turns out that their ability to act on it will be limited by what God has already done in giving Jericho and Ai to Israel.

The initial focus here is on the king of Jerusalem,[1] Adoni-zedek, and his response to two key pieces of news – the fall of Ai and the covenant between Israel and the Gibeonites. Both issues cause problems for him. Israel's defeat of Jericho and Ai[2] means that they now control significant points in the area from the Jordan valley to the hill country immediately to the north of Jerusalem. The covenant with the Gibeonite tetrapolis puts more pressure on Jerusalem as it means that Israel's control now covers the region to the north-west of the city. Exacerbating the problem is that Gibeon was a major city, far more significant than Ai, and he might perhaps have thought of it as a potential ally – especially because of its military reputation. Instead, his access to the north is cut off by Israel and their ally, and so he needs to contact the kings in the south if he is to form an alliance. Accordingly, he forms a coalition with the kings of Hebron, Jarmuth, Lachish and Eglon, all cities to the south-west of Jerusalem, with the express purpose of attacking Gibeon.

Why attack Gibeon and not Israel? The answer can only be inferred. Militarily, it might have given greater access to the coast, something now made more difficult by Gibeon's position. Perhaps, though, we see in this a further hint of the fulfilment of God's

[1] Boling and Wright, *Joshua*, p. 278, point out that this is the first time the city is named in the Bible (though note 'Salem' in Gen. 14:18).
[2] Which may have included Bethel.

promise to Israel that no-one would be able to resist them.[3] Adoni-
zedek's fear of Israel is a manifestation of God's promise to Israel,
and a first hint that God is indeed still with them as they continue
into the land. The God who promises is the one who continues to
fulfil his promises, a theme that will become more important as the
book progresses.[4]

2. Victories over the Amorites (10:6–28)

a. Victory at Gibeon (10:6–15)

Confronted by an attack from the Amorite kings, the Gibeonites
immediately contact Joshua, summoning his assistance against the
southern coalition. Joshua here has the opportunity to find a loophole
that might allow Israel to escape from their earlier promise. Promising that the Gibeonites could live could be taken simply to mean
that Israel will not kill them. After all, that was the specific concern
they had raised with Joshua after their identity had been revealed.[5]
So Joshua could see this as a simple way of getting out of a difficult
situation, letting the Amorites do what Israel no longer can. David
would face a similar challenge when, with Saul helpless before him,
Abishai offered to kill him so that David would not have to go back
on his vow not to kill Saul.[6] But just as David there saw that he
would not be guiltless simply because he had found a loophole, so
also Joshua recognizes here that the promise to the Gibeonites cannot
be set aside that way. This is because the Gibeonites have effectively
committed themselves to Israel and thus to Yahweh. They were
certainly far less effusive in their confession of faith than Rahab, but
the reality is the same. Making a covenant with Israel has set them
against the rest of the Canaanite peoples, and accepting them means
that Israel have a duty to protect them just as they have also done
for Rahab.[7] Accordingly, Joshua takes his fighting forces with him
from Gilgal to Gibeon.

It is only at this point that we hear again from Yahweh, the first
time he has spoken since he directed Joshua in the battle of Ai.[8] Here
Yahweh tells Joshua not to be afraid of the southern coalition because
he has given them into Joshua's power and none of them will be able
to resist. This word of reassurance addresses Joshua's immediate

[3] 1:5.
[4] Cf. 21:45; 23:14.
[5] 9:24.
[6] 1 Sam. 26:8–11.
[7] 6:22–25.
[8] 8:18.

concern, but does so by reasserting the promise made in 1:5. Israel can enter this battle because, in spite of all that has happened, the promise that Yahweh made will continue to be honoured. Joshua, and the army with him, may well have been greatly afraid as they set off, knowing that their arrangements with the Gibeonites were not all that they should be. As such, they faced the question of whether they were about to enter a situation similar to their first assault on Ai or whether they could go with confidence that Yahweh was fighting for them. This word of assurance makes clear that they can go with confidence because Yahweh is indeed faithful to his promises. However – and this is vital – Yahweh here shows himself faithful to his promises only after the people of Israel have shown themselves faithful to theirs. God expects faithfulness on the part of his people, and that includes in their relationships with others as well as in their relationship with him. Or, as Jesus puts it, we should be people whose 'yes' and 'no' mean exactly that, so that all can trust us.[9] Looking for loopholes in order to break a promise is not how God acts, and neither should it mark the life of his people.

With this reassurance, Joshua takes his troops on a night march in order to launch a sudden attack on the southern kings. This is illustrative of something often seen in Scripture: just because we have the promises of God, that does not mean we should set aside a sensible approach to a situation.[10] However, just as happened at Jericho, it is again Yahweh who will fight for Israel, this time sending large hailstones to strike their opponents. Large hailstones in this area are a known phenomenon, with instances of hailstones the size of cricket balls being recorded.[11] It is not clear whether it is Yahweh or Joshua who then pursues the Amorite kings to Azekah and Makkedah, though of course if Yahweh is fighting for Israel both are possible. In any case, it is Yahweh's involvement that is stressed so that we realize that, as with Jericho and Ai, it is really Yahweh who wins this battle. The pursuit of these kings also takes Israel out of the highlands for the first time as both Azekah and Makkedah are probably located in the lowlands to the south-west of Gibeon.

That this is Yahweh's victory is then stressed in the comments provided on the battle that emphasize that the hail killed many more than did Israel. Yahweh's involvement is stressed even more in the remarkable statements of verses 12–14. Here we have a record of Joshua's prayer, at least part of which appears to be a quotation from an old poem from the Book of Jashar, a book also said to contain

[9] Matt. 5:37.
[10] Similarly Butler, *Joshua*, p. 115.
[11] See Pitkänen, *Joshua*, p. 224, for details.

David's lament over Saul and Jonathan.[12] There is considerable dispute about where the quote begins and how it is to be interpreted,[13] much of which cannot be considered here. However, as with most translations it seems reasonable to assume that the quote itself begins halfway through verse 12, with the first half of the verse setting the context in which Joshua spoke it to Yahweh. Although Joshua is speaking to Yahweh, however, it is clear that the poem itself addresses the sun and moon directly, not Yahweh. Although it was clearly incorporated into the Book of Jashar at a later time, it is still quite possible that Joshua cites an earlier poem that remembers another time when the nation's enemies were defeated, and since the sun and moon are under Yahweh's control, Yahweh is addressed indirectly through the poem. But is Joshua here asking for the sun and moon literally to stop? Although many have argued this, suggesting that Joshua wanted a longer day in order to complete the defeat of the Amorites, it seems unlikely. If the sun is over Gibeon and the moon over the Valley of Aijalon, then the sun is in the east, so it is morning. If so, Joshua does not yet know he needs additional time. This makes it unlikely that we are looking for evidence of a change in the earth's rotation or anything of the like, and indeed Howard shows that claims that science has found this supposedly 'longer day' are really just a form of Christian urban myth.[14] It is more likely that the language here is intended to be figurative, so that just as other battle victories won by Yahweh are described in terms of the involvement of sun, moon and stars[15] without meaning their actual physical involvement, so here the language is pointing out that all creation was involved in Yahweh's victory.[16] The poem and the direct comment from the narrator thus affirm the same thing: it was Yahweh who won the victory, and he won in a dramatic way. Indeed – and this is what amazes the narrator – Yahweh won the battle because he responded to Joshua's prayer; indeed, he *obeyed* the prayer (14). This perhaps points to the sheer audacity of Joshua's prayer, since we normally ask God in prayer but in response obey him. This time, Yahweh obeyed Joshua. Surely we too ought to be stunned by this, while at the same time remembering that Joshua could be audacious in prayer precisely because his prayer was rooted in God's promises to him. Of course, this was a unique moment in Israel's story, but it reminds us that we can indeed be

[12] 2 Sam. 1:17–27.
[13] For a helpful summary, see Howard, *Joshua*, pp. 238–251.
[14] Howard, *Joshua*, pp. 241–242.
[15] E.g. Judg. 5:20; Hab. 3:11.
[16] Similarly, Howard, *Joshua*, pp. 247–248; Hubbard, *Joshua*, p. 297.

audacious in prayer when our requests are grounded in God's promises to us, just as Jesus also promised his disciples.[17]

Whatever the poem means, the basic point remains: Yahweh has proved faithful to his promises as he has seen Israel act in faithfulness to theirs. In so doing, he has also validated Joshua's decision of how to treat the Gibeonites.[18] God's 'yes' is just that, and he expects the same of his servants. So God here heeds the voice of his servant Joshua and fights for his people, something that we are told had never happened before or since at the time of writing. God does indeed honour those who honour him,[19] and in particular those who honour him in their dealings with others.

b. Defeating the kings (10:16–28)

After the extraordinary events just described, these verses can feel a little disorientating, as if we are encountering material we have previously covered. After all, did we not just hear about these kings fleeing to Makkedah? Indeed we did, but such repetitions are a common device in Old Testament narrative, in this case providing the narrator with the chance to focus more directly on how Yahweh's involvement changed things for Israel. It is as if, having painted out the whole landscape before us, an artist then comes back and starts to fill in elements of detail so that we can see more clearly what the various parts of the landscape are. In this case, we know that Yahweh is keeping his promises, but what does that look like in detail?

So we are back at Makkedah, nearly twenty miles south-west of Gibeon. It has been a long flight for these kings who have set themselves against God, and now they have hidden themselves in a cave there. Unfortunately, effective hiding requires that no-one knows where you are, and it seems that not only did these kings pick the wrong fight, but also they are not terribly good at hiding; Joshua is soon told of their whereabouts. Joshua quickly realizes that defeating the kings themselves is not the whole story, so having blocked them by rolling large stones over the entrance of the cave and having also appointed guards, he directs the rest of the men to continue their battle against the Amorites. In the context of a story that emphasizes Yahweh's involvement, Joshua's words are particularly important. He recognizes that the victory so far is one that Yahweh has won, and that its completion is also something that Yahweh is giving to Israel. After all, Joshua can see that he is proving faithful to his promises. Therefore, the men are to continue their pursuit of the

[17] E.g. John 14:12–14.
[18] 9:27.
[19] 1 Sam. 2:30.

stragglers to prevent as many as possible from entering fortified towns. Of course, the battle at Jericho has already shown that walls cannot keep Yahweh out, though many of these towns will be more heavily fortified than Jericho. And though a remnant do make it to fortified towns, the victory is clearly won so that in the end no-one can even speak against Israel.

When the troops return to Makkedah, Joshua orders the cave to be opened and the five kings to be brought out to him, with all five listed rather like roll being called. The crucial element here lies in Joshua's message to the troops as he summons them to gather and put their feet on the kings' necks. This is a clear statement of victory, the sort of thing that victorious kings would do; but Joshua here defuses any sense that Israel have won the battle themselves, although they have clearly been involved. Rather, his speech echoes God's words to him in 1:9. There, Joshua was told to take courage and not be afraid because he meditated upon Yahweh's word. Here, he directs the troops not to be afraid but to take courage because what they are doing symbolically to all their enemies, Yahweh will do in reality. Meditation on God's word is not mentioned this time, but the troops clearly have to know that God is here fulfilling his promises, and the reality of God's teaching is something that Joshua is able to mediate to them. It is because Joshua is aware of this that he can pass on this advice to the troops. It is this, reflecting on Deuteronomy 7 and 20, which then shapes his directions to the troops to execute the kings,[20] treating them just as he had the king of Ai,[21] and also leads to the capture of Makkedah and its destruction, with the key note that Joshua does to the king of Makkedah what he had done to the king of Jericho.

Although the book of Joshua is not written as a textbook on leadership, important themes about the nature of leadership emerge in this passage. Joshua is not always a model leader – the previous chapter has shown him to be someone who can make mistakes, as also was clear in the initial assault on Ai – but even so there are two important elements here. First, Joshua is able to pass on to the troops the essential content of God's instruction. This was not a context in which people had free access to God's word, and only a few such as Joshua would have had access to it in writing. In passing on his directives to the troops, Joshua passes on key elements from parts of Deuteronomy while also encouraging them. In doing so, he helps them to realize something they might not otherwise have understood, which is that this was a victory given to them by God. It was

[20] Fulfilling Deut. 7:24 and thus preparing for 11:1–20.
[21] 8:29.

not a matter of their own strength, even at those points where they indeed had to pursue the enemy. As one who was called to reflect on God's teaching, Joshua had the responsibility to show how this applied to the troops. Today, even though we live in a world where many have free access to the Bible, it remains a key task of Christian leadership to help people make connections between what they experience and God's Word. This requires continued reflection on the Bible, but it also means paying attention to the world and interpreting it through the Word. This is not an easy task, and we must beware of making facile connections. Nevertheless, if God is at work and fulfilling his promises to his people, it is the task of leaders to help people see what these promises are and how they are being fulfilled, and therefore how they should respond to them.

But, second, the clear references to the kings of Ai and Jericho mean that we are to read this passage in light of those two stories. As we have seen, they operate to interpret one another, with Jericho showing Israel the importance of obedience and Ai showing both the dangers of sin and also the possibilities of repentance. The covenant with Gibeon shows Israel potentially making new mistakes – even if this one will receive God's approval. What is clear here, though, is that Joshua is learning from prior mistakes, both his own and also those of the people as a whole. In shaping his directives he is clear that the people of Israel are to remain faithful to God's word and also that they are not to repeat their previous mistakes. Israel will not prove to be faultlessly faithful through the book, but Joshua here demonstrates that leadership is about creating a context for faithfulness through learning from previous mistakes.

3. The southern conquests (10:29–43)

The listing of the remaining conquests in the south can be a little off-putting for readers today who find the accounts repetitive because of their similarity, and of course that is not greatly helped by the fact that few of us have a clear idea where these places are. This is therefore definitely one passage where a Bible atlas will prove useful. Broadly, having pursued the Amorite kings to Makkedah, Joshua then goes about seven miles south to Libnah and then continues in the same direction for much the same distance to Lachish. There he also defeats the king of Gezer (who had travelled some distance from the north to aid Lachish), though without capturing that city, before heading south-west to Eglon, a city at the point where the lowlands meet the coastal plain. He then heads east into the highlands again to Hebron before turning south once again to Debir. Since other southern towns are mentioned in chapter

12,[22] this is probably meant to be a representative list. Apart from the encounter with the king of Gezer, whose city is not captured at this point, the pattern is broadly similar in each case: the city is captured, its inhabitants are put to the sword and its king is executed. There are minor variations in each account, but the key element in the pattern is made clear in the accounts of Libnah and Lachish as it is noted that it is Yahweh who gives the cities into Israel's power. Although this point is not repeated with the other cities, it is clear that we are to read them too as examples of Yahweh being faithful to his promises and giving Israel the land. Joshua had directed the people in terms of what God required of them, and he in turn was faithful to them in keeping his promises.

Indeed, the faithfulness of God to his promises is something that is again emphasized in the closing verses of the chapter, which indicate that Joshua *struck the whole land* (40), covering the hill country, the Negeb (or wilderness to the south of the land) and the Shephelah (or lowlands) and its slopes along with their kings. 'All the land' at this point is hyperbolic if we take it to mean the whole of the land promised by Yahweh, because the next chapter will cover events in the north where more victories will be won; but if we understand it to cover the south it is a more sober statement. Of course, defeating armed opponents and actually occupying the land are not exactly the same thing, as will be made clear in 13:1–7; but Joshua has been able to gain control of the south. That this involved devoting all to destruction is probably meant to refer to those who engaged in armed resistance, since later chapters will show many alive and well in these regions. For example, although Hebron and Debir are apparently completely destroyed in verses 36–39, both still need to be taken when the land is allocated to Caleb.[23] If so, this again points to the fact that, as with the Gibeonites, the issue of devotion to destruction was ultimately about whether or not people set themselves against Yahweh's purposes for his people. In other words, those destroyed were those who continued to oppose what God was doing and would themselves have chosen to destroy Israel. So this was not random violence; those who did not set themselves against Israel, and who probably fled their towns during battle, were not destroyed or hunted down. Throughout this chapter it is notable that although Israel is an invading people, the battles themselves were initially defensive – Israel had to overcome those who chose to attack them. All that Joshua did in taking control of the south is said to have been in obedience to Yahweh's command, while the narrator

[22] E.g. Hormah, 12:14.
[23] 15:13–15.

makes clear that Joshua won because Yahweh fought for Israel. Thus Joshua could then return to the security of Gilgal.

The chapter, though it covers many difficult matters, holds an important balance. The people of Israel start it in a position of uncertainty. Has their covenant with Gibeon put at risk their relationship with God? Will they still know the certainty of his promises? Theirs is a position of ambiguity because it is unclear whether or not their actions towards the Gibeonites will be assessed positively. What emerges through the chapter, however, is that God is indeed faithful to his promises, and he indeed reaffirms them in giving the south to Israel. But the people of Israel only discover the faithfulness of God to his promises as they too are faithful to their promises. And as they are faithful to their own promises so the chapter shows them finding more opportunities to be faithful in turn to the commands of God, through which they continue to find God faithful.

The church today has no right to claim any land as its own, least of all by force of arms, because the promises of God to us in Christ do not come in that form. The occupation of the land was meaningful in that sense only for Israel at this time. With that caveat, there is much here for reflection. We know that God is indeed faithful to his promises, but we face the challenge today of compromise and perhaps wonder whether a church that compromises stands in the place where God's promises can be meaningful for us today. Certainly as later generations of Israelites read these stories they would have been reminded of the fact that at this time God acted against the wickedness of Canaan, and therefore they would have been challenged to ask where they stood with God. Perhaps the word of reassurance we need to hear here is that where our choices have been made with good intent, as we live in faithfulness to those choices so God still opens up for us the chance to discover how his promises continue to find their 'yes' in Christ.[24] The God who was faithful to his people at the time of Joshua continues to be faithful to us today.

[24] 2 Cor. 1:20.

Joshua 11:1 – 12:24
10. Obedient to God: the northern campaign

Where Joshua 10 had emphasized God's faithfulness to his people, these chapters now put a much stronger emphasis upon Israel's obedience to God's commands as the reason why they were able to occupy the land of promise. This is particularly important because Joshua 7 – 9 has shown ways in which Israel could have put the promises of God at risk because of disobedience – most obviously through Achan's sin[1] but also through their covenant with the inhabitants of Gibeon.[2] Chapter 10, by contrast, has shown that God remained faithful to his people through the campaign in the south. That chapter recorded a miraculous victory won by Joshua as he overcame the alliance of southern kings who had opposed Israel because of their agreement with Gibeon. Indeed, that Yahweh responded to Joshua's prayer as to no other[3] makes it a particularly remarkable victory, a clear demonstration that he had not rejected Israel because of their covenant with Gibeon.

But does God only work through and for his people by miraculous means? In other words, can we only point to the work of God when we can see something that stands outside of normal experience? If we listen to testimonies given at some Christian meetings, we might gain the impression that the only times we can know God has been at work are when we can point to the miraculous, and indeed one of the problems we face today is that when we ask for testimonies it is usually the miraculous (or at least the unusual) that we seek. Actually, however, Joshua has for some time been emphasizing the theme of obedience, stressing that it is by obedience that God's people progress. God does indeed work miraculously, as the previous

[1] Josh. 7.
[2] Josh. 9.
[3] 10:14.

chapter has shown, but there is something more basic than this at the heart of so much that God does: simply put, God works through the obedience of his people. In Joshua 11 especially we see the importance of obedience, and we shall find that this theme is also present even in what seems a rather dull listing of places and kings that Israel defeated in Joshua 12. What might surprise us, though, is the particular shape that obedience takes here, though throughout we continue to see the faithfulness of God.

Before we look at these chapters in more detail we need to pause and get our bearings again, as with these two chapters we reach the mid-point of the book, and although we have some new material here it is shaped by concerns that the book has been developing up to this point. In particular, we need to note links between these chapters and the material in Joshua 1, 5:1–12 and 10, because these help us understand the message of these chapters.

Two key themes in Joshua 1 are important for understanding these chapters. There we saw the importance of Joshua's continued reflection on God's instruction as revealed through Moses. This was to be his guide to all he did, and he was to meditate on it continually.[4] We noted earlier that Deuteronomy especially is presented as the text that guided Joshua, but this theme comes to particular prominence here in chapter 11 as we are told that Joshua did everything that Moses commanded, eventually taking the land Yahweh had promised to Moses.[5] Obedience, the second theme, was thus required from Joshua, and it was through that obedience that Yahweh provided the land. Obedience was also required from the people, especially from the tribes who were settling east of the Jordan, since they could not return to their land until those who would live within the originally promised boundaries were also settled.[6] As we move into the listing provided in chapter 12 we see how Yahweh had indeed provided the opportunity for the other tribes to claim their inheritance, meaning that the trans-Jordan tribes had been obedient. Chapter 12's list thus serves to close off the first half of the book by demonstrating that the obedience required of the eastern tribes had played its part in Yahweh giving the land to the other tribes – though we will return to this matter in Joshua 22.

Joshua 5:1–12 also insisted on the priority of obedience at the point when Israel had first entered the land and were about to begin to take it, requiring them to circumcise the men and then celebrate Passover prior to any action against Jericho. The obedience required was then shown at Jericho, though the effects of disobedience were

[4] 1:8.
[5] 11:12, 15, 20.
[6] 1:12–18.

also demonstrated in the events at Ai. The return to this theme here at the end of the accounts of conquest means that it bookends the battle accounts. We are thus reminded of the importance of obedience at the commencement of these accounts and then again at their conclusion.

Finally, there is a very close link between chapters 10 and 11, though of course these also reach back to chapter 9, where the motif of the Canaanite peoples' 'hearing' also refers back to 5:1. What is particularly notable is that the structures of these chapters closely parallel one another so that chapter 11 is a 'literary mirror' of chapter 10.[7] Both begin with an alliance of kings who oppose but are defeated by Israel (10:1–15; 11:1–9), then report the capture of cities (10:16–39; 11:10–15) before offering closing summaries (10:40–43; 11:21–23). Their close parallels are also important for showing how they differ. Most obviously, in Joshua 11 we have now moved to the far north of Israel, whereas the previous chapter had started in the middle and moved to the far south; and it is notable that chapter 11 provides far less detail than chapter 10. The more important distinction, however, is in how Yahweh gives the land to Israel. In chapter 10 it is by means of a miracle, albeit one where Israel still needed to have its forces moving to the site of battle. In this way Joshua 10 echoes the fall of Jericho in chapter 6, since that was also miraculous. The repeated emphasis here in chapter 11, though, is that Yahweh has given Israel the land because of their obedience. So, whether by miracle or by obedience, it is Yahweh who has given Israel the land. And it is given here through obedience.

1. Northern conquests (11:1–15)

a. Overcoming the northern alliance (11:1–9)

The close parallel between this chapter and chapter 10 is particularly evident in the opening verses: the opening sentence of each is almost identical, with the main change being in the insertion of the relevant kings who have heard about Israel. Since 9:1–2 has described a similar response, we need to see this as part of a continued process whereby Israel are attacked by the peoples already in the land, an extension of the problems caused by Achan's sin at Jericho,[8] demonstrating yet again that the effects of sin linger far longer than we might imagine. This gathering of towns continues a motif from the previous chapter, though now we have moved to the north of the country.

[7] Nelson, *Joshua*, p. 151.
[8] 7:1.

Again, though, it is an alliance of kings who will oppose Israel, this time organized by Jabin,[9] king of Hazor, though this appears to be a much larger alliance than they have previously faced. Hazor was a major city in the region, about twelve miles north of the Sea of Galilee. As it was close to the main trade road it became wealthy, a fact that is borne out by excavations which reveal a site which in total exceeds two hundred acres. As a result, it was a city that would naturally be worried by Israel's emergence, especially if their control of the south might threaten the trade routes which ran to the coast and then down to Egypt.

Hazor on its own would be a formidable opponent, but Jabin appears to be aware of the failure of the southern kings and so here gathers a grand alliance of the north against Israel. The location of all the towns listed here is not known with certainty,[10] but the alliance seems to cover a semicircle, with Hazor more or less at the centre, from the region of Mount Hermon at the south of the Lebanon range to the north, across to the coast at Naphoth-dor and then to Madon, a little west of the lower part of Chinneroth, to the south. That these are representative of the towns included in the alliance rather than a comprehensive listing is indicated by the fact that we are also told that six of the peoples of Canaan are included, and their kings will also be among those summoned by Jabin. The extent of Israel's challenge is made explicit in verse 4, which not only compares the numbers of their opponents to the sand on the seashore – a proverbial phrase in the Old Testament for a huge number[11] – but also adds that they had *very many horses and chariots*. These pose a major challenge for Israel because they represent a form of warfare that Israel has not previously encountered, and indeed chariots would later cause the people of Ephraim to fear the Canaanites on the plains[12] – though of course at the crossing of the Sea Pharaoh's chariots had not helped him against Yahweh.[13] Nevertheless, chariots still represented a significant piece of military hardware, offering a quick mobile platform from which archers could shoot at the opposition. As these forces come together at the waters of Merom – an unknown site but perhaps a stream that flows into the north-west side of the Sea of Galilee – the people of Israel face a mighty challenge on a military

---

[9] Possibly a hereditary title rather than a personal name – note that there is another Jabin who is 'king of Canaan' in Judg. 4:2. Similarly, Howard, *Joshua*, p. 265; Woudstra, *Joshua*, pp. 187–188.

[10] For a helpful overview see David Merling, Sr., *The Book of Joshua: Its Theme and Role in Archaeological Discussions* (Berrien Springs: Andrews University Press, 1997), pp. 139–145.

[11] E.g. Gen. 22:17; 32:12; 41:49; Judg. 7:12.

[12] 17:16.

[13] Exod. 14:25.

scale quite unlike what they have faced before. One might think that a miracle is precisely what they need. However, this Canaanite dependence on horses stands in contrast to Deuteronomy 17:16's insistence that any Israelite king is not to acquire many horses,[14] and in this there may be a hint of where Hazor's grand alliance might fail. Indeed, the temptation to depend on horses seems to be a particular problem that is challenged in this account.

However, a miracle is not to happen – at least, not if by 'miracle' we mean something supernatural that might match the hailstones of 10:11 or Yahweh's response to Joshua's prayer in 10:14. Nevertheless, there are still close parallels here with chapter 10 as in verse 6 Yahweh again tells Joshua not to fear his enemies because he is giving them over to Israel,[15] while in verse 7 Joshua again launches a sudden attack, possibly having chosen a site where chariots will be ineffective.[16] However, where Yahweh had previously assured Joshua that no-one would stand before him,[17] this time his promise is that Israel's opponents will be *give[n] over ..., slain, to Israel* (6). How that will happen is not specified, but what matters is that Israel are to hamstring the horses and burn the chariots. In other words, even though Israel at this point do not have a king, the people are still to avoid the temptation to accumulate power for themselves and trust in military resources that might make them forget that Yahweh is their real source of strength. It is notable that David also follows this pattern after defeating another northern king.[18] Hamstringing the horses probably involved a process that rendered them useless for military activity but would still permit their use in agriculture.

Thus Israel, like the church today, were not to imagine that they gained power through adopting the practices of the nations around them. Rather, Israel's weapons were focused on their faith and obedience to Yahweh, something that Paul takes up in his discussion of the whole armour of God,[19] also stressing that the strongholds against which we battle are not those of flesh and blood.[20] Nevertheless, there is a continuing temptation for the church to accumulate political power so that our source of strength is something visible. Hamstringing the horses and burning the chariots was to be a visible sign for Israel that they were not to follow this pattern.

[14] Howard, *Joshua*, p. 267.
[15] Cf. 10:8.
[16] Cf. 10:9.
[17] 10:8.
[18] 2 Sam. 8:4.
[19] Eph. 6:10–20; 1 Thess. 5:8.
[20] 2 Cor. 10:4.

That obedience was the key to victory is made clear in verses 7–9. Joshua's surprise attack again shows that there is no contradiction between trusting God and acting wisely, but the victory that was gained was still Yahweh's because Joshua acted on the basis of God's promise. The battle itself is therefore barely described, with the focus instead on the extent of their pursuit of survivors as far as the coast at Sidon in the south of Lebanon or Misrephoth-maim south of Tyre, and of others as far to the east as the Valley of Mizpeh in the Hermon range. Again the defeat is total, though once more those killed are clearly those who continued to resist. That obedience was central is emphasized by the statement of verse 9. Joshua did exactly what Yahweh had commanded, hamstringing the horses and burning the chariots. Israel gained victory by trusting in the promise of Yahweh; why would they, or we today, want anything else?

b. Capturing the cities (11:10–15)

With the kings defeated, Joshua then turns to take the cities of the north. Just as happened in the south, defeating the armies did not mean that the cities had been captured. However, where the account of the southern cities took time to provide a roll call of their capture,[21] this time the capture of Hazor is sufficient, with the other cities mentioned only in summary. Although the king of Hazor was killed there is no indication that he was executed; he could well have been killed in battle. However, consistent with the southern accounts, Joshua again devotes the inhabitants of the towns captured to destruction, leaving no survivor. Hazor is, unusually, also burned, and is noted as the only city treated this way.[22] We are given no reason for this, but in light of the resistance to the trappings of royalty and human power in general, we are perhaps to understand this in terms of a further extension of this policy. The capture of a city as powerful as Hazor could well lead Israel to trust in its fortifications, and just as they were not to depend on attacking weapons apart from those given by God, neither were they to trust in other defences. The presence of God, and that alone, remains sufficient for the people of God, something today experienced through Jesus' promise to be with his disciples[23] and the presence of the Spirit.[24]

[21] 10:28–39.
[22] Excavations show a destruction layer at Hazor which can be dated to the time of Joshua.
[23] Matt. 28:18–20.
[24] Acts 1:8.

But what of the apparent violence that is described here? How does this fit with the peaceable kingdom of Jesus?[25] Devoting to destruction, as we have seen before,[26] meant leaving nothing behind, though there were degrees to which it could be applied as only at Jericho was the taking of spoil prohibited. Walter Brueggemann has argued that the only normative element in this passage is the command against horses and chariots,[27] but this seems to adopt too narrow a view; certainly the subsequent comments about Joshua's obedience to everything Moses had commanded seem to imply that he has applied the requirements of Deuteronomy 7. So, although Brueggemann's insights about the egalitarian nature of the alternative society Israel was constructing are helpful (since at least one of the fundamental problems with Canaanite structures was their agglomeration of power and wealth into very few hands), I do not believe we can marginalize these later statements. A better solution is to hand when we note that in chapter 10 we saw that it was those who continued to resist Israel who were placed under the ban: that is, Yahweh's judgment was on those who continued to resist his purposes. Devotion to destruction was something that was permitted only in the context of Israel taking the land and needs to be understood as Yahweh's judgment on sin for the specific purpose of allowing Israel to flourish as his people. When these sections are read within the larger narrative arc of the book, however, we realize that it did not have to be this way. This remained a sorrowful action for Yahweh just as it is difficult for us today; it was not God's intention for anyone then any more than it is now.

The centrality of obedience is again reinforced by the concluding statement of verse 15, which insists that Joshua did everything just as Moses had commanded, leaving nothing undone. In light of the preceding narrative, this might seem surprising. After all, should Joshua have entered into a covenant with Gibeon? Indeed, Deuteronomy 7 seems to leave no room for anyone to survive, but we have seen that Joshua only destroyed those who continued to resist Yahweh. Likewise, Deuteronomy seems to allow no room for any plunder to be taken, but this has clearly been applied only in Jericho; elsewhere, plunder has been permitted. It is no surprise, then, that Hawk finds this statement to be 'problematic'.[28] Actually, however, this points to a remarkable aspect of the nature of obedience that needs teasing out. Although Deuteronomy 7 and 20 make clear

[25] Isa. 11:6–9.
[26] 6:17–18.
[27] Walter Brueggemann, *Divine Presence Amid Violence: Contextualizing the Book of Joshua* (Milton Keynes: Paternoster, 2009), pp. 33–41.
[28] Hawk, *Joshua*, p. 172.

that the peoples under the ban are to be devoted to destruction, the same law also prohibits intermarriage with them because of a concern that they will lead the people of Israel away from faithfulness to Yahweh.[29] Clearly one cannot intermarry with people who are dead, so Deuteronomy already contains a seed that points to the fact that it describes a *maximum* that could happen, though in its typical hortatory style it does not express this directly. Joshua, then, has not only known the content of the law that he might obey it, but his continued meditation on it means that he has also understood the fact that obedience is always mediated by context. In other words, a law in Deuteronomy such as that of the ban can direct Israel in what is expected, but it always needs to be interpreted if it is to be applied in a specific circumstance. Joshua has thus seen that Deuteronomy's core concern is with anything that will lead Israel away from faithfulness. Where necessary, because of continued resistance, devotion to destruction is required; but where such resistance does not take place, such destruction is not required. So Brueggemann is right – Scripture has to be contextualized if it is to be applied. However, our approach to contextualizing Joshua has to happen through understanding how Joshua has contextualized Deuteronomy. In turn, that means that not only do we need to know the content of Scripture – though that is an essential starting point – but we also need to understand what it was doing in its own context. Then, and arguably only then, can we begin to consider how that applies in our own time and place. This means that obedience to God's Word is more complex than is sometimes suggested, but understood in these terms we recognize that it is always applicable. These things were indeed 'written for our instruction'.[30]

2. Campaign summary (11:16–23)

We now have presented for us three summaries of the campaign up to this point. The first highlights the way in which the land was taken, and it once again does so by highlighting the obedience of Joshua.

We are first given a general summary of the whole of the campaign in verses 16–20. It repeats briefly much of what has been covered in the preceding chapters, though through its listing the land by its various regions we appreciate that God has been faithful in giving Israel all the land. Indeed, although the land is described in generalized geographical terms,[31] these broadly follow the route recorded for the campaign to this point. After crossing at Gilgal, Israel had

[29] Deut. 7:3–4.
[30] Rom. 15:4.
[31] Though admittedly the reference here to *the land of Goshen*, v. 16, is obscure.

moved into the hills before the campaign in the south which went down towards the Negeb, covering both the lowlands towards the west and also the Jordan valley. Subsequently, as recorded in this chapter, they moved into the hill country to the north – here described as the *hill country of Israel* (16), which reflects later terminology which would have been more understandable for the first readers. The south is marked again by reference to Mount Halak, which as somewhere towards Seir is probably to the south of the Dead Sea, while Baal-gad, near Mount Hermon, is in the far north. Joshua has thus taken the land – though as is also clear, there is a great deal of difference between taking the land and occupying it.

That Joshua recognizes this distinction is seen in the statement of verse 18 that insists that this was a long campaign. We might imagine that the book has described a rapid process in which Israel swept in and claimed the land. Deuteronomy 7:22, however, has already made clear that the campaign could not be too quick because that would desolate the land. Thus, as Joshua has obeyed God's command to him, so also God has been faithful to him, ensuring that the land is taken in a way that will enable Israel to flourish. Obedience is thus shown to be the means of discovering God's best for his people. In this case, this even includes the fact that the Gibeonites make peace with Israel, though the hardening of the hearts of the other nations is deliberately reminiscent of Pharaoh in the exodus. The summary, though, makes its point in verse 20. It was God who was waging war – and even leading the Canaanites out to war, so that in many respects Israel was waging a defensive campaign[32] – so that he might judge them for their sin. Canaanite disobedience is thus contrasted with Israelite obedience, showing that it was their rebellion which led to their armed resistance and ultimately their destruction,[33] since their hardening of heart was really God giving them reason to follow their own foolish inclinations, just as Pharaoh had done.[34] The victor was always Yahweh, and never Israel alone. However, that is not the whole of the emphasis, for it was also an action that involved faithful human response – and all that was done was in accordance with what Yahweh had commanded Moses. The advance came through obedience.

This point is highlighted again in the second campaign summary, in verses 21–23, where we read of how Joshua defeated the Anakim. The Anakim were the people who had terrified Israel at the point of their first approach to the land in Numbers 13:33, leading to the rebellion of the Israelites so that all apart from Joshua and Caleb

[32] Cf. Jerome F. D. Creach, *Joshua* (Louisville: Westminster John Knox, 2003), p. 96.
[33] Hess, *Joshua*, p. 218.
[34] Hubbard, *Joshua*, p. 339.

would perish in the wilderness.[35] This in turn led to the forty years of wandering in the wilderness. The Anakim were a fearsome foe renowned for their great size, but they too were defeated, with only those in the coastal plain towns of Gaza, Gath and Ashdod (where Joshua does not record Israel going) still surviving. The plain lies within the boundaries promised earlier,[36] so the survival of these Anakim points to something that was still to happen, making clear that although God had indeed given all the land, much still remained to be taken.[37]

The Anakim were also defeated by Yahweh, again as Joshua was obedient to his command. On that basis, the land could then experience *rest* (23). As Hebrews makes clear, this was not a final rest for God's people,[38] and indeed there would be continual warfare for many generations. Nevertheless, it was a real rest in the sense that the campaign had come to an end. Now, rather than battling to gain control of the land, the emphasis can be upon its apportionment among the people, and it is this that will dominate chapters 13–21.

3. Captured territory and defeated kings (12:1–24)

The third campaign summary is then provided for us in chapter 12. This is, admittedly, not a chapter that immediately swells the breast with warm devotional thoughts! It is here to provide a roll call of God's faithfulness that points to him overcoming the kings of the land. Of course, *king* here does not have the sense it typically has in the West today of a ruler of a recognizable nation; more probably it refers to someone who was chief in a town, though there was probably a hierarchy of kings, so that some (such as those in Jerusalem or Hazor) reigned over lesser kings. The list itself is divided into two parts. First, in verses 1–6 we have a listing of the territory captured under Moses east of the Jordan. This is the land occupied by the tribes east of the Jordan who had left that land behind to join in the campaign. This is then followed in verses 7–24 by a listing of the kings defeated by Joshua, not all of whom are mentioned earlier in the book, pointing again to the summary nature of the narratives that we have. Joshua is thus once more affirmed as Moses' successor, again linking this chapter with the opening verses of chapter 1. As with the summary in 11:16–20, the northern and southern boundaries are Baal-gad and Mount Halak, with the listing broadly following the pattern of the narratives that have preceded

[35] Num. 14:30.
[36] 1:4.
[37] 13:1–2.
[38] Heb. 4:1–13.

it, so that we start with Jericho and the central highlands, move to the south and then to the north, though ending with Tirzah brings us back to the central highlands.

We might wonder about the value of a text like this – but it is a roll call of God's faithfulness. The land had rest because Yahweh won the battle, and he won the battle because of the obedience of the people. This list is the evidence of that outcome, showing that Canaanite kings have no place in God's purposes, and that indeed God alone is now king. More than this, it is also a roll call of God's faithfulness in the context of his people's obedience. All the tribes, including those from east of the Jordan, had to commit themselves to God's purposes for them, and as all obeyed, all then enjoyed the rest mentioned at the end of chapter 11. Moreover, although the territory east of the Jordan was not part of the initial promise it has now become part of the land, so that a united people who have obeyed God live in the blessing of his peace. It will not stay that way, but it is held out to us as a sign of what a people who are obedient to the faithful God can experience. God does indeed work through the miraculous, but this list is one more pointer that the more normal path is through the obedience of his people.

Joshua 13:1 – 14:15
11. Living the promise

As is apparent to most readers, we enter a new section of the book of Joshua at this point. Chapter 12's sonorous listing of towns and kings acted as a closing summary of the first part of the book, and here we commence the second, which runs through to the end of chapter 21. It is clearly very different from the material that has gone before. Where, with the obvious exception of chapter 12, the bulk of the book to this point has provided readers with a series of tightly focused accounts that explain how Israel was able to take control of most of the land Yahweh had promised, this new section is notable for an almost complete lack of narrative. There *are* brief narratives, most of which are concerned with how issues from the period of the wilderness wanderings will be resolved, but for the most part we are provided with lists of borders and towns that most readers today find almost impenetrable in their mind-numbing detail. I have known many Christians who could recite some of their favourite verses in the Bible, quite a few of which came from the Old Testament; but I don't think I have ever met anyone whose favourite verse came from these chapters. These are chapters that have defeated many an earnest believer's attempt to read through the whole of the Bible, and they are often either omitted or treated very briefly in Bible reading notes that seek to provide guidance on what the Bible has to say to us today.[1] This is also borne out by the decision of the editors of some editions of the New English Bible to print them in a smaller font in order to indicate that they would probably not be of interest to the general reader. In short, these are chapters that many of us find difficult and, if we're honest, more than just a little dull. Perhaps this is why the first time I preached through the

[1] To give one example, Jerome Creach's otherwise very helpful commentary on Joshua devotes some 78 pages to chs. 1–12 while giving only 8 to chs. 13–21.

141

book of Joshua I decided to treat the whole of chapters 13–21 in a single sermon.

If you are reading this hoping that I am about to reveal a means of making these chapters instantly interesting, I am afraid you will be disappointed. The simple reality is that these chapters are hard work, and they pose some quite particular problems for the interpreter, quite apart from the obvious challenge of showing how they speak to believers today. We do not have to consider some of those issues in any detail here, though it is important to realize that there are often significant text-critical challenges in these chapters and also that some of the lists may well have been updated over time. For us, it is enough to consider the more basic hermeneutical issues. In short, what is the function of chapters like these, and do we really need to read them?

We can answer these questions in reverse. Yes, we do need to read these chapters (though we don't need to enjoy them in the same way as we might enjoy some other parts of Joshua). The book of Joshua is not complete without them as they provide the evidence that Yahweh was indeed fulfilling his promises to Israel. Joshua's subsequent claims about Yahweh's faithfulness to his promises[2] depend upon what is said here, though that much of the land remains to be claimed also provides the foundation for Joshua's final messages to the people.[3] So we do need to read these chapters; and that we need to do so comes from their function. They are the key evidence that Yahweh had indeed given the land, and, more than that, that every clan could understand that the land where they lived was theirs. Just as title deeds today provide information about a property that most of us cannot understand without a solicitor or surveyor because they are much more precise than our own ways of giving our address, so these chapters provide Israel with their title deeds.[4] They are not easy to read precisely because of their function, but perhaps that in itself is sufficient reason for us to read them carefully today.

As we read chapters 13–14 we will note some central issues. Most importantly, we quickly see that although Joshua 13:1–7 encourages us to think about the future action of distributing the land, we almost immediately encounter the record of the tribes in the east with a summary of the land they have already received.[5] As we read 14:1–5 it again seems as if we are about to begin the main distribution of the land, only to focus instead on the story of Caleb and his claim of Hebron, an account which is rooted in the events of Numbers

[2] 21:45; 23:14.
[3] Josh. 23 – 24.
[4] I owe this analogy to Howard, *Joshua*, pp. 321–323.
[5] 13:8–33.

13 – 14.[6] Both chapters thus have a structure which begins by focusing on the distribution of all the land, only to retard that to explain how past issues have been resolved. Discussion of the main distribution of the land therefore begins only in chapter 15, which suggests that, although they describe the allocation of the land on both sides of the Jordan, these two chapters need to be read together as a prelude to the main distribution. In this way we see that they provide a model for Israel's future, and indeed for our own. The distribution of land to the eastern tribes makes clear that God does indeed provide for his people as he has promised, while Caleb then models what it means to claim what God has promised, a claim that derives from obedient discipleship and a willingness to continue to trust God. Both the past (through the eastern tribes) and the future (modelled through Caleb) point to this fundamental pattern. Only with these points established can we move to the actual allocation of the land in the subsequent chapters.

1. Directions for Joshua (13:1–7)

Although age has not previously been mentioned as an issue, from this point on it is, both for Joshua and for Caleb.[7] Mention of Joshua's advanced age introduces this section and later also his farewell speeches.[8] The key difference is that in the latter case it is Joshua himself who recognizes the limitations of his age, while here it is Yahweh who needs to point it out to him. As Caleb will show, age is not itself a limitation for claiming a small portion of the land, but the implication is that Joshua has now reached the stage where he can no longer continue to lead the nation in claiming the land. So although one of the key motifs through the book is how Joshua becomes like Moses, eventually sharing the title 'the servant of Yahweh' with him,[9] he still differs from Moses in that he reaches a point of effective retirement, whereas Moses continued to lead the people until his death. Moreover, Joshua's 110 years leave him short of Moses' 120.[10]

Achieving a great age was considered a blessing in the Bible, much as most people today would see it. However, the contrast that is drawn between Joshua and Moses at this point is instructive. It is clear that there is no particular age at which people become too old to serve God, and of course even after the allocation of the land

[6] 14:6–15.
[7] 14:10.
[8] 23:2.
[9] 24:29.
[10] Deut. 34:7.

143

Joshua would still lead the people, albeit in a different way, until his death. For Moses, there was no point at which age diminished his ability to lead. On the other hand, for Joshua, his age did mean that there were limits on what he was able to do, but this did not mean he suddenly ceased to serve God. Perhaps the simplest observation to make on this is that there is no universal pattern for understanding the relationship between age and effective ministry. Some, by God's grace, will be able to continue in effective leadership well past the age that our societies have determined is the point of retirement, perhaps because their love of ministry and sense of vocation are such that they derive real energy from that, energy which can clearly be traced to the work of God in their lives. Yet for others, the demands of their earlier labours are such that they are unable to continue as they once did. This in no way belittles them because God's gifting and call differ for each. It is unlikely that any of us today will match Moses in his extraordinary vitality, but I have known and been blessed by the ministry of those who have served well beyond 'retirement age'. Indeed, as a student minister I learned a great deal from working with a much older man, though perhaps like many younger people I did not fully realize it at the time. Yet, as we see here, there will be times when older leaders will need to recognize their limits – even if, like Joshua, they may need God to make it clear to them. As many Christian denominations now face the problem of ageing clergy and fewer people coming through for training, it may prompt us to rethink the resources that we have in our older leaders, asking ourselves how best we can use what God has given us in them and through which he continues to bless us, rather than assuming there is a fixed point or form of 'retirement' – even if pension schemes tend to make us think in those terms!

Beyond Yahweh's declaration of Joshua's age, much of what follows is rather liable to make the eyes of contemporary readers glaze over. Nevertheless, it makes explicit what was already hinted at in the listing in 11:16–23 of 'all the land' that had been taken. Already it was clear that, although Joshua had led the nation in a so-far successful campaign, the actual area taken was relatively small, and in fact Israel would need to retake some of the places,[11] making clear that there is an important distinction between taking the land and occupying it. So while it is important to note that much of the land had indeed been taken, much still remained to be taken. Israel had received the promise of God with the land, but the fullness of the promise was still ahead of them, and this meant an ongoing

[11] For example, Hebron is taken in 10:36–37, but it will need to be retaken in 14:10–15.

process of occupation. We are not helped by the fact that the identification of some of the places mentioned here is uncertain, but it seems that the description starts in the south and gradually moves to the north. If so, the Geshurites were resident in the area of the Negeb[12] rather than the region in Bashan mentioned in 12:5. The list then moves across to the coastal plain, which was being occupied by the Philistines at about the same time as Israel, mentioning all five of their traditional towns, though the identification of the Shihor River is uncertain beyond the fact that it was towards Egypt. In verse 4 the list moves further up the coast, skipping the area whose capture was described in 11:1–15, and on to an area around Sidon. Verse 5 then heads inland to the east, listing areas in the Lebanon around Mount Hermon, which of course featured as a northern boundary to the account of 11:1–15.

The goal of this listing becomes clear in verses 6–7. Joshua is told that he is to allot the whole land, including that which has not yet been taken. Thus the distribution of the land is also an act of faith on his part. Accordingly, there is an important link here with 1:2–9. There, as the conquest accounts were about to begin, we saw that Joshua, and Israel as a whole, had to trust God to lead them through the land so that they might take it. Now, it is as Joshua and the people look back to what God has already done on their behalf that they are to look forward to what he will continue to do. By being told to allot the land at this point, the whole nation are therefore to understand that they need to continue to trust in Yahweh's provision, a provision that will need to take a new form given the apparent limitations of Joshua's age. What is more, they have to realize that although it is Joshua who will divide the land into the portions for the nine and a half tribes who have not yet received their inheritance and who will be listed in the subsequent chapters, it is still Yahweh who is removing the existing inhabitants and giving it to them. So the means by which Yahweh will act on Israel's behalf will change, but the fundamental nature of what he will do will not. Yahweh will keep his promises to his people, and they go forward only by realizing that.

Obviously, the Christian church is not bound to any land today. The church is, by its very nature, something that transcends all national boundaries, so we must be careful not to associate the promise of land with any particular land or nation today. That is not something God has promised us. We do, however, need to see this promise within the framework of the mission of God.[13] God's

---

[12] Mentioned in 1 Sam. 27:8.
[13] Most helpfully laid out by Wright, *The Mission of God*.

purpose is to bring creation back to himself, and Israel's existence within the Old Testament was part of this. The form that this role took changed over time, though without changing the fundamental purpose. Most obviously, this changed as the covenant relationship between Yahweh and Israel developed through the main covenants in the Old Testament, but there are also points where we see subtler changes taking place, and this is one of them. God is here continuing to fulfil his promise of land to Israel, but the means by which he is fulfilling it has changed. No longer will the land promise be fulfilled through the presence of a central leader; rather it will now find its fulfilment in the faithful action of the whole of God's people. There are many points of connection for Christians today, but perhaps the most important for us to note is that the promise of God's continued presence with us as we join him in his mission remains.[14] It is clear, however, that in different seasons the work of this mission has at times depended more on the presence of important leaders and at other times more on the continued work of the church as a whole.

One minor analogy might help make the implications of this clear at the local level. When my wife and I worked in Zimbabwe we assisted in a church plant in a high-density township. The initial work of the church plant depended very much on an influential leader who could galvanize those present to join the work. The leader was essential to the work of planting the church. However, it became clear over time that the church flourished when the work did not depend on a central leader, but rather when the congregation as a whole took responsibility for joining God in the work that he was doing. The mission we had to that community was the same, but the means by which it was fulfilled and by which we claimed the promise of God's empowering presence with us changed over time. This was a pattern we saw repeated at a number of other places. Indeed, these churches were in many ways released once they no longer depended on a central leader, even though their initiation depended on one. Here, then, for Israel to flourish they needed to see that they all had to join God in his mission and not simply depend on the work of a prominent leader, no matter how revered that leader might have been. The same is true for us today.

2. The eastern tribes revisited (13:8–33)

Following the directives given to Joshua we expect that he will begin to allocate the land, but in fact that is delayed while we are given a listing of the land occupied by the tribes who had claimed their

---

[14] Matt. 28:18–20; Acts 1:8.

territory in the area east of the Jordan – Reuben, Gad and half of Manasseh (the other half of Manasseh will receive their land within the promised boundaries in ch. 17). And if the listing in verses 2–5 is difficult for readers today, this one is a real nightmare (though worse is still to come!). Again our difficulties are compounded by uncertainty about some of the places mentioned, though we know enough of what is described to have the general area reasonably clear. Nevertheless, for all the difficulty a passage like this generates, we need to understand its function here. By deliberately delaying the allocation of the land under Joshua and looking back to the allocation of the land east of the Jordan under Moses, two key things are achieved. First, we see that Joshua will again continue the ministry of Moses. Just as Moses allocated the land to the eastern tribes, so Joshua will allocate the land to those in the west. Again we see the pattern of transitions within God's mission that was already hinted at in the opening verses of the chapter, and recognize that as God has already shown his faithfulness to his people, he will continue to do so, albeit in a slightly different way. Second, we are reminded again of the unity of Israel, so that although the Jordan is a physical barrier (admittedly one that, apart from when it is in flood, is not too difficult to cross), Israel as a people are not divided by it.[15] God's mission will continue to include and be carried out by all God's people. This carries on the theme of the unity of God's people established in 1:10–18 and which was also shown by the listing of territory captured on both sides of the Jordan in chapter 12.

The listing itself begins in verses 8–12 with a general summary of the region and once again outlines the area as covering the kingdoms of Sihon and Og,[16] so broadly matching the territory described in 12:1–6. The concluding note of verse 13, however, makes clear that there is still territory to take, though this time Geshur (along with Maacath) is in the region of Bashan. After this, the list is divided into three main sections which move in a broadly south-to-north direction. First, the territory of Reuben is described in some detail in verses 15–23; a shorter listing is then provided for Gad in verses 24–28; and an even briefer listing is given for the eastern half of Manasseh in verses 29–31. Much of the territory of Reuben and Gad would later become part of Moab, while the Ammonites would raid and claim much of eastern Manasseh. However, at this time it is land that Israel can look back to and see as something that Yahweh has indeed given, and in giving it he has provided a paradigm for the rest of the people.

[15] This will, though, become an explicit issue in ch. 22.
[16] See comments on 2:10.

147

This list is not, however, simply a matter of historical interest. Rather, it serves to show that just as Yahweh has been faithful in the past, so he will continue to provide for his people, doing so not only at the level of the tribe but also at the more local level of the clan – which we might think of as a group of villages within a tribe – since the allocation of the land is consistently made clan by clan. This provision is seen not only in the claiming of the land, but also in the brief note about Balaam which is inserted into the list of Reuben's territory, along with mention of Sihon and his Midianite allies. Balaam's story of ultimately blessing Israel rather than cursing them is recounted in Numbers 22 – 24. Later, however, he was apparently involved in the process by which Midianite women seduced Israelite men, leading to Yahweh's punishment of Israel which was stopped by the zeal of Phinehas,[17] with Balaam eventually being killed when Israel took vengeance on Midian.[18] His brief mention here is not accidental. Rather it points to a different type of adversary from those that Israel have so far faced in the land. Throughout Numbers 22 – 24, the people of Israel are apparently unaware of the attack that is being attempted through Balaam, and yet Yahweh protects them and even sees them blessed. So not only has God given them land, he has also protected them through all attacks – something his people can therefore trust that he will continue to do.

The list is also bounded by two references to the tribe of Levi and the fact that they did not receive an inheritance among the eastern tribes.[19] This is because Levi, as the tribe set aside to serve Yahweh,[20] would not receive an inheritance of their own but rather would be scattered through all the tribes. Indeed, as the list of tribal allocations comes to a close we return to Levi in chapter 21, where we see them receiving towns on both sides of the Jordan. Moses could not allocate towns to Levi because the whole of the land had not yet been taken, though Joshua will allocate many of their towns in faith. Looking back to what God has done is thus an encouragement about what God will continue to do, a pattern that abides today.

3. Caleb and the first land claimed in the west (14:1–15)

As we commence chapter 14 it seems as if we are to begin the allocation of land with Joshua working alongside Eleazar, the priest who had succeeded his father Aaron.[21] This, indeed, will be the process

---

[17] Num. 25.
[18] Num. 31:8.
[19] 13:14, 33.
[20] Exod. 32:25–29.
[21] Num. 20:22–29.

that is recounted from chapter 15, but again we look back briefly in verses 3–5 to what Moses had done as the pattern that is to be followed, then from verse 6 look at the actions of Caleb. Caleb's story will be the first of five 'land grant narratives'[22] that look back to promises about the land first made in the wilderness period and which are to be resolved now. We see through them that God not only keeps the large-scale promise of land, but he also remembers his promise to particular families, again reminding each clan that they are living in the particular land God has given them.

Caleb's story is linked to the people of Judah, though beyond their initial mention in verse 6 we hear no more of them as Judah's wider allocation will be made in chapter 15. But although there are disputes about Caleb's background,[23] he is remembered as being Judah's representative among the spies[24] who, together with Joshua, had brought back a good report about the land.[25] For this reason Caleb and Joshua were the only two from their generation not to die in the wilderness, and it is notable that the allocation of land begins here with Caleb and ends with Joshua,[26] apart from the concerns of the cities of refuge and towns for the Levites.[27] For the rest of Israel, these two faithful individuals offer a model that is held out to all as those whose faith is acknowledged by Yahweh.

In this vignette Caleb clearly shows continued faith. He begins by reminding Joshua of the events of Numbers 13 – 14 at Kadesh-barnea and how he had remained wholehearted in his trust in Yahweh. Although it is not mentioned in Numbers, Moses apparently swore an oath to Caleb that he would receive some of the land because of his faithfulness,[28] something mentioned three times.[29] Moses' oath is actually a representation of Yahweh's commitment, because it was Yahweh who would give him the land. However, Caleb's faithfulness was not just something that happened forty-five years previously (indicating that the conquest so far has taken some five years); rather, it is something he continues to demonstrate. And neither is he going to be put off because of his age. Advancing years may have limited Joshua's future role, but they will not prevent Caleb from claiming his inheritance in the land. Like Moses, he retains considerable vigour into his old age, and he will not be put off by

---

[22] Nelson, *Joshua*, p. 177. The others are in Josh. 15:18–19; 17:3–6, 14–18; 21:1–3.
[23] See the discussion of 15:13–19.
[24] Num. 13:6.
[25] 14:6–9.
[26] 19:49–50.
[27] Josh. 20 – 21.
[28] See Num. 14:24; Deut. 1:36.
[29] 14:8–9, 14.

the Anakim who so troubled the people when the spies had gone through the land. Indeed, the area he requests is an area where they are known to be. So Caleb's faithfulness continues to be demonstrated as he claims the area of Hebron. Instead of being known, as in former times, for its association with the terrifying Anakim, it will henceforward be known for its association with the faithfulness of someone who served God and trusted in his promises, again pointing to the rest the land would have from war.

Caleb's story is undoubtedly placed here precisely because of the encouragement it offered to Israel, and continues to offer to us today. This story insists on the reality of God's promises, promises that we receive in the face of real challenges but which continue in Jesus Christ to sustain us and give us hope. For Caleb, those challenges came in the form of fearsome adversaries; for us, in the Western world today, we face difficulties in terms of our witness because of the rise of militant atheism which claims to be the default position and which is therefore, often unthinkingly, accepted by many. The challenges we face are thus significantly different from those of Caleb, and yet in some senses their nature is the same: they seek to discourage us through their appearance of power. Caleb, however, saw through that and so was able to claim God's promises for himself and his family. The same holds true for God's people today.

Joshua 15:1–63
12. Judah's allotment

If reading Joshua 13 – 14 is challenging, Joshua 15 is even more so as it records the allotment given to Judah. No other tribe's allocation will receive this much detail, and this lengthy listing of place names therefore provides an ongoing challenge to readers who wonder what God has to say to them through it. To make matters worse, it even seems to repeat itself at some points.[1] We might, of course, take some comfort from the fact that the evidence of minor slips by the scribes charged with copying this text could suggest that even ancient readers did not find a listing like this intrinsically exciting, or at least that they found it difficult to retain their concentration.[2] Indeed, some of the verses in this chapter simply give three or four place names without any action involved, so one can easily understand a scribe losing his place.

Yet in spite of the challenges a chapter such as this poses for readers ancient and modern, this remains an important passage within Joshua. As we noted, in chapters 13–14 we are led to expect the point where the allocation of the land west of the Jordan will begin, but apart from the note about Caleb claiming Hebron – a story that will be revisited here – the focus is on the land east of the Jordan, the territory that had been claimed prior to Israel entering the land. Only

---

[1] For example, a town called Ashnah is mentioned in both v. 33 and v. 43, though this may be an instance of two places with the same name. Given that place names are often descriptive of their locality, it may be that these towns were in similar types of locations; but since we are unsure what the name means we cannot say what that location might have been like.

[2] For example, LXX includes an additional eleven cities and their villages in v. 59, and is accordingly included in the main text of REB and in the footnote of HCSB. Since a scribe's eye could easily slip across lines in a list like this it is likely that this is original, though it would have fallen out of the text before the standardization work of the Masoretes. Note the number of variations listed by Boling and Wright, *Joshua*, pp. 379–380.

now does the allocation proper begin, though somewhat ominously chapter 15 will conclude with reference to Judah's inability to expel the Jebusites at Jerusalem, so that they continued to dwell with the people of Judah through to the point when this list was compiled. This note stands in contrast to the continuation in 15:13–19 of Caleb's story from 14:6–15. Caleb stands as one who recognizes not only Yahweh's gift of the land but also that it needs to be claimed by faith. The closing note of chapter 15, however, shows that in spite of some exemplary individuals, Judah was unable to claim God's promise in full. Taken together, these elements point to God's faithfulness and the possibilities that human faithfulness can experience in response, while recognizing that the exemplary is not universal. God remained faithful, but a people who did not live faithfully in response would not fully enjoy God's blessing. The blessing was there – as was clear from the fact that Judah was in the land – but the continued presence of the Jebusites indicated that there could be more. Indeed, that there could be more is made clear by the fact that, compared with the listings for the other tribes, so much more space is given to the listing of the towns that Yahweh was giving Judah, because God always fulfils his promises – but God's people sadly do not always live fully in them.

1. The allotment described (15:1–12)

Having been deferred in chapters 13–14, the description of the allotment of the land finally begins here. Right from the outset we are reminded that this is Yahweh's apportionment of the land. Although the noun 'allotment' is absent from Yahweh's instruction to Joshua in 13:6,[3] it is clear that the land is to be divided as Yahweh allots it, and the noun will then recur some twenty-six times in the land-allocation chapters,[4] and always in reference to how Yahweh is dividing the land. As the people of Judah are given this description of the boundaries of the land, they are therefore reminded that they are not taking just *any* land, but the *particular* portion of the land that Yahweh is giving them.

It is worth noting that the allotment is not just for the tribe of the people of Judah, but for them *according to their clans* (1). Reference to the clans creates a literary boundary for this section which itself describes the boundaries of the tribe.[5] The exact divisions between the various levels of the family within ancient Israel are not always

---

[3] The verb used, hiphil of *npl*, is typically used for the casting of lots, which was the means by which Yahweh would allot the land.
[4] Josh. 13 – 21.
[5] Cf. 7:1, 14.

easy to discern, in part because the divisions were somewhat fluid, but the clan[6] was always part of the tribe, with the clan then made up of individual households. Clans could be relatively small, as would seem to be the case when Rahab's clan was saved at Jericho,[7] but in other instances might have constituted several villages that were located close to one another. However, whatever its relative size, the clan was a smaller group that was made up of households that lived reasonably close to one another and which constituted the more immediate family commitment for most. Marriage usually took place within the clan since this would represent a reasonably local process. Indeed, in the case of the daughters of Zelophehad in Numbers 36:5–9 we are specifically told that they, as their father's heirs in the absence of any sons, were to marry within their clan because his inheritance could not pass outside the tribe, and marrying within the clan would ensure this did not happen.[8] Given this factor, land allocated within households could over time move around within the clan and occasionally outside the clan, but was not meant to transfer outside the tribe.[9] Functionally, therefore, in allocating the land the clan was the lowest level of family for which the allocation needed to be made since it was the lowest level at which the land allocation could remain fairly stable.

That the concern in allocating the land went to this level is significant. It makes very clear that God's interest in his people was not simply at the macro-level. In other words, God was interested not only in ensuring that Israel as a whole received the land he was giving them; that very clearly was a concern that he had, but his interest went further than that and took up the issue of each tribe and clan. So as the members of each clan within each tribe in Israel looked at the land where they were, they could affirm not only that Israel as a whole had received the land, but also that the members of each clan were where they were because God was concerned for them. God's provision thus reached down to the basic structures of Israel's

[6] Somewhat confusingly, some versions (e.g. NIV) have inconsistent translations for the terms for different levels of family. The word translated 'clans' in 15:1 is translated as 'family' in 6:23, but a different phrase (literally 'house') is translated as 'family' in 7:14.

[7] 6:23.

[8] We shall return to their story in 17:3–4.

[9] In practice, because the boundaries between the tribes were not always clear there was some transfer between the tribes, as is perhaps illustrated by the fact that these lists appear to have been revised at some points. So Jerusalem appears as a boundary for Judah (15:8) but not Benjamin, yet it is included in the cities for Benjamin (18:28) but not Judah. Evidence of revision can be seen in the times when a site is mentioned by the name it was initially known by but a brief note is attached indicating the name that was current later (e.g. Jebus is Jerusalem).

society, ensuring that all could understand themselves as recipients of the promise of land.

Obviously the church today as the people of God is not structured on the kinship model that defined Israel as a particular people in a particular time – although it is notable that the New Testament often makes use of kinship patterns when defining how Christians relate to one another as the family of God, while also seeing us as recipients of God's promise to Abraham. For example, Paul's argument in Romans 9 insists that the 'children of the promise' are Abraham's true descendants[10] before picking up on Hosea 1:10 to show that Gentiles and Jews alike can be God's children.[11] So, although we are not necessarily related to one another, one of the dominant metaphors for the church in the New Testament is the family of God.[12] Perhaps most radically, Paul in Ephesians 2:19 points out that in the reconciling work of Jesus, Jew and Gentile are the one 'household of God', and it is also notable that his addressing fellow believers as 'brothers'[13] also draws on this theme.[14] In using this family language, the New Testament writers are consciously drawing on the kinship pattern of the Old Testament to highlight at least one aspect of what it means to be the people of God. The church is not only the 'Israel of God'[15] but also the family of God. Just as in the Old Testament it is possible to think of Israel as a people as a whole and yet also as a collection of tribes and clans, so also we can think of the church as both the people of God as a whole and yet also as a group that understands itself as a family in its local expression.

Although one might make many connections here, the one which is perhaps important from this context in Joshua is the reminder that although God is interested in the church as a whole, he is also interested in and cares for the local expression of the church. So, just as each Israelite clan could know that the expression of God's care and concern for them reached down to the simple fact of where in the land they lived, so also Christians can be encouraged to remember that God's concern is expressed in the gathering of each local church. Although it is a much abused promise (bearing in mind that it is

[10] Rom. 9:6–8.

[11] Rom. 9:25–26.

[12] See Robert Banks, *Paul's Idea of Community: The Early House Churches in their Historical Setting* (Homebush West: Lancer, 1979), pp. 61–71. Note especially the subtitle in David Watson, *I Believe in the Church: The Revolutionary Potential of the Family of God* (London: Hodder & Stoughton, 1978).

[13] E.g. Rom. 12:1.

[14] It is unfortunate that NRSV normally translates this as 'believers', thus obscuring the family link. One can translate inclusively and still maintain the family language by using 'brothers and sisters'.

[15] Gal. 6:16.

given in the context of church discipline!), Jesus' assurance that he is present where two or three are gathered together is surely an expression of this.[16] God is concerned not only with what is happening overall, but also with every local expression of his people.

That local expression here takes the form of a description of boundaries, a description that is not helped by the fact that we don't know exactly where some of the places mentioned are.[17] What is perhaps surprising to readers today is that the description of these boundaries is presented almost in the form of a story, with a set of eight verbs describing each movement of the boundary. It reminds me of some programmes showing reconstructions of Roman battles which my sons and I watched on television a few years back: the camera seemed to fly across the terrain, but in so doing it gave us a much better understanding of what was happening than any static map, let alone a description on its own. Obviously, the Old Testament's writers lacked the sort of computer graphics that would enable this to happen, but the description here does its best to present the boundaries in those terms. It is as if we have a 3D map in front of us and then watch a line as it snakes across the territory, going across hills and valleys to define Judah's boundaries. In this way, we see the landscape not simply as a group of marks on a map but rather as a living environment. Thus we begin with the southern border, moving west from the Dead Sea to the Mediterranean,[18] before a short statement is made that the eastern border is the edge of the Dead Sea.[19] A lengthy description of the northern boundary is then provided,[20] perhaps because it would later prove to be the most complex; it is mostly replicated in the description of Benjamin's southern border.[21] Within this is a brief note about Jerusalem, known here as Jebus. Although nothing is made of it at this point, it is preparing us for the comment with which the chapter will end. Finally, the western border can be described quite simply as the Mediterranean coast.[22] All of this is Judah's territory according to their clans – a territory that comes alive as the people occupy it and live in it as the place where they can serve God, and yet a territory where – hints are already dropped – God's people will not always be as faithful as they should. The church, both local and universal, lives within the same tension, knowing that it comes most fully alive

[16] Matt. 18:20.
[17] See Hess, *Joshua*, pp. 249–255, for possible identifications.
[18] 15:2–4.
[19] 15:5a.
[20] 15:5b–11.
[21] 18:15–19.
[22] 15:12.

when it lives and serves God where it is, but wrestling always with the knowledge that we are not as faithful as we might be.

2. Caleb again (15:13–19)

With the general borders of the land outlined, we now pick up Caleb's story from 14:6–15. There we had learnt about the general area that Caleb was to inherit around Hebron, and here we also learn about his acquisition of Debir, a town generally thought to be located about ten miles further south towards the Negeb. Although this story follows the general pattern of the other land-grant stories scattered through chapters 13–21, each is placed where it is because of the way it highlights the main themes of the land allocation and how they were worked out locally within each of the tribes.

Having already shown Caleb to be a man of active faith, this narrative can pick up on the previous one, safe in the knowledge that readers already understand that he is an example showing what those who trust God's promises can receive.[23] In other words, Caleb trusts God to fulfil his word, and thus receives what is promised, something which by implication is possible for all believers. This point becomes even more important if Caleb's designation as a Kenizzite indicates that he is not Israelite,[24] so that he, like Rahab, shows that faith matters more than anything else, and indeed shows the very faith that many in Israel did not show. Nevertheless, there is another important element brought out in his negotiations with Achsah, which is that the land is apportioned on the basis of need and that human consideration therefore needs to be applied to the question of how God's gifts can most effectively be deployed. Faith here, then, is not an unthinking assumption that God will provide, but a thoughtful consideration and acceptance of what God has given that understands the identity of the giver and also reflects on how best to use what God has given. The model that Caleb offers is thus extended beyond that seen in the previous passage.

The story itself can be broken down into three sections, each of which is important for appreciating what is being communicated here. First, we note that the land was allocated through Yahweh's command to Joshua. We have no record of that command elsewhere but there is no reason to doubt it here, even though there has not previously been mention of Debir. The importance of this is found

---

[23] This story about Caleb is repeated in Judg. 1:10–15 in what appears to be a reprise of this account, though it is also possible that chronologically the position in Judges is more appropriate given the thematic interests which govern these chapters.

[24] The Kenizzites appear to be descended from Kenaz, a grandson of Esau (Gen. 36:11, 15, 42).

in the simple fact that there was a real reason for trusting that this was indeed God's promise and it could therefore be claimed by faith. God had spoken through Joshua, someone who though not generally thought of as a prophet clearly fulfilled this role,[25] and this provided a secure basis for action. The parallel today must surely be found in the promises of God's enabling presence in Scripture, an enabling presence that is most obviously seen when we have committed ourselves to joining God in his mission – bearing in mind that the occupation of the land by Israel is something the Old Testament always sees as part of God's mission.[26] For example, we can confidently claim the enabling power of the Holy Spirit as we bear witness to Jesus.[27] This is a claim rooted in Jesus' promise to us, and thousands can attest to its validity today. By contrast, there is sometimes a danger of having faith more or less in faith itself. I have often sat in meetings where, in the face of various challenges, someone has asserted that we 'just have to trust that the Lord will provide'; but we cannot make such a generalized claim about every circumstance, because without clear evidence that God is indeed sustaining something we make the mistake of putting our faith in the wrong place, no matter how spiritual it might sound. Of course, there is no easy rule to guide us on specific matters, beyond the important point that where we trust God it must be in terms of his mission rather than the agendas we set for ourselves.

Second, having received the promise from Yahweh, Caleb still had to act on that promise. It was a promise which made sense only in terms of an active commitment to what God was doing. For Caleb, this meant driving out the three sons of Anak, the very people who had terrified the rest of Israel when the spies went through the land.[28] There is something rather appropriate about the spy who had insisted that with God's help these people could be overcome being the very one who drove them out here. In addition, he went up against Debir, a city previously mentioned in 10:38–39 and here referred to by its former name of Kiriath-sepher. As with Hebron, it is most likely that we should assume that the earlier description is of the defeat of the people who remained to oppose Israel, which is why Caleb needed to go up and take this city as well. In this case, Caleb decided to offer his daughter Achsah in marriage to whoever claimed the city. We cannot know his reasons for doing this, though we should guard against assuming that Achsah was being treated as some form of possession because she clearly acted on her own. Marriage customs

[25] Most explicitly in 24:2–13.
[26] Grounded especially in Yahweh's covenant with Abram in Gen. 15:7–21.
[27] Acts 1:8.
[28] Num. 13 – 14. On the Anakim, see comments on 11:21–23.

then were very different from our own, but it is not impossible that at least one reason why Caleb made this offer was to provide a husband for his daughter who would live out faith in the way he had. That this is at least possible is evident from the fact that the one who married her needed to show the same sort of faith that Caleb had in claiming Hebron. As it happened, the person who would do this was Othniel, someone known to him and Achsah as a member of his own clan, the son of his brother Kenaz. Othniel will later be introduced as one of the saviour figures in the book of Judges,[29] though there his work will be in the north of Israel, whereas here it is in the far south. Othniel, like Caleb, was someone who was prepared to act on the basis of God's promise even though he knew that claiming this promise would happen in the face of serious opposition. This is a point worth stressing for believers today: God's promises can be trusted, but that does not mean we receive them without struggle and opposition. To go back to the promise of the Spirit as we join in God's mission, perhaps we should note that it is in those times of struggle that we most truly need the power of the Spirit – or at least we are most conscious of his enabling at those times.

Third, having taken the town Caleb still needed wisdom in how he dealt with God's provision. This is clear from Achsah's request in verses 18–19. Although there are some linguistic difficulties in the passage, it seems that Achsah initially *urged*[30] Othniel to ask for an additional field. However, we then find Achsah asking her father not just for a field but also for some *springs of water*. Achsah apparently dismounted from her donkey,[31] presumably a gesture of politeness before her father. She then asks for a blessing which takes on the specific form of springs, or pools, of water. Caleb has earlier been blessed by Joshua[32] and he in turn now shares a blessing with his daughter. There may also be a pun here in that the consonants that spell 'blessing' can also mean 'pool' with different vowels, though that is not the word used here for the springs. Caleb does indeed give his daughter the blessing she requests, and in doing so models another aspect of faith. Here he has received the promise of God, but he also needs to make a decision about the best way to use that

[29] Judg. 3:7–11.

[30] The verb used here, *sût*, usually means 'incited' in a negative sense, but perhaps we are to understand it here as indicating the force with which she urged her husband to request something he might not otherwise have requested.

[31] 'Dismounted' is a best guess from the context for a verb that occurs elsewhere only in Judg. 1:14 and 4:21. Since 1:14 is the parallel to this verse, the only other example is really Judg. 4:21, where the meaning 'dismount' is hard to sustain, though some downward motion is implied. See Butler, *Joshua*, pp. 180–181.

[32] 14:13.

promise. This is because Debir is closer to the Negeb than Hebron, it is in a drier region, and so water is particularly important. So, rather than holding the valuable water for himself, Caleb chooses to share that resource so that it now belongs to his daughter and her husband. God's gifts have been received, but they are not simply for Caleb to hold for himself. Rather, they are to be shared in the way that means they are most effective for enabling God's people to live the life to which he calls them. Again, this is a pattern which is laid before the ancient readers of the book as an example to follow, and it is one which should continue to challenge us today as we ponder how to use the resources God has given to the church. Fundamentally, whatever we hold from God, we hold so that it can be committed to his mission, and like Caleb we are called to weigh up how we contribute what God has given most effectively to this.

3. The towns of Judah (15:20–63)

After Caleb's example we return here to a listing of the towns which make up Judah's allocation. Verse 20 acts as a hinge, joining this list to what has gone before so that we see that this is not separate from the previous list but a filling out of the places involved. There are problems with the list as we have it now, most obviously in that the running totals given throughout do not match the actual number of towns listed[33] – though given the other indications of problems with copying the list we should probably accept that a degree of corruption has crept in over time. Although this is not an easy list to read, and many of the towns mentioned here occur nowhere else in the Bible, it is worth noting that it is organized into four basic groups, though with only minimal comments on each one. Verses 21–32 thus focus on the towns in the far south, heading towards the Negeb, thus joining this list with the earlier story of Caleb, though these towns were further south again.[34] Then in verses 33–47 the towns of the lowlands are listed, covering the area in the Judean foothills heading towards the coastal plain. Within this group is a listing of the Philistine towns in verses 45–47 which serves to move the list all the way to the coast in the west.[35] Then another short title indicates

[33] See Howard, *Joshua*, p. 340.

[34] It is in this section that the discrepancy between the number of towns listed and the number given occurs – after this, the running totals all agree with the number of towns.

[35] However, 19:43 assigns Ekron to Dan. Perhaps, like Jebus (among others), some border towns could be considered as shared by tribes, or at least some of the pasturage described by the town might belong to a tribe different from the one actually allocated the town.

159

that we have returned to the mountains in the east of Judah's allo-cation in verses 48–60, with the towns more or less listed from south to north. Finally, a rather vague group is said to be *in the wilderness* in verses 61–62, here describing places in the region heading down towards the Dead Sea. Although it is perhaps not the most exciting text to read, this list drives home the point illustrated through Caleb that these were all the places that Judah could indeed occupy through faith – though presumably that faith was meant to follow Caleb's pattern and make appropriate judgments about how best to make use of them.

At the end of this list, however, there is suddenly an editorial note that brings us up short: Judah could not drive out the Jebusites, and they accordingly continued to live with the people of Judah until the time when this list was compiled. Obviously, this changed after David's capture of Jerusalem,[36] and in a sense therefore David became the next example of someone who lived out faith in Yahweh's promise on the model of Caleb. We are not told why they could not displace them, but given the confident note shown in Caleb, the implication is that Judah as a whole did not exercise faith in the same way. So until David's success, this brief note is a sharp reminder that just because God has promised something, it does not mean we live in the reality of that promise unless we have the faith to do so. Given the limited information here we cannot say more than that, but it is an important reminder of the continuing importance both of knowing what God has promised and then of living it by faith.

---

[36] 2 Sam. 5:6–10. However, 2 Sam. 24:18–25 shows that some Jebusites continued to live there even after David's capture of the city, though we ought perhaps to think of Araunah on the same model as Rahab, as a Canaanite who accepted Yahweh's reign.

Joshua 16:1 – 17:18
13. Joseph's allotment

After the allotment for Judah we move to the allocation for the two half-tribes descended from Joseph. Although they were technically one tribe – something noted here by the fact that both 16:1–4 and 17:14–18 treat Joseph as a whole – they also functioned as separate tribes. This is evident from the fact that 16:5–10 is concerned with the territory of Ephraim and 17:1–13 with the territory of Manasseh, so that each receives its own territory.[1] Nevertheless, as becomes clear in the complaint of the people of Joseph to Joshua in 17:14–18, they have received only one allotment in the allocation of the land among the tribes, albeit (like Judah) an extensive one.

Why should Ephraim and Manasseh be treated this way? The answer is found back in Genesis, and this in turn prepares us for one of the key themes of these chapters (and of the land allocation overall), which is that the allocation is itself a fulfilment of what God has previously promised. To appreciate this we have to go back to Genesis 37 – 50. Although often referred to as 'the Joseph narrative', it is more accurate to describe it as the story of Jacob's sons.[2] This is particularly important if we are to recognize the significance of Judah in the allocation process since, after Joseph, Judah is the most prominent of Jacob's sons in those chapters. None of the sons comes off particularly well in this story, including Joseph, but through it all God was fulfilling his promises to Abraham that through his descendants all the clans of the earth would find blessing.[3] Near the end of that story, as the family was reunited, Joseph presented his sons Manasseh and Ephraim to his elderly father Jacob.[4] There, Jacob claimed Ephraim and Manasseh as his own, equal to his other sons, rather than as his

---

[1] Though 16:9 indicates that the distinction was not absolute.
[2] This is suggested by the heading to the whole of that section in Gen. 37:2.
[3] Gen. 12:2–3.
[4] Gen. 48.

grandsons. When Joseph presented them to his father for blessing, Jacob deliberately reversed their order so that he gave the greater blessing to Ephraim, the younger son, rather than to Manasseh. The prominence of the younger son is a common theme in Genesis[5] and seems to point to God's willingness to go against social convention to achieve his purposes. In blessing Joseph, Jacob extended his blessing to Ephraim and Manasseh while continuing to recognize that the fundamental tribe was that of Joseph. As we continue into the blessing of Jacob's sons in Genesis 49 it is notable that by far the most space is given to Judah[6] and Joseph.[7] We understand from these chapters, therefore, that Judah and Joseph are to be the most significant tribes, and that Joseph will function as two half-tribes, Ephraim and Manasseh, but with Ephraim always given prominence. The previous chapter, with its extended focus on Judah, has begun to show how the story of Genesis is being worked out, while the focus on Joseph here continues that story. The point is not simply that this is land being allocated, but rather that the land which God had promised Abraham and his descendants is being allocated in line with more specific elements which emerged through time. God may surprise us by choosing those we would not,[8] but he remains absolutely faithful to his promises and their place within his mission. Accordingly, this allocation of land for Joseph fulfils not only the promise of land made to Abraham for his descendants overall,[9] but also the more specific promises made through Jacob to Joseph and his sons.

Nevertheless, although these chapters show God acting in faithfulness to his promises, there continues to be a hint that the tribes are not claiming those promises fully. Where for Judah this was seen in the brief note about the continued occupation of Jerusalem by the Jebusites,[10] here we have more extended notes about how both Ephraim[11] and Manasseh[12] fail fully to occupy their land, and indeed even express discontent at the extent of their allocation. The actions of the tribe as a whole are contrasted with the faith of the daughters of Zelophehad, who, like Caleb,[13] show faith to claim their inheritance in accord with Yahweh's promises to them.[14] So we see both

[5] Isaac is younger than Ishmael, Jacob is younger than Esau, and Joseph is younger than most of his brothers.
[6] Gen. 49:8–12.
[7] Gen. 49:22–26.
[8] Note how Paul riffs on this theme in 1 Cor. 1:26–31.
[9] Gen. 15:18–21.
[10] 15:63.
[11] 16:10.
[12] 17:12–13.
[13] 14:6–15; 15:15–19.
[14] Num. 27:1–11.

God's faithfulness – faithfulness which is concerned once again with particular clans and not just the nation as a whole – and a lack of human faithfulness, along with hints of what this means for the longer term. Thus the balance which has been consistently struck since Joshua 1, where the land is both a gift from God and something to be claimed, continues here.

1. The allocation to Joseph (16:1–4)

It is immediately evident that the account of the allocation to Joseph is considerably briefer than that for Judah, and that the listing of the towns within the allocation is missing, making this the only tribe for which this is the case.[15] In addition, although the description of the boundaries for Joseph here follows the pattern for Judah so that the boundary line is portrayed rather like a line being traced on the map before us, it is again much briefer than in the account for Judah. However, like the description of the allocation for Judah, there are also allusions here to the period of David (and Solomon) which remind us that, although these allocations were given by Joshua as something which looked forward to what Israel could do, later generations in Israel could also look back to them and see something significant for their own setting as they worked out in practice what it meant to be God's people then. In other words, although these chapters may be hard going for us today (and no doubt were for many ancients as well), they were always seen as a word of enduring significance for later readers. Their significance may be less obvious for readers today, but these chapters have always been an example of God's word as something 'living and active'.[16] So, although they are not easy to understand, they remain an important word for us today.

The description of the allocation in these verses is actually of the southern border for Joseph, and this broadly matches the description

[15] Pitkänen, *Joshua*, pp. 299, 304, is open to the possibility that there may once have been such lists after 16:8 and around 17:9–11. If so, these must have been deliberately removed because it is difficult to imagine that exactly the same text-critical error occurred for both Ephraim and Manasseh. The text here is certainly difficult, which could point to somewhat awkward editing, but there are numerous difficulties throughout these chapters, and tracing the various boundaries is exceedingly problematic, reducing the probability that these particular difficulties are signs of editing. And, of course, it is not clear why an editor would have done this to Joseph alone. None of this makes the suggestion impossible, but in the absence of positive evidence it is probably better to assume that those responsible for maintaining this tribal allocation did not retain a city list, just (minimal) boundaries, with the exceptions being those towns which were across the boundaries but allocated to a particular group.

[16] Heb. 4:12.

of the northern border for Benjamin.[17] The border is traced in a line moving more or less east to west, starting at the Jordan at a point just above the Dead Sea and then passing the edge of Jericho but including a spring there, perhaps Ain es-Sultan, then moving westward through Bethel, and then to Luz,[18] before heading south-west to Ataroth and moving on to Gezer and then the coast. The small number of towns mentioned means that the border is described in general terms rather than with any great specificity. As such, the references to two groups in this area, the Archites and the Japhletites, stand out. Unfortunately, we do not know anything more about the Japhletites[19] so can only speculate on the reason for their mention, but the Archites are mentioned elsewhere. If they are the descendants of Ham's son Canaan,[20] they are another Canaanite group that would be incorporated into Israel, perhaps because they were not one of the nations devoted to destruction. We do not have a story that tells us how they were included, as we do for Rahab and the Gibeonites, but by the time of David one of his closest advisors, Hushai, was an Archite.[21] Readers at the time of the monarchy would thus be reminded that God's plan in calling Israel was always to include people in his purposes, and Hushai is a clear example of how this happened, and indeed of someone whose service contributed much to God's mission. As much as anything else, this should serve to warn us against the common habit of treating the Canaanites en masse. More than this, though, it also emphasizes that even in what was mostly an act of judgment on the sinful in Canaan, God did not give up on his primary purpose of bringing all to himself, and that where judgment was necessary it was only because those who were judged had placed themselves completely outside of God's purposes because of their opposition to them. So, even as the land is being allocated, there is a gentle reminder of God's greater purposes. There is, even here, a wideness in God's mercy.

[17] 18:12–13.

[18] Luz is usually given as an alternative name for Bethel, following Jacob's renaming of it (Gen. 28:19), and this is the case in Josh. 18:13, though it is to be distinguished from a second town with this name mentioned in Judg. 1:23. But here they seem to be discrete locations. NIV's 'Bethel (that is Luz)' reconciles the texts but is hard to defend linguistically, unless we emend the text. There is no easy solution here, and emendation may be needed unless we follow Woudstra, *Joshua*, p. 258, in thinking of Bethel as originally the place where Jacob lay and whose name was subsequently applied to the nearby town, meaning that they might still to some extent be distinguished.

[19] 1 Chr. 7:30–40 mentions a group with this name, but as descendants of Asher, so different from that mentioned here.

[20] Gen. 10:17.

[21] 2 Sam. 15:32–37; 17:1–16.

2. Ephraim's territory (16:5–10)

Having initially presented Joseph as a united people, the focus is now on Ephraim and Manasseh as separate groups. Because of the prominence given to Ephraim in Genesis, their territory is described first. As with the description of the southern boundary for Joseph as a whole we are again to imagine a line snaking around the map, moving from Ataroth-addar in the east to Upper Beth-horon to the west and out to the sea. This is an abridged version of Joseph's southern boundary, with verses 6–7 then moving to Ephraim's northern boundary, which goes east from Michmethath[22] before heading towards the Jordan and more or less following it down as far as Jericho – though since most of these places are difficult to identify with any certainty our map lacks precision for readers today. However, the northern boundary heading west seems more precise since it appears to refer to what is known today as Wadi Qanah. As was the case for Judah,[23] the allocation for Ephraim is for the clans and not just for the tribe as a whole, again emphasizing the fact that God's concern is with ensuring that every group is allotted their place within the land. Nevertheless, although Ephraim's territory could be described, it seems that at least some of their towns were within the territory of Manasseh, though we are not told which towns these were.[24]

The description of the borders for Ephraim might lead us to expect that they occupied all this territory, but just as was the case with Jebus for Judah,[25] so Ephraim were unable to drive out the Canaanites who lived in Gezer, though this too was a town that Joshua had earlier defeated.[26] Indeed, this town would remain outside of Israelite control until the time of Solomon, when Pharaoh captured it to give to Solomon as part of his daughter's dowry.[27] According to the account in Kings, it was Pharaoh who killed the remaining Canaanites there, though it seems that the net effect was that Solomon was able to raise some of his forced labour teams from there. Given that this emerged from a failure on Israel's part to carry out what was commanded here, it probably shines a negative light on Solomon's

---

[22] This was perhaps a little to the east of Shechem. However, since the word takes the definite article (i.e. 'the Michmethath') it may not be a name as such, though since we do not know what the word means we do not know what type of geographical feature it might describe.

[23] 15:1, 20.

[24] Note, though, that according to 17:9–11 Manasseh also inherited some towns in other tribal areas.

[25] 15:63.

[26] 10:33.

[27] 1 Kgs 9:16.

activities. In this setting, however, it perhaps also points to a negative reading of Ephraim's actions. Since the people resident in Gezer are expressly called *Canaanites* (10) they, unlike the Archites, stand under the ban and so are to be devoted to destruction. Ephraim, though, has not done this here and has instead found a way to put these people to *forced labour*. We might think this refers to slavery – and it might; but the account of Solomon's actions in 1 Kings 9:15–22 shows that not all forced labour was slavery. As an analogy we might think of countries which employ conscription for their armed forces. Those conscripted are still paid and have their period of service determined in advance so they are not slaves, though neither can they choose whether or not they are in the armed forces. According to Kings, Solomon did not enslave his Israelite forced labour, only the remaining Canaanites. So forced labour, however harsh, was not equivalent to slavery. Given that Ephraim continued to live with these Canaanites, and that Solomon's actions seem to be something new, it seems that what is intended here is less than slavery. In effect, the people of Ephraim have treated Gezer like a city outside the land that has made peace with Israel,[28] something which is clearly not the case here. Ephraim's actions here thus seem to be viewed more negatively than Judah's failure with Jebus, because they not only failed to drive out the Canaanites, but also have effectively entered into an arrangement with them. Where Judah's failure to remove the Jebusites stood as a spur to further action that would ultimately lead to the capture of the city, Ephraim's failure has led to an accommodation that stands outside of God's purposes for Gezer. Although the hint is a small one, and this situation will only reap its fruit more fully at the time of Solomon, it is a reminder of the damage that even seemingly minor compromises will ultimately do to God's people. So, although the presence of the Archites, and perhaps the Japhletites, is a reminder that God's purposes are often bigger than we imagine, the inclusive nature of those purposes does not mean that judgment is set aside. That we have to take seriously both these elements is surely why the summons to repentance remains such a vital element of the proclamation of the gospel: God's purpose is to bring people in, but those who become part of God's people are called to conform their lives to God's purposes.

3. Manasseh's territory (17:1–13)

The allotment for Manasseh follows that of Ephraim, the order consistent with the events of Genesis 48, so that even though Manasseh

[28] Deut. 20:10–11.

was Joseph's firstborn, the tribe's allocation can be recounted only after that of Ephraim. The pattern of blessing that God established there continues to shape the presentation of the tribal allotments. That Manasseh was Joseph's firstborn is acknowledged here, though the initial concern is with the status of Machir as Manasseh's first-born. The allotment in verse 1 looks back to the events in Numbers 32:39–40 which recount how Machir captured Gilead, aptly fitting the description of him as *a man of war* here (1). So this refers back to the earlier allocation of the land east of the Jordan to half of the tribe of Manasseh, meaning that the rest of this passage refers to the part of Manasseh which is in the main part of the land. According to Numbers 26:28–34, Machir was Manasseh's only son. However, Genesis 50:23 indicates that Machir's sons were to be treated as Joseph's own sons, meaning that we then trace the allocation through Machir's sons. Gilead, however, was his only son, with the other descendants listed here in verse 2 therefore being his grandsons. Nevertheless, faithful to Joseph's earlier decision, the allocation of the land west of the Jordan is divided among Machir's six grandsons. The focus here is particularly on Manasseh's clans, with this being the only tribe where the clans are specified. This is because the story of the daughters of Zelophehad will represent a particular example of what it meant to allocate land to specific clans. The clans here match those in Numbers 26 except for a slight change of order.[29]

The story of the daughters of Zelophehad signals an important change in the process of inheritance that also draws on events recounted in Numbers. The genealogy in Numbers 26:33 had already indicated that Hepher's son Zelophehad had no sons, only daughters. Since the assumption was that only males would inherit, this caused a problem for his five daughters. Accordingly, they had presented their case to Moses, pointing out that although their father had died in the wilderness, this had happened only because he was part of the generation that died there.[30] They therefore asked to receive his inheritance, something that Yahweh confirmed to Moses – though this was later modified to require that they marry within their clan so that the inheritance might not be broken up.[31] Nevertheless, it was an important step in the ancient world to allow for women to inherit as this certainly was not the norm.

It is against this background that we need to read the allocation to the daughters of Zelophehad. They, like Caleb,[32] approach Joshua

---

[29] In Num. 26:30 Gilead's eldest son is called Iezer, whereas here he is called Abiezer, but these are variants on the same name.

[30] Num. 27:1–11.

[31] Num. 36.

[32] 14:6–12.

and Eleazar, the priest, and raise the issue of the promise made while still in the wilderness. Like Caleb, they are to some extent outsiders from the normal patterns of leadership, but because of the promise of Yahweh they will become leaders of their clans because they are faithful to claim that promise. However, where Caleb could claim Yahweh's promise to him on the basis of his prior faithfulness – faithfulness that he now applied to the context of life in the land – the daughters of Zelophehad claim their promise solely on the basis of the fact that their father was no worse than the rest of the generation which had perished in the wilderness. Of course, these women needed persistence to ask for their inheritance, a persistence that would change the ability of women in Israel to inherit,[33] but their claim was still for a general part of the inheritance of their tribe, not for some special allocation, as with Caleb. What mattered most, though, was that Yahweh had promised that they would receive their allocation and they therefore claimed it. One does not need to be exemplary in faith to claim God's promises to all his people; one simply needs to know what God has promised and then live in light of that. Mention of these women, therefore, is still intended to point to them as examples of faith, as those who claim the promises; but at the same time they are more typical of ordinary believers than Caleb in that they have no extraordinary basis for claiming their promise, merely the persistence to keep bringing those promises before God. In this case, these women became like the other clan heads in Manasseh, each receiving their portion within the allotment to the whole tribe. They therefore provide an important point of balance, because many believers today continue to make the mistake of thinking that God's promises are only for those who live an exemplary life in some way. The simple reality seen in these women, though, is that it is merely a matter of knowing God's promises and being willing to ask for them in Christ Jesus, in whom they all find their fulfilment.[34]

After the account of the daughters of Zelophehad, verses 7–11 return to Manasseh's allotment in general by describing the southern boundary, with the details of the border here largely repeating the information given earlier[35] for the northern border of Ephraim. Again, we see in verses 9–11 that the tribal boundaries were not exact divisions, since there were some towns within the general boundaries of Manasseh that belonged to Ephraim. This is not altogether un-surprising in that both Ephraim and Manasseh make up Joseph, but

[33] Hawk, *Joshua*, p. 209, points out that they personify the fact that Israel could not be defined solely in male terms.
[34] 2 Cor. 1:20.
[35] 16:5–9.

we are also told that there were towns assigned to Manasseh in both Asher to the north and Issachar to the east, though the boundaries for these tribes are not given here.[36] So although the land was allocated according to the tribal divisions, Israel was still to see itself as a whole and not simply a collection of tribes, so that the resources that the land offered were for the whole nation rather than to be broken up piecemeal, even if local conditions still needed to be taken into account. The same principle needs to be applied to the resourcing of the church in its work: there remains a need to apply resources locally for work which is being done in a particular place, but we still need to see that all resources are ultimately given to the whole of the church, and our stewardship needs to take both elements into account.

In spite of the clear example of the daughters of Zelophehad, however, Manasseh were like Ephraim[37] and unable to possess those cities allocated to them. Manasseh did not drive out the Canaanites either, and like Ephraim decided ultimately on a course of compromise. Like Ephraim, it seems that their actions are held up to us as a failure to do as God had directed, so that they too never fully realized what God's promises could mean for them. Whereas for Ephraim it was only a failure to take Gezer, the failure of Manasseh was more widespread, so that their life was an enduring example of compromise that could not be squared with God's purposes, and so an enduring failure to live fully in the promises of God, even when they later had the opportunity to do so. Compromise, it seems, can have its own seductions which are hard to break.

4. Expanding Joseph's territory (17:14–18)

After recounting the allocations for Ephraim and Manasseh separately, the narrator closes this section by once again thinking of Joseph as a single tribe. Indeed, the issue that is raised here is that Joseph is a large tribe, and they have only received one allocation – the same as all the tribes. Although their initial approach to Joshua has the veneer of faith, attributing their great size to the blessing of Yahweh, it soon becomes clear that they are speaking in the language of convention rather than from genuine faith on their own part. This becomes evident in Joshua's response as he twice picks up on their claim to be a numerous people, and the reply from the people of Joseph makes clear the perspective from which they are really operating. Moreover, as Howard points out, the previous claims for

---

[36] Though their territories are given in 19:17–23 for Issachar and 19:24–31 for Asher.
[37] 16:10.

land allocation have been made on the basis of the promise of Yahweh, but this time there is no promise to be claimed.[38] Instead, this is Joseph's own perspective, the people's own belief that they need more land than God is allocating.

In his first response, Joshua starts with their claim to be a numerous people, suggesting that they therefore can go into the hill country and clear some of the forest there for themselves. Exactly where Joshua intends them to go is unclear, but later references to the forest of Ephraim in the Jordan valley might suggest they are to head in that direction, though remaining within the hill country. The reaction from the people of Joseph is telling: they do not see the *hill country*[39] as being sufficient and instead want the area of the plains. Yet they do not believe they can capture them because the Canaanites there have chariots of iron, ignoring the fact that Yahweh has previously defeated a massive force with chariots.[40] Joshua's proposal has thus brought out the unstated position of Joseph, one which gives the appearance of operating from the perspective of faith but which in reality trusts only in human resources.

It is this perspective that Joshua has to challenge as he again takes up the point of Joseph's size in verses 17–18. Nevertheless, it is also notable that Joshua says nothing about Yahweh. Instead, he speaks only in terms of Joseph's size, saying that they are large enough to claim the additional territory, irrespective of the power of these Canaanites. However, it is clear that this is not seen as something that Yahweh will give them – it is solely something that they will hold by their own power, just like any other people. So they will indeed claim the additional territory Joshua has mentioned, clearing the forest and defeating the Canaanites and their chariots. As has often happened during Christendom, the church is sometimes able to achieve things through political positioning and manoeuvring, but it does not mean that God is in it. It is easy to confuse these things and believe something represents the blessing of God when it was simply the achievement of our own strength, and the claims of Joseph here are a reminder of that possibility. Rather, it is only as we are rooted in the promises of God that we can truly see how he is at work.

---

[38] Howard, *Joshua*, p. 356.

[39] *Hill country* (v. 16) might also be just 'Mount Ephraim', which could explain why they think the area is too limited.

[40] 11:1–9.

Joshua 18:1 – 19:51
14. Seven more allotments at Shiloh

Where the previous tribal allotments appear to have been made at Gilgal,[1] for these chapters we move about fifteen miles north-west to Shiloh, a town in the central highlands of Ephraim. Indeed, the importance of the location is stressed by the fact that these chapters begin and end with reference to it.[2] Although no reason is given for the move, it is clear that it had at some point in the process of land distribution become the site of the central sanctuary. As such, the other key theme about this location is that the allotments to the remaining seven tribes could be made in Yahweh's presence.[3] This is not to deny Yahweh's involvement in the previous allocations, but rather it stresses the fact that it has now become possible for Israel to be united around the central sanctuary that was required by Deuteronomy 12. Thus, although these chapters are generally not seen as especially inspiring by readers today, they represent a key point in the message of the book of Joshua. Yahweh has been faithfully fulfilling his promises such that the whole nation can now be gathered around him in worship, so that the goal of Israel being a worshipping community in the midst of the nations has now been fulfilled. However, a nation that is united in worship must also be a nation that is united in claiming the promises of Yahweh and so claiming the balance of the land. Accordingly, these chapters carefully gather together key themes that have been developing through the book and bring them to a climax in the context of worship. The pattern that is established for Israel here continues to be important for the church today, in that as a people we are to be united in worship – though of course for believers today, Jesus himself

---

[1] 14:6.
[2] 18:1; 19:51.
[3] 18:6, 8, 10; 19:51.

represents the temple,[4] our point of access to the heavenly sanctuary.[5] At the same time, our unity in worship is meant to result in us living out the promises of God to us in Jesus, so that what Israel models for the land of promise in its gathering at Shiloh, the church also lives out in its witness to the nations.

1. The gathering at Shiloh (18:1–10)

a. The gathering (18:1)

The short narrative recounted here is full of key theological themes around which the book of Joshua is built.[6] It emphasizes once again the unity of the whole of Israel, a theme which we noted was particularly important in chapter 1 and again in chapter 13, and which will become important again in chapters 22 and 24. So as we move through each stage of Israel's occupation of the land we come back once again to the importance of their unity, perhaps because the very process of occupation of the land will also lead to the people being scattered across the whole of it. This unity of the people continues to be essential if the promise of the land is to be actualized in the nation's experience because the land remains both something which Yahweh is giving and something which still needs to be taken. The crucial addition here, though, is the place of worship at the centre of the nation's life. In Joshua 1 we see the centrality of God's instruction in the Torah in Joshua's own life, though as a leader this was also something that he was to model for the people as a whole. Worship was implicit in this (and if Deuteronomy especially forms the background there, it was worship at the central sanctuary), but it is something that is only made explicit here. However, rather than directing the nation to be a people in worship, these verses instead model the importance of worship as something in which the whole life of the people of God is shaped. It is worship which unites the people, it is worship that sends them out to claim the promises, and

[4] John 2:21–22.
[5] Heb. 10:19–23.
[6] H. J. Koorevaar, *De Opbouw van het Boek Jozua* (Heverlee: Centrum voor Bijbelse Vorming-Belgie, 1990), pp. 229–234, has shown that this narrative is at the centre of an extended chiasm that runs across the whole of chs. 13–21. Indeed, he also argues (p. 240) that it is the point around which the whole theological message of the book is suspended, thus fulfilling the hope expressed in Lev. 26:11 of Yahweh dwelling among Israel (p. 255). In my judgment, this claims a little too much for this one passage, and it is better to see this as a point where themes developed so far are brought together and prepare readers for what is to come. He has, however, rightly stressed its importance, something most readers today are likely to miss.

it is worship which brings them back to understand how those promises will be experienced.

The importance of these elements is immediately established for us in the first verse, which has been described as 'one of the most theologically pregnant in the book'.[7] The whole congregation has gathered at Shiloh, with the language of gathering already typical of Israel as a worshipping community. That they gather at Shiloh might be a surprise since the sanctuaries of Gilgal[8] and Mount Ebal[9] have previously been important, whereas Shiloh has not been mentioned before. Moreover, though Shiloh will subsequently become important,[10] Shechem will also be prominent.[11] Shiloh would, however, later be the place where Israel came to worship,[12] even if it would in time be replaced by Jerusalem. The history of the central place of worship in Israel need not detain us here, but it is worth noting that, although Deuteronomy 12 stipulates that Israel's sanctuary was to be at the one place that Yahweh would choose, it does not prohibit worship in other places, even if all sacrificial worship was to be at the central sanctuary. Neither does the fact that there was to be only 'one place' mean that that place would be the same for ever. What mattered was that Israel worshipped God in the place that he chose. We are not given any indication here as to how or why Shiloh became the central sanctuary, but since we are later assured that Joshua and his generation served Yahweh[13] the assumption is clearly that in making Shiloh the central place of worship they were faithfully doing something that Yahweh had directed but which did not need to be recorded for the purposes of the book of Joshua. We need to remember that, although Scripture faithfully records the past, it does not give a comprehensive treatment of that past. Indeed, these chapters will end by referring to Israel's faithfulness to another command of God's that is not recorded elsewhere – the granting to Joshua of a town as his own inheritance.[14] What the Scripture records is sufficient, but not comprehensive.

The more important point for the writer of Joshua, then, is that the balance of the land allocation takes place within an authentic act of worship. This is immediately evident from the fact that the people *set up the tent of meeting there.* The exact identification of this tent

[7] McConville and Williams, *Joshua*, p. 73.
[8] 5:1–12; 14:6.
[9] 8:30–35.
[10] 22:9, 12.
[11] 24:1.
[12] 1 Sam. 1 – 3.
[13] 24:31.
[14] 19:50.

is complicated by reference to another temporary tent that Moses used in the wilderness and which he called 'the tent of meeting';[15] yet the tabernacle, the portable shrine used in the wilderness, was also called 'the tent of meeting',[16] and it is the tabernacle that is meant here since this is the place at which Israel gathers. As the tabernacle was the place where Yahweh's presence with Israel was made manifest in the wilderness, it is clear that erecting the tabernacle here symbolizes Yahweh's presence with them.

The erection of the tabernacle thus symbolizes two key and related points. First, it makes clear that Yahweh is indeed with Israel. They have undoubtedly made mistakes up to this point – such as Joshua's failure to inquire of Yahweh when approached by the Gibeonites[17] – but this does not mean that they have therefore been abandoned by Yahweh. Rather, Yahweh remains with his people even when they have not been as careful in following him as they might. Second, it provides a context in which the upcoming allocation of the remaining land can clearly be approved by Yahweh. Although Judah and Joseph are the main tribes west of the Jordan, the remaining tribes are not simply to receive their share of the land through a grab of what is left. It is to be an orderly process which is overseen by Yahweh. Indeed, the comment that *the land lay subdued before them* points to what he has already done while providing for what he will do. So Israel's past and future hope were all centred on Yahweh's presence with them. Christians today find God's presence with them in Jesus, our 'Immanuel' (which means 'God with us'), and we can indeed be reassured by the fact that he will never leave us or forsake us.[18] Knowing this can, however, encourage the practice of a highly individualized faith, whereas we need to recognize that Jesus' presence is most clearly evident when believers are gathered together. However, we too can draw comfort from the fact that he does not abandon us when we make mistakes, and also we can be assured that the fulfilment of God's promises to us are found in Jesus. This, therefore, ought to remind us of the importance of gathering for worship and, in that gathering, discovering both restoration for our past sin and hope for a future of which Jesus is at the centre.

b. The commission (18:2–7)

Once the people are gathered, attention is given to the seven tribes who have not yet received their allocation. Of course, there were

---

[15] Exod. 33:7.
[16] Exod. 29:42–43.
[17] 9:14.
[18] Heb. 13:5, though of course quoting Josh. 1:5.

still eight tribes, but the priestly tribe Levi would not receive a particular territory, though they would receive towns and pasture scattered throughout the land.[19] There is an immediate challenge for these tribes from Joshua as he asks them how long they will delay taking possession of the land that Yahweh has given them. Once again, there is the balance between the land as a gift, something that belongs ultimately to Yahweh and which he is giving to Israel, and the land as something to be taken. More importantly, however, there appears to be a note of frustration on Joshua's part that these tribes have not yet claimed their inheritance. The examples of Judah and Joseph, and perhaps more particularly of Caleb[20] and the daughters of Zelophehad,[21] showed that the land could indeed be taken. It appears, therefore, that some time has passed for this to have become a problem, and it could even be the reason why everyone has gathered at Shiloh, though it is equally as likely that Joshua is taking advantage of the situation to bring this challenge. Whatever the circumstances, it is clear that these tribes have not claimed the land. God's promise has been made to them and they have seen clear evidence that God is fulfilling that promise, but they have not acted upon it. Unlike the spies who had earlier been terrified of the giants in the land,[22] no reason is given for this failure. Instead, they are perhaps emblematic of a wider laxity that can also affect churches today, whereby the effort involved in living out God's promises to us, remembering that they remain both gift and challenge, leaves us in a sort of limbo in which these promises (such as growth in holiness) remain distant from our actual experience. Here Joshua challenges these tribes to make their experience and the promises one and the same, a challenge that needs to echo through the life of the church today.

Accordingly, Joshua directs them to appoint three men from each tribe who will act as surveyors of the land. Allowing for the tribes which have already received their inheritance, and for the fact that Levi will not have a specific territory, the task of these surveyors is to make a written report of the land (something that might well form the basis for the allocation list that follows), including a division into seven portions which are presumably more or less equal, and then bring it back to Joshua. They can also go out with the assurance that they are doing what Yahweh has previously directed since he had promised that he would give all the land where their foot trod.[23] Joshua will then cast lots for the land before Yahweh at the

[19] Josh. 21.
[20] 14:6–15.
[21] 17:3–6.
[22] Num. 13 – 14.
[23] 1:3. Cf. Hawk, *Joshua*, p. 215.

tabernacle,[24] and each tribe will receive its portion. In point of fact, each grouping so far had received their land in a slightly different way – the east of Jordan tribes had received theirs following their request to Moses since it was technically outside the promised boundaries,[25] while the allotments for Judah and Joseph were made without any formal survey.[26] However, as these tribes had not yet acted to claim their allotment a survey was apparently needed.

It is important to note that, although the land was subdued before them, it was not yet fully taken.[27] So the act of the surveyors journeying through the land was indeed an act of faith in that it was still occupied land. They still had to trust God for his protection as they journeyed and made their report. However, they would also know when they returned that the allocation of the land was something controlled by God, and perhaps they would have greater confidence in this because of their journey. At the same time, by referring to the fact that both the east of Jordan tribes and Judah and Joseph had received their allocations, Joshua subtly reminds them that these promises can indeed be received. So, as Davis reminds us, God's promises throughout Scripture were meant to be a stimulant to the faithfulness of God's people to live within them.[28] Joshua's task was to encourage these particular tribes to live out the promises, a task which continues for all Christian leaders today. And just as Joshua, in order to encourage these people, was able to point to what God had already done, so also those of us in leadership have a responsibility to discern the ways in which God is at work and to encourage our people to live in the promises, often by providing practical ways in which they can discover the reality of God's faithfulness to us.

c. The allotment (18:8–10)

Because the focus of these chapters is on the allotment of the land, no attention is given to the experience of the surveyors. Rather, it can simply be reported that they went out with Joshua's words of commission and assurance of the coming allocation ringing in their ears and that, having done as they were directed, they returned to Joshua and the camp at Shiloh. There, and in the presence of Yahweh, Joshua cast lots for them and apportioned the land. So the people here are gathered in worship, are sent in worship, return in worship and there discover how God's promises are to be fulfilled

[24] Though 19:51 makes clear he actually did this with Eleazar the priest.
[25] Num. 32.
[26] 14:1–6.
[27] 13:1.
[28] Davis, *No Falling Words*, p. 142.

for them as each tribe receives its allocation. As we gather in worship today, may we too discover that same reality!

2. Allocations for the seven tribes (18:11 – 19:48)

With the allocation having been made, it remains only for the inheritance of each tribe to be reported. Apart from that of Benjamin, whose report is somewhat longer than the others – perhaps because their territory fitted neatly into a gap that had been left between Judah and the Joseph tribes – each report is fairly short and in some cases not much more than a list of towns.[29] Beyond that, there is no clear rationale for the order in which the tribe allocations are reported, though it is perhaps worth observing that the initial allocations west of the Jordan (Judah, Joseph, Benjamin, Simeon, Zebulun, Issachar) are made to the descendants of the children of Jacob's wives, though not in birth order, and that the remaining tribes (Asher, Naphtali and Dan) are descendants of the children of his wives' maids, though again not in birth order. There is also a general move to the north, though again it is not particularly structured, and in the case of Dan we discover both their initial allocation on the coastal plain to the south and the fact that they ended up in the far north.

a. Benjamin (18:11–28)

The account of Benjamin's allocation is the most complete, containing both a description of the border in verses 11–20 and a listing of towns within the allocation which is divided into two groups in verses 21–28. In this way it most closely resembles the description of the allocation for Judah, though in this case there is no note of a failure to overcome any of the remnant Canaanite groups. Indeed, where this failure was highlighted for Judah and for the Joseph tribes, it is notable for its absence in the whole of the allocation accounts for these seven tribes, with the exception of Dan, who were unable to occupy their land[30] – though in their case there is no reference to remaining Canaanites. Since we know from elsewhere in the Old Testament that each of these tribes failed to possess their territory completely,[31] we should not read too much into this silence but rather understand this allocation as laying out before these tribes what they could possess with Yahweh's assistance, not what they would fully possess.

[29] E.g. Issachar, 19:17–23.
[30] 19:47.
[31] Judg. 1:21–36.

As noted, Benjamin's territory lay between Joseph (12–13) to the north and Judah to the south (15–19). The border description is again best understood by tracing an imaginary line across the central mountains. It here more or less repeats both Judah's northern boundary[32] and Ephraim's southern boundary.[33] The western border (14) was in the foothills, leaving room for Dan's initial allocation on the coast, while the eastern border (20) was at the Jordan. The boundaries are then filled in by two city lists, with the eastern towns listed in verses 21–24 and the western ones in verses 25–28. Much of this is simply a listing with no comment until we come to the closing note in the second half of verse 20, a note which is repeated in the second half of verse 28. Here we are reminded that this is not simply a description of a piece of real estate; it is not just a survey. Rather, it is an inheritance given to them by Yahweh. What was presented to Benjamin was the possibility to discover how their inheritance could truly be lived, and their territory was a concrete opportunity for this to be experienced. Christian readers today do not have an inheritance in any land, but we do have an inheritance that is 'imperishable, undefiled, and unfading'[34] through the resurrection of Jesus Christ. Although our inheritance is not one of real estate, the basic principle holds true: the inheritance is both something that we already have and something that we need to claim. Just as a physical inheritance was outlined for Benjamin as something which existed in reality but which could only be experienced by claiming the promise, so the reality for us is that Jesus Christ is indeed risen, and we therefore share in this inheritance[35] as a people made up from all nations[36] who only experience what that means by faith, faith which is both an initial response to Jesus and also a life lived in faithfulness to him.

b. Simeon, Zebulun, Issachar, Asher, Naphtali, Dan (19:1–48)

Since Benjamin's allocation provides the paradigm for the remaining west of Jordan tribes, we can treat them more briefly. This is because, with the notable exception of Simeon and Dan, what is given here is largely just a description of the borders of each tribe (e.g. Zebulun, 10–16) or a listing of towns within the territory (e.g. Issachar, 17–23). For each, there is an opening statement indicating that their territory was given by lot (1, 10, 17, 24, 32, 40) and a closing

[32] 15:5–11. I understand Geliloth (v. 17) to be a variant for 'Gilgal'.
[33] 16:1–4.
[34] 1 Pet. 1:4.
[35] Eph. 1:14.
[36] Eph. 3:6.

statement declaring that this was the particular tribe's inheritance (8, 16, 23, 31, 39, 48). So, although these allotments are recorded more briefly than that of Benjamin, the basic pattern established there continues here: this is the land that Yahweh has allotted to each particular tribe and for each it is an inheritance to be claimed. Since the reports of Simeon and Dan's allocations deliberately vary from this pattern they draw attention to it, something given more force by their placement at either end of the list – even though for Dan it means breaking from the general south-to-north pattern of the allocations to reflect what actually happened.

The southernmost tribe is Simeon. There is a small variation in their report in that we discover that their territory is within that of Judah, with a scattering of towns in Judah's south. The reason for that given here is that the portion allotted to Judah is too large for them,[37] the implication being that Yahweh is concerned to ensure that the allotments are made so that no particular group has a greater share of the land, and therefore of the resources of the land, than is appropriate for its size. In other words, the land is allocated so that all have enough – something that may also represent an oblique criticism of the demand of the Joseph tribes for more land.[38] We need to bear in mind that one goal of Israel's life was, in effect, to become a living theatre before the nations, who would be astonished by the nation's wisdom, though Israel was to understand that this was not just wisdom but an expression of Yahweh's justice.[39] We ought, perhaps, to reflect on this in terms of contemporary church life, in which some congregations are able to hold a great range of resources in reserve (both financial and, perhaps more importantly, people and their gifts) while others struggle. If we do not work to ensure an equitable distribution of the resources that God has given us in Jesus Christ, both locally and globally, we should not be surprised if those outside the church cannot always see anything distinctively different about us.

But why should Simeon be the one to share when the others received a grant? According to the census list in Numbers 26 Simeon was roughly half the size of the next whole tribe, and even Ephraim (half of Joseph) was roughly 50% bigger. Thus it may simply be a matter of size, with the largest tribe helping the smallest. However, Howard also points back to Jacob's blessing of the tribes in Genesis 49:5–7, where Jacob declared that Simeon and Levi would be scattered through the nation because of their violence against

---

[37] 19:9.
[38] 17:14–18.
[39] Deut. 4:6–8.

Shechem in Genesis 34.[40] Although Levi's dispersal would take on a different character because of their priestly status[41] it seems that a concern here is to show how God's purposes are being worked out. If so, we see a profound paradox in which God takes the outworking of human sin and makes it the basis on which he is able to show his righteousness.

The allotments for Zebulun (10–16), Issachar (17–23), Asher (24–31) and Naphtali (32–39) show no major variations from the main paradigm.[42] As noted already, it is largely a question of whether the description of the allotment focuses on the borders or the towns[43] within the territory. The variation may depend on the nature of the survey of the area that was brought back to Joshua. Although the exact borders of these northern tribes are difficult to pin down, we can note that Zebulun and Issachar are north of Manasseh, with Zebulun to the west towards the Mediterranean and Issachar to the east, running to the Jordan. Asher is further north again, on a coastal strip which runs up to Tyre and Sidon, while Naphtali is on the east, with its territory running north of the Sea of Galilee along the upper Jordan. In reality, much of this territory would never be taken, but the point here is that as Yahweh's allotted inheritance for them it could have been.

The main variation then occurs with the tribe of Dan, who are allotted land on the southern end of the coastal plain in the territory that would be occupied by the Philistines, a people who may have been attempting to enter the land very soon after Israel. However, although they clearly attempted to take this land,[44] we are simply told here that their territory *went out from them* (47).[45] How they lost it is not said, merely the fact that they did. Although this chapter is not interested in noting the failure of the various tribes to fully possess their allotment, in the case of Dan it is necessary to mention it because they ended up migrating to the far north, taking a city called Leshem[46] and renaming it Dan. The city itself appears to be outside the territory Yahweh had promised. If so, then Dan compounded their failure to take their allotment by initiating a war

[40] Howard, *Joshua*, p. 366.

[41] Though this was only achieved later, according to Exod. 32:25–29.

[42] There are slight variations in the wording of how the lot was cast which are smoothed by most translations, but these need not detain us here.

[43] A summary with the number of towns occurs on this pattern, though it is usually not easy to match this to the names given, indicating that there are probably some corruptions in the text.

[44] Note that Samson, who was from the tribe of Dan, was active in the allotted region in Judg. 13 – 16.

[45] HCSB mg.

[46] Called Laish in Judg. 18.

against a people who did not stand under Yahweh's judgment. Although Dan would then function as the northernmost point of Israel, it seems that through this they began a history of sin that would shape their life from that point on, indicating how easy it is for sin to become an entrenched pattern in whole communities. In the West today we often treat sin in a highly individualized way, but the reality seen here is that sin can also be communal. When this happens it forms in the life of that community deep roots which only the gospel can change – though if Paul's troubles with the Corinthians are any guide we should also note that changing these deep-rooted patterns of sin still takes time, reflecting again the important balance between knowing what God has promised and actually living out those promises.

3. An inheritance for Joshua (19:49–51)

Finally, and somewhat surprisingly, we have a brief narrative of a land grant for Joshua. This is surprising because although reference is made to a command from Yahweh, we have no record of this command. Since Joshua's allotment falls within the territory already allotted it needs to be given by the rest of Israel to him, but it is also a gift that comes from Yahweh to him. Its placement here means that these verses close off not only the land allocation at Shiloh in chapters 18–19 but the whole of the west of Jordan allocation in chapters 14–19, since allocations to Caleb and Joshua, the two faithful spies from Numbers 13 – 14, frame the section. In Joshua's case, his continued faithfulness is seen not only in his leaving his own allocation to the end,[47] but also in the fact that having received his allocation he then rebuilds and settles the city. Together, Joshua and Caleb stand as a reminder of what Yahweh's servants can achieve, reminding all who read this text that it is trusting faith in Yahweh's promises that matters. Joshua and Eleazar had allotted all these portions before Yahweh, and just as Caleb and Joshua received their inheritance, so all since then might receive theirs.

[47] Hess, *Joshua*, p. 277.

Joshua 20:1 – 21:45
15. Taking God at his word: cities of refuge and the allotment for Levi

Readers who have battled their way through chapters 13–19, with their seemingly endless lists of place names that are difficult to pronounce and often even more difficult to locate on the map, may feel a sense of disappointment as they turn to these chapters. Did not the ringing declaration that 'they finished dividing the land'[1] mean that we could now move on from such lists? Can we not go on to something looking more like the gripping stories of chapters 1–11 once more? As it happens, we will indeed soon return to such narratives, but those who have read the preceding chapters attentively will have noticed that although the division of Joseph into two groups – Ephraim and Manasseh – means that the land has been allocated to twelve tribal groups, one important tribe has not been mentioned. Simeon's allocation within the tribal territory of Judah[2] means that one part of Jacob's declaration in Genesis 49:5–7[3] has been fulfilled – Simeon has been scattered throughout Israel and will struggle henceforward to have a clear tribal identity. However, the same was also said of Levi, and no mention has yet been made of this tribe in the allocation. Of course, in their case the fact that they were subsequently ordained as the priestly tribe[4] means that their scattering will work rather differently from that of Simeon, but for the writer of Joshua it is important that this word be seen to be fulfilled.

Indeed, although Jacob's pronouncements about his sons were not originally a word directly from God, the book of Joshua treats them

[1] 19:51.
[2] 19:1–9.
[3] Commonly called the 'blessing of his sons', even though these particular words can hardly be called a blessing!
[4] Exod. 32:25–29.

as such, suggesting that its authors regarded them as scriptural and so as a word from God which needed to be fulfilled. Indeed, although at one level these two chapters are concerned to explain what happened to the tribe of Levi and how they were allocated land across Israel, there is a larger purpose that runs through them: to stress the importance of taking God at his word both in the actual doing of what he requires and in the acceptance of the promises he has made. These two chapters are actually crucial to the whole structure of the book of Joshua as they ask us as readers to look back to earlier passages in the Pentateuch and see how God's word is being worked out, as well as directing us to earlier parts of the book of Joshua to see how this pattern continued to be demonstrated. So, however much we might long for more exciting narratives, these chapters are theologically loaded with material that stresses the importance of taking God at his word. It is this theme which is implicit in the first two sections of them, and which becomes explicit in what is essentially a doxology in the third, opening up their abiding significance for readers today. Moreover, this doxology shows that taking God at his word is both a reflection of what God has done and a preparation for how we are to live in response – which is precisely what these chapters now begin to model.[5]

1. Cities of refuge (20:1–9)

Although the whole of these chapters is finally concerned with the allocation to Levi, they begin by describing the setting aside of six cities of refuge. Each of these cities is taken from Levi's allotment and so will reappear in chapter 21 when the full list of Levitical cities is given. The book of Joshua here assumes that readers are familiar with a number of texts from the Pentateuch which provide the background to this. However, before noting those and how they help us understand this chapter more clearly, it is worth observing that the cities of refuge are listed before all of the cities in Levi's allocation.[6] We are given no reason in Joshua why this should be, but an important distinction in how these two chapters begin might provide a clue. Here in chapter 20 we are told that Yahweh spoke to Joshua, with the opening verse of the chapter then strongly reminiscent of numerous passages in the Pentateuch where a new law was given through Moses.[7] Indeed, apart from the change of name to 'Joshua'

---

[5] Similarly, Hubbard, *Joshua*, p. 451.

[6] Given that Num. 35, which lies in the background for the whole of chs. 20–21, treats them in the reverse order, the order in Joshua is more notable since it is not expected.

[7] By contrast, ch. 21 recounts a response to a previously given law.

there is no difference here from these passages. In this instance, the most obvious parallel is provided by Numbers 35:9, which begins the section outlining the law of the cities of refuge.[8] Although there have been many points throughout the book where Yahweh has spoken to Joshua,[9] this is the first time that he is spoken to on exactly the same model as Moses, introducing a fresh directive for God's people, even if in this instance it is the completion of one given earlier. At the start of the book, Joshua was Moses' 'assistant'[10] and Moses was still Yahweh's 'servant',[11] but by the end of the book Joshua will have assumed the title of Yahweh's 'servant',[12] effectively marking him as Moses' successor. By this introduction, the narrator subtly flags for us that this transition has taken place. There has been no single moment when Joshua grew in his role as a leader to occupy the same status as Moses, but the transition has happened nonetheless. For the book of Joshua, it is perhaps important to raise this point before the allocation to Levi proper, since Eleazar the priest will be equally involved in that. Joshua's authority as a leader needs to be made clear before that happens.

Today's readers of Joshua might therefore reflect on the nature of leadership and how the most effective leaders are often those who are given the opportunity both to exercise some leadership and yet at the same time to grow into all that this involves. This pattern is perhaps most important in the training of those called to positions of leadership within the church. One approach which has been particularly prominent over the last century or so has been to take those called out of local churches and send them to colleges and universities, where their learning is largely separate from the experience of the local church, with only a few placements which are often simply a foray into the local church before a retreat to the place of learning. I do not wish to disparage this model – many highly effective leaders have been trained this way, and it does have the immense benefit of allowing students to be immersed far more in their learning, especially of the Bible and theology more generally. However, the model of Joshua, and perhaps also of Jesus' disciples, is closer to that of an apprenticeship in which learning does happen, but it does so in the context of ministry. Joshua grows in his status because he is always both learning and doing. How we balance these aspects is always a challenge, and it is not helped by the financial constraints

[8] Num. 35:9–34. The law is repeated, with some developments and abbreviations, in Deut. 19:1–13, though both derive to some extent from Exod. 21:12–14.
[9] E.g. 1:1; 4:15; 5:9; 7:10; 8:1; 13:1.
[10] 1:1.
[11] 1:2.
[12] 24:29.

that often drive what we do more than a theology of formation; but this does represent an important model that needs to be considered as we take theological education forward. Beyond this, Joshua has also continued to develop in his leadership as he has exercised his ministry, a salutary reminder that the best leaders are those whose lives and discipleship come from growing maturity.[13]

There is also a second reason why we might focus on the appointment of the cities of refuge first: in this way the text emphasizes the importance of the Levitical cities in terms of service to the whole community of Israel and the exercise of their ministry rather than simple possession. When the tribe of Levi was ordained it was to the 'service of the LORD'.[14] As we begin to move into the allocation to Levi, an allocation which is deeply rooted in the earlier passages in the Pentateuch which have allowed for this, we are reminded that the resources that Yahweh is giving to them are given so that they might serve. This is actually true of all their cities, but it is particularly true of the cities of refuge because of their special role in Israel. The interesting element here, however, is that although these cities will be drawn from the Levitical allotment, Joshua is directed to speak to all Israel and tell them to *give yourselves cities of refuge*,[15] whereas Numbers 35:11 had said simply that they were to 'select' them. These verbs are not contradictory, but they do suggest a subtle difference in emphasis. For although the people of Israel are here being directed to do what Yahweh has previously said, and they are clearly having to select the cities, they are also to see what they are doing as giving themselves a gift.[16] Faithfulness to what Yahweh has commanded turns out to be in itself a gift that is to be enjoyed, though of course it only makes sense in the context of a larger commitment to what God has said. It is understanding God's instruction as a gift that leads the psalmist to declare, 'Oh how I love your law!'[17] This is not a mode of reading that Christians have traditionally appropriated, and laws like that of the cities of refuge have often been treated as matters of little interest for us, but it in fact represents a far healthier approach to understanding these texts. What God has given us he has given for our good, and seeing his instructions as given for our good helps us appreciate them in a

[13] R. W. L. Moberly, *Old Testament Theology: Reading the Hebrew Bible as Christian Scripture* (Grand Rapids: Baker Academic, 2013), p. 210, though discussing Jonah at the time, puts it pithily: 'Good pedagogy sees learning and life as belonging together.'
[14] Exod. 32:29.
[15] 20:2, my translation.
[16] Similarly, Howard, *Joshua*, p. 381.
[17] Ps. 119:97.

healthy way. Indeed, the wider concern of the laws associated with these cities – that justice needs clear formal practices which prevent vengeance spiralling out of control – ought to be a spur to continued reflection by Christians today.

The process of the allocation and role of the cities of refuge is laid out for us in verses 2–6. Much of Numbers 35:9–34 and Deuteronomy 19:1–13 is assumed here, and readers would be well advised to look at both these texts. For example, according to Deuteronomy 19:3 Israel was to measure the distance between the cities so that any who had committed manslaughter could flee to one. That can be assumed here, as can the role of the avenger of blood, the kinsperson who was to execute blood vengeance for murder. Under Israel's penal system, murder incurred the death penalty,[18] but someone who had unintentionally killed (manslaughter in most Western systems of justice – death in warfare is not envisaged here) could flee to the city of refuge. The assumption, drawn from Deuteronomy 19:3, is that the person should be able to get there in a day and so reach a place of safety before the avenger could catch them and thus prevent what was meant to be a form of judicial practice becoming simple vengeance. The killer still had to make a case for admission (4), and perhaps stand a more formal trial too (6) to ensure that justice was done. Once they were there, however, and provided the person was guilty of unintentional killing, the city was a place of refuge and the killer could not be reached by the avenger. However, a human life could not be taken without there being some penalty, so the killer would remain in the city until the death of the high priest, which seemed 'symbolically to terminate the punishment'.[19] This, in effect, made the city a form of open prison in which the person could live and work, kept safe from blood vengeance, but still paying the penalty for what had happened. For the Levites, this was an important reminder of Yahweh's commitment to justice as something that was actively practised and not simply spoken about, and thus that their larger role of ministering to the people of Israel had to deal with real, and costly, issues of daily life. Their cities were the means by which Yahweh resourced them, and, through them, the whole of Israel. Put simply, God resources some of his people in special ways, but he does so in order that they serve the whole community of his people. In this particular context, it is a clear evidence of the fact that the people of Israel were not simply receiving a homeland; they were

[18] Num. 35:30.

[19] Hess, *Joshua*, p. 279. Some, e.g. Davis, *No Falling Words*, pp. 151–152, have speculated that the high priest's death therefore functions as the mode of atonement for the killer. This is entirely possible, but it is not something any of the texts actually say, so it is perhaps wiser not to press this point.

receiving a land where they could establish Yahweh's justice, a land where the violence of retaliation could be limited.[20]

Verses 7–9 then recount quite simply that Israel as a whole did as Yahweh had said through Joshua, setting these cities aside. This time the verb used indicates that the setting apart of these cities was an act of making them holy, showing that they truly belonged to Yahweh. Three cities west of the Jordan are listed, running from north to south, and then three east of the Jordan, this time running from south to north, though the latter have already been noted in Deuteronomy 4:43–44. No details beyond this are given here because it is enough to note that the process was properly followed. But there is the interesting comment in verse 9 that the city of refuge was not only for the Israelite, but also for the *stranger sojourning* among them. These foreigners were referred to previously at the ceremony at Mount Ebal,[21] but their mention here is still slightly surprising, though it once again demonstrates that the vision of Israel in the book of Joshua is an inclusive one, in which all who commit themselves to Yahweh receive the benefits of being among his people. This is what God's word has required, and taking God at his word has meant doing it.

2. The Levitical cities (21:1–42)

Having been introduced to the allotment to Levi through the cities of refuge, we now move to the general allotment for Levi. Where the cities of refuge were seen as fulfilling a requirement from God, albeit a requirement that was itself a gift, the allocation of these cities to Levi is presented as an act of claiming what God has previously promised. The actions of Levi as a tribe, therefore, are closely modelled on those of Caleb[22] and of the daughters of Zelophehad[23] in that they approached Israel's leaders to request their allotment. The link with Zelophehad's daughters is particularly strong in that, like them, the family heads of Levi approached Eleazar and Joshua, whereas Caleb is said to have approached only Joshua. However, as 19:51 has already indicated that Eleazar could have been involved without prior mention, this distinction is not to be pressed. What matters for the family heads is the point they make in verse 2 – that Yahweh had previously commanded Moses that the Levites be given cities to occupy along with their associated pastureland to graze their livestock. In effect, this recognizes that although Levi did not receive

[20] Cf. Creach, *Joshua*, p. 103.
[21] 8:33, 35.
[22] 14:6–15.
[23] 17:3–4.

a tribal allotment as a designated region, they would need places of their own to live, and these places should provide them with their living. Being called to serve God should not mean having to beg; rather, appropriate provision should be made for those called to such work, and one function of this allocation of cities and pastureland is just that. As Paul would later put it when discussing church leaders, drawing on both Deuteronomy 25:4 and Jesus' own teaching,[24] 'The labourer deserves his wages.'[25] For the leaders of Levi, the more immediate reference is to Numbers 35:1–8, which had specified that the Levites would receive forty-eight cities, of which six would be the cities of refuge. It had also specified that the pastureland associated with the city was to extend to about 500 yards in each direction from the city. In this case, taking God at his word means that the Levites ask that they receive their full allocation of forty-eight cities.

As with the allocation for the seven tribes mentioned in chapters 18–19, this happens at the sanctuary at Shiloh, meaning that the casting of the lot which will assign the cities to the Levites is conducted in Yahweh's presence. Just as this had guaranteed that the previous seven allotments[26] were exactly as Yahweh intended, so also here the allotment to Levi is shown to be the means by which Yahweh does indeed fulfil his word for the tribe. What is slightly surprising in light of Numbers 35:8's note that each tribe would give cities to the Levites in accordance with their relative size is that, with only two exceptions, each tribe gives four cities. Because they are mixed into one another, the allocations from Judah and Simeon[27] cannot be completely separated but together they give nine cities, whereas Naphtali gives only three.[28] Given that the towns are allotted by Yahweh, we are reassured that the allocation was indeed fair, though a glance at a map will also show that the towns are not distributed particularly evenly across the land. Readers might also be surprised by the note that Shiloh is *in the land of Canaan* (2), since the Old Testament's narrators do not tend to include redundant information, and this is something we already know; so why mention this fact here? The answer again is probably rooted in the earlier directions given in Numbers which had indicated that the allotment to Levi was to come from 'the possession of the people of Israel'.[29] The subsequent list will indeed give the cities to Levi from this possession, though at this stage it is still spoken of as an inheritance.

[24] Luke 10:7.
[25] 1 Tim. 5:18; cf. 1 Cor. 9:14.
[26] 18:11 – 19:48.
[27] 21:9–12.
[28] 21:32.
[29] Num. 35:8.

The reason for this is that although the land of most of these tribes has been allotted, it has not yet been claimed. Rather, it is (for the most part) an allotment to Levi of towns that are currently possessed by Canaanites, meaning that although they are taking God at his word in asking for the cities, they too must recognize that they have a part to play in claiming these towns and their pasturelands. Once again, we see that characteristic balance that runs through the book as a whole, where the land is both something that Yahweh is giving because it is his to give and yet at the same time something to be claimed. The narrative thus subtly indicates that for Levi, as indeed for us today, taking God at his word is not simply a matter of waiting to be given what he has promised. It is not something in which God's people are passive. Rather, we simultaneously accept the wonder of God's gifts and strive with all we are to make those gifts real in our experience.

The process of the allotment of Levi's inheritance is presented in a standard pattern, but with Levi broken up into four main groups, with these divisions first mentioned in verses 4–7. The first group is the priests, those members of Levi who were descended from Aaron. Technically, they were one part of the larger clan of the Kohathites; the balance of this clan is noted as the second group. The third and fourth groups are the other two clans, the Gershonites and the Merarites. The whole of the allotment is summarized here and then recorded in detail in verses 8–42. The order of presentation for the groups within Levi is broadly linked to their association with the sanctuary. So, rather than follow their order as given in Numbers 3, where they are listed in order of the age of their ancestor,[30] it is the order of Numbers 4 that is followed for the clans in terms of their responsibility. Thus the priests who are most involved with the sanctuary are listed first. The Kohathites, the largest clan, were particularly responsible for the transportation of the tabernacle and those items such as the altar that were associated with sacrifice after they had been prepared by the priests.[31] The Gershonites, who are listed second here, were responsible for the tabernacle's coverings and curtains,[32] while the Merarites were responsible for the tabernacle's frames and pegs.[33] In the wilderness period, the Gershonites and Merarites would take the tabernacle and set it up before the Kohathites brought in the holy things.[34] Ultimately, once the central sanctuary was established in Jerusalem, this would mean that the greatest responsibility would rest with the priests and the Kohathites.

[30] Num. 3:17. The order there is Gershon, Kohath, Merari.
[31] Num. 4:1–20.
[32] Num. 4:21–28.
[33] Num. 4:29–33.
[34] Num. 10:21.

JOSHUA 20:1 – 21:45

That being so, it is interesting to observe that the allotments locate the priests and the Kohathites closest to Jerusalem: the thirteen cities associated with the priests are all taken from the allotments of Judah,[35] Simeon and Benjamin. The ten cities for the rest of the Kohathites are then drawn from the allotments to Ephraim, Dan and west Manasseh, though the cities from Dan are all from their original allotment, land they never possessed. The Gershonite allotment is further north, with their thirteen cities drawn from east Manasseh, Issachar, Asher and Naphtali, with the twelve cities for the Merarites drawn from Zebulun, Reuben and Gad and so being the furthest north. Each of the cities of refuge is also mentioned, ensuring that once again the listing encourages reflection on both the cities as a gift to be claimed and a responsibility to be exercised.

That God could indeed be taken at his word is reinforced by the summary statement in verses 41–42. Once more we are told that forty-eight cities were allocated to Levi along with their pasturelands. As Jacob had indicated, Levi was indeed scattered across Israel,[36] but as had been promised through Moses, they were indeed allotted forty-eight cities and their pasturelands.[37] Levi's allotment was, somewhat paradoxically, both a judgment in that they were scattered throughout Israel, and a provision in that this enabled them to carry out the ministry to which God had ordained them. We might find it difficult to keep both these elements together, and there is no doubt that those God calls today should emphasize his provision for them; but the important point here is that what God said had indeed come to pass. Thus there is in this closing summary already a moment of doxology, a moment when looking to see how God's promise had been fulfilled and was being fulfilled led to praise. Perhaps it would do the church good to pause and do the same today.

3. Every promise fulfilled (21:43–45)

The doxology that began in noting the fulfilment of God's promise for Levi reaches a glorious crescendo in these verses which simultaneously serve to close off the section dealing with the allocation of the land and also show that the promise of claiming the land in Joshua 1 has been fulfilled. God has indeed been faithful to his word throughout, and this needs to be observed, not just by reporting it but also by rejoicing in it.[38]

---

[35] Though as v. 12 makes clear, this involved careful negotiation of the areas already allotted to Caleb.

[36] Gen. 49:5–7.

[37] Num. 35:1–8.

[38] Davis, *No Falling Words*, p. 158.

This summary operates in two stages. First, in verse 43 it looks back over the whole of chapters 13–21. As we have noted at several points, these are not easy chapters for most readers today, though there is little reason to think that ancient readers found them especially gripping either. Perhaps that is why the book needs to come to this point of doxology, in order to remind us that this is not simply a listing of distant towns, many of whose locations were possibly as unknown for the first readers as they are now; rather, it is a ringing declaration of the faithfulness of God. In Genesis 15:18–20 Yahweh had promised Abraham a particular land, a promise repeated to Isaac[39] and Jacob.[40] That had been a long time before, more than half a millennium, and yet God had fulfilled his promise: Israel both possessed the land and had settled there. Second, verse 44 refers back to the more recent promises that Yahweh had given Joshua in chapter 1: Israel had indeed been given rest[41] because no enemy had been able to resist them.[42] Thus, as the book of Joshua looks back on the issue of taking God at his word, it is able to declare that both those promises which reached back to ancient times and those which were more recent had been fulfilled. Hence the chapter closes with the glorious affirmation that not one promise had failed; *all came to pass.*

Readers might, however, wonder about this. Although chapters 13–21 have shown that the land has indeed been allocated, it is also clear that much of the land remains untaken; indeed, the references to Dan in these chapters have even alluded to the fact that this tribe would not occupy its allotted land but would move further north. So, although the affirmation here is consistent with earlier statements in the book,[43] is it not contradicted by those texts which affirm that much land remained to be taken?[44] The answer is that the book has consistently emphasized both the fidelity of God to his promises and the need for his people to lay claim to those promises. This balance is highlighted by the fact that the allocation to Levi is recounted last, because there we see both God's absolute fidelity to his promises in allotting the cities, and the need for God's people to claim those promises. It is important to recognize that a human failure to claim God's promises for his people does not invalidate

[39] Gen. 26:3.
[40] Gen. 28:13–14.
[41] 1:13, 15; 11:23.
[42] 1:5.
[43] 10:42–43; 11:16–20, 23; 12:7–24.
[44] So Robert Polzin, *Moses and the Deuteronomist: A Literary Study of the Deuteronomic History. Part 1: Deuteronomy, Joshua, Judges* (New York: Seabury Press, 1980), p. 132, who sees this as an irreconcilable problem; or Coote, 'Joshua', p. 701. See Josh. 13:1–6; 15:63; 16:10; 17:12–13; 19:47.

them, and indeed may provide part of the background to the claim
of the writer to the Hebrews that the failure of Joshua's generation
to find rest was resolved only in the work of Jesus.[45] God's promises
did not fail and would indeed be fulfilled, but that does not mean
that everyone experienced the blessing of this in full. Joshua holds
this tension in place.[46] And in light of all that had happened it
could be truthfully claimed that none of God's promises had failed.
Taking God at his word, then as now, leads to doxology, while also
challenging us to ask whether the promises have indeed become
reality in our own experience.

[45] Heb. 4:1–10, though drawing on Ps. 95.
[46] See also 23:4–5 which reflects directly on this.

Joshua 22:1–34
16. Keeping together

The section dealing with the allocation of the land had concluded with a marvellous note about how God had been faithful to his promises,[1] promises that had been important for the whole of the land allocation in chapters 13–21 but were of particular importance for the designation of the cities of refuge and allotment to the Levites in chapters 20–21. There we saw a strong emphasis on the theme of taking God at his word. However, that concluding celebration of God's faithfulness contained within it a challenge to later generations concerning the importance of continuing to live within the framework of God's promises. As we move into the last three chapters of the book of Joshua, it is this issue which is particularly central, with each chapter in turn exploring a different aspect of it. Along the way, they prepare us further for the designation of Joshua as Yahweh's servant, a designation matching that of Moses and which we have noted was hinted at previously.[2] This is particularly notable in that each chapter provides us with a farewell speech from Joshua,[3] first to the east of Jordan tribes,[4] then to the leaders,[5] and then to the nation as a whole.[6] The speeches are increasingly more detailed, with the second roughly twice as long as the first, and the third roughly three times as long. Joshua himself thus becomes more important as we proceed through these chapters. However, this is not so much to elevate him personally as to show that God has indeed raised up someone to follow Moses. These chapters are also linked to the declaration of 21:43–45 by their emphasis on rest – something

[1] 21:43–45.
[2] 20:1.
[3] See Howard, *Joshua*, p. 401.
[4] 22:1–8.
[5] Josh. 23.
[6] 24:1–27.

which these verses assert Yahweh has given, to which Joshua refers in addressing the eastern tribes here,[7] and to which the narrator will again refer in the next chapter.[8] Beyond this, the central theme of Yahweh's faithfulness to his promises will be picked up again by Joshua in the next chapter,[9] while this chapter's surprising use of an altar as a witness for Israel will be matched by the erection in chapter 24 of a large stone as a witness to the people of their covenant relationship with Yahweh.[10]

As this chapter begins to wrestle with the issue of taking God at his word as the model for how to live in the future rather than simply as promises from the past to be claimed, it focuses on the particular question of how to know that God is among his people. That is a question that many of us could pose. We might reasonably suppose that a number of different answers could be given. Some might say that God is among us when we see signs of numerical growth. Others might stress answers to prayer, especially in terms of the miraculous. Still others might wish to cite evidence of the work of the Holy Spirit among us. All of these would, to some extent, be valid expressions of what it means to say that God is present. However, this chapter takes a rather different approach, one that varies from those which dominate much contemporary discussion; namely, that God is recognizably present among his people when they understand that they can work together in spite of their differences in perspective. In particular, these differences emerge from different stages in the life of God's people, as the allocation of land to the eastern tribes in Numbers 32 and the central sanctuary of Deuteronomy 12 are brought together. God has been faithful and demands faithfulness in the future, and though the general framework for this has been outlined, the exact means by which this is to be achieved needs to be negotiated, perhaps because no single rule can cover every circumstance. To take a musical analogy, we might say that although God has indicated the key and the general form of the melody that Israel is to play in its common life, he expects Israel to improvise within this structure. The people of Israel are not free to change the key or the melody's theme, but as long as they are true to these they are free to work out what it means to be faithful, to integrate different elements of both God's prior faithfulness and the faithfulness he expects. This is quite unlike some modern perspectives on church life in which our own emphases and needs are often seen as being most important, so that people often leave a church to

[7] 22:4.
[8] 23:1.
[9] 23:14.
[10] 24:26–27.

find (or even establish) a congregation that suits their particular preferences. Rather, this chapter emphasizes the importance of the unity of God's people. It is a unity in the midst of diversity, but one which insists that there are certain non-negotiable points which are pivotal for retaining unity. Thus this chapter reminds us not only of the importance of the unity of God's people, but also that such unity in spite of their differences is a sign of the presence of God.

1. The return of the eastern tribes (22:1–8)

After the seemingly endless lists of the previous chapters, it is no doubt refreshing to come back once again to a story – though one that may sound a little strange to many of us today! Nevertheless, this is an important chapter in that it introduces the final section of the book; it is a chapter which begins to outline what is expected of the people of Israel now that they are in the land. In other words, given that Yahweh has proven himself to be absolutely faithful, how are Israel to live in response? These issues are vitally important, and the unity of the people is one that is addressed at the outset.

The key to understanding this chapter lies in Joshua's charge to the eastern tribes as they prepare to return to their territory across the Jordan. However, although unity will emerge as a crucial element in the story, it is only hinted at in these opening verses. Nevertheless, from Joshua's very act of summoning the tribes of Reuben and Gad and the half-tribe of Manasseh (here understood as that part which dwelt east of the Jordan) it is clear that attention is being given to a group which stood outside of the main body of Israel. As we noted before,[11] the fact that these tribes dwelt outside the land of promise as a result of a special allocation by Moses in Numbers 32 meant they were something of a special case. It was because they already possessed their land that Joshua needed to exhort them to remember their prior commitments in order for their compatriots to occupy their land.[12] So, although it is only hinted at, the possibility of a division between the tribes on both sides of the Jordan is recognized, though the general assumption was that the western tribes would need to remind the eastern tribes to remain faithful.

Apart from during the spring thaw,[13] the Jordan is not itself a huge barrier and has a number of crossing points. However, it represented a significant psychological and spiritual barrier precisely because it represented a boundary of the land as promised, and the eastern tribes all lived outside that territory. So, when Joshua gives them

[11] See comments on 1:12–18.
[12] 1:13–15.
[13] 3:15.

their parting charge here, he does so as an occupant of the land that was promised, west of the Jordan. In doing so he is conscious of the need of these tribes, as they return to their land, to build on the faithfulness they have shown in joining their compatriots in claiming the land. Joshua thus recognizes the possibility that the eastern tribes might falter in their faithfulness when they return to their homes. This reflects the idea that the eastern tribes were in some way at greater risk of falling away from Yahweh because they lived outside the promised boundaries of the land. This risk is particularly focused in the narrator's reference to Manasseh as a tribe that occupies both sides of the Jordan,[14] because as a 'bridge people'[15] they embody the problem of how Israel can be faithful both within and without the promised boundaries of the land.

Joshua's speech thus builds on the record of the faithfulness they have already shown, noting that just as they had earlier promised, they had not forsaken their compatriots[16] while claiming their land. They had therefore been faithful to the charge of Moses[17] that they join their compatriots in claiming the land west of the Jordan; but this was also an expression of their obedience to Joshua, who had likewise challenged them to be faithful in claiming all the land.[18] Their faithfulness to Yahweh, then, was expressed in their faithfulness to their compatriots.

Although the conquest was a one-off event, the idea that faithfulness to God is expressed through faithfulness to the community of his people is something that is found frequently in the Bible. For example, we can note that, in the Ten Commandments, the fifth to tenth commandments all express a commitment not to act in a way that damages one's community. This is in itself an expression of the worship of God that is at the heart of the first four commandments. Although most of the commandments prohibit behaviour that damages community, we can see the actions of the eastern tribes as a positive expression of this in which they, knowing what God has done for them, take that as a basis for working for the well-being of the rest of their community. At the same time, Joshua knows that past faithfulness does not always lead to future faithfulness. This is why he charges them directly to live out their continued faithfulness to all that Moses commanded them by loving Yahweh, walking in his ways and holding to him with wholehearted faithfulness. Indeed, that Joshua is drawing on Moses' own directives is clear from the

[14] 22:7.
[15] Nelson, *Joshua*, p. 247.
[16] 1:16–18.
[17] Num. 32:28–31.
[18] 1:13–15.

similarity between the language here and in a number of passages in Deuteronomy.[19]

Joshua's charge has thus directed the eastern tribes to continue taking God at his word, living out what they have already experienced as they journey with God into their shared future. The blessing he gives them as they return home is probably shaped by this, though it no doubt also includes sharing out the spoil with these tribes.[20] The wealth they take with them is a reminder that God has provided for them, just as he had also provided for the generation who had left Egypt in the exodus.[21]

2. Conflict and investigation (22:9–20)

That the eastern tribes are leaving the land as promised is hinted at again as their return is described, for we are told that they not only depart from the sanctuary at Shiloh, but they also leave the Israelites who are in the land of Canaan; that is, they leave the land that was promised. Even though God has granted them their territory east of the Jordan, it is not the land promised to Abraham. On the way, something strange happens – the eastern tribes build an altar which is of *imposing size* (10) by the Jordan. At this stage we are not told why they should do this, principally because we are meant to experience the shock of the western tribes as they see it and as it then becomes the basis of rumour and report among them. Then, suddenly, the western tribes are ready for war.

We might find that a little strange. To understand this response we have to remember that Deuteronomy 12 prohibited the practice of building altars wherever anyone wanted. An altar could be built only where Yahweh would choose – otherwise, one would be treated like a Canaanite and be liable to destruction.[22] In light of that, the emphasis in this chapter on the fact that the tribes had been at Shiloh suddenly becomes especially important. Since Israel had set up the tabernacle there in 18:1 Shiloh had been the site of the central sanctuary. Given its presence, the eastern tribes were not free to initiate an alternative altar for themselves.[23] The shock of this for the

[19] E.g. Deut. 10:12–13.

[20] Elsewhere, only Caleb is blessed by Joshua (14:13).

[21] Exod. 12:35–36.

[22] This law is most commonly understood as prohibiting any altar other than the central one, though as Peter C. Craigie, *The Book of Deuteronomy* (Grand Rapids: Eerdmans, 1976), p. 217, notes, this is not actually the issue addressed. As Woudstra, *Joshua*, p. 320, observes, prior to Josiah's reforms Israel does not seem to have been particularly troubled by multiple sanctuaries.

[23] Butler, *Joshua*, p. 246, stresses that the accusation is that the eastern tribes made the altar 'for themselves', which suggests that it is the lack of divine initiative that is the issue.

western tribes is that it seems as if, almost immediately after being
sent back by Joshua, the eastern tribes have transgressed Yahweh's
commandments. It appears that the very thing Joshua had urged
them not to do is what they have done. Thus, suddenly, one un-
explained action has placed the whole unity of the body of God's
people under threat.

Fortunately, it is recognized that the people's unity is under threat,
and before warfare can begin a party is sent with a specifically recon-
ciliatory purpose – a group led by Phinehas, the son of the then high
priest, Eleazar. Their task is to investigate what the eastern tribes
have done, and to see whether or not they will repent. At one level,
Phinehas might seem an odd choice to stop violence since it was he
who had speared an Israelite man and woman while they engaged in
the worship of Baal at Peor and to whose family Yahweh had sworn
a covenant of perpetual priesthood.[24] In that case, though, it was his
quick action to prevent the spread of an indisputable rebellion that
was recognized, whereas here the narrator has been careful to shield
the intent of the eastern tribes from us. So Phinehas is despatched
with ten tribal elders to investigate, the number ten apparently
covering the nine tribes entirely in the land plus one from Manasseh
as a tribe with members either side of the Jordan.

It is immediately apparent that the group has assumed from the
outset that the eastern tribes are guilty of having sinned. Although
it is not the principal purpose of this chapter to model patterns for
resolving conflict, it does so incidentally here by showing, in essence,
what *not* to do. The accusatory tone of the question posed by
Phinehas' party on behalf of the western tribes in verse 16 makes
this clear. With the other western tribes gathered for war it seems
that they have been despatched to resolve the problem without
warfare, but their question immediately serves to heighten the
tension since it makes no effort to find out what has been done or
why. Rather, it first excludes the eastern tribes by claiming to be a
message from *the whole congregation* of Yahweh, with the clear
implication that the eastern tribes are not included. More than this,
it then accuses them of acting as infidels who have turned from
following Yahweh in building this altar. In a context of heightened
tensions this is not the way to proceed, since there is seldom a more
effective way of generating defensiveness than by such a direct
accusation.

Nevertheless, like a good many mistakes, this one is built on
something that is actually true, which is that sin can infect a whole
community from a small beginning. Two examples of this are given.

[24] Num. 25.

The first is the sin of Peor,[25] when Israel forgot to be faithful to Yahweh and became involved with Moabites and their worship. Only Phinehas' zeal prevented the plague then from being worse. The point is that rebellion in the wilderness had dire effects for the nation as a whole, some of the implications of which were still being worked out. Given that Phinehas is the leader of this delegation, it is perhaps an unsurprising example. The implication Phinehas' group derive from this is that the eastern tribes should leave their homes and move to the area west of the Jordan where the tabernacle, and hence the only appropriate altar, stands. The second example is that of Achan from Joshua 7, when the sin of one man damaged the whole community. This second example uses the same verb to link the eastern tribes' act of infidelity with that of Achan,[26] suggesting that the building of this altar is as significant a sin as the theft of the devoted items from Jericho.

Taken together, these two examples serve to drive home the point: the sin of one group affects the whole of the nation, and that sin places them all in a situation of rebellion before God. This, of course, is why unity in faith is so important. The problem, however, as we shall discover, is that although their theology of sin is correct (because the sin of an individual or group *does* affect the people as a whole), it is a truth that is misapplied. They properly recognize the importance of the whole of God's people remaining together, but by failing to discover what is actually happening they misapply that truth. However, before we accuse this group too quickly, we should perhaps note how the narrator has carefully refrained from giving us more information, meaning that we as readers are likely to be equally as outraged by what seems to have happened; the text thus holds up a mirror to us as readers and reminds us of how easily we can jump to wrong and possibly damaging conclusions on the basis of limited evidence.[27] Failing to give proper heed to all involved can never be the appropriate way for Christians to resolve areas of disagreement.

3. The reconciliation (22:21–34)

After all these accusations, though, the narrator suddenly reveals a deliberate irony: the eastern tribes had not meant any of the things with which they have been charged by the western tribes. Indeed, the whole problem of the altar stems from a misunderstanding of what they were trying to do. Nevertheless, the report of their response

[25] Num. 25.
[26] 7:1; 22:16, 20.
[27] Prov. 18:17 is apt: 'The one who states his case first seems right, until the other comes and examines him.'

carefully holds back the reason for their actions until the end of the speech, so that we understand the passion with which they speak, and emphasizes the importance with which they view the nation's unity.

a. The eastern tribes' response (22:21–29)

We feel the sudden and complete shock of the eastern tribes as they respond to these charges by twice invoking a series of names for God, perhaps a means of swearing an oath, while pointing out that Yahweh is indeed all-powerful.[28] In essence, it is this declaration that shows why these tribes belong within Israel.[29] Most importantly for these tribes, it is clear that Yahweh already knows why they built the altar and that they have not broken faith or acted with infidelity, but this has not been understood by the rest of Israel. Thus it is the western tribes who must know what they have done and, more importantly, why. Indeed, they are even prepared to accept any just punishment if they really have rebelled against Yahweh, whether by encouraging the worship of other gods or by the inappropriate worship of Yahweh – though of course their reason for stating this is that they believe they have acted faithfully.

The irony lies in the ways in which the altar was viewed. The western tribes saw it as a sign of division, a sign of the unfaithfulness of the eastern tribes, a sign that they could not be trusted. The eastern tribes, on the other hand, saw it as a sign of faithfulness, a sign to indicate to the western tribes that although they lived outside of the technical boundaries of the land, they were still a part of the people of God. This is rather like viewing a work of art without any context for its interpretation – we will tend to see expressed in it those themes that we expect, though they may not at all be those intended. Thus an altar that was intended by one group to be a witness to faithfulness and unity was seen by the others as a sign of faithlessness and disunity. Perfectly appropriate and well-intentioned acts can easily be mis-understood, with the unity of God's people thereby put at risk.

In fact, the reason for the construction of the altar is explicitly stated as being a means of preventing the descendants of the western tribes ever convincing the eastern tribes that they have no place among the people of promise and so not regarding them as legitimate worshippers of Yahweh. The Jordan, the crossing of which was so important early in the book,[30] thus remains an important barrier to perceptions of who is included among God's people. Indeed, it

---

[28] Hess's suggestion, *Joshua*, p. 292, that this might be translated 'The LORD is the greatest God' well captures the force of their declaration.
[29] See Creach, *Joshua*, p. 112.
[30] Josh. 3 – 4.

becomes a crucial point for different understandings of what it means to be Israel – is it defined on the basis of geography or kinship?[31] Or is there a deeper way of understanding what it means to be God's people? It is perhaps notable that at this point only are Reuben and Gad mentioned, perhaps because Manasseh has clans on both sides of the Jordan. The point, as they develop it, is that the altar is meant to be a replica of the real thing – it was never intended to supplant Shiloh or wherever the central altar would be. However, standing on the west side of the Jordan, this was obviously difficult to see. Understanding the unity of the people of God thus requires an effort on the part of all concerned because this unity is so easily damaged and imagined transgressions can be established in the popular tradition and so entrenched. The declaration of the eastern tribes here shows how keenly they felt this issue, and it is one which continues to be important today. It is why Paul emphasizes the unity of all believers in Christ in spite of our diversity.[32]

Nevertheless, the statement of the eastern tribes brings the unity back by reconciling the parties. It achieves this by highlighting the fact that they are, in fact, being faithful to the command of God through Joshua as well as to the law. The people of Israel really are together in the land because, in spite of the differences in perspective, they are united in their worship and what it means to be faithful to God in that worship. They have had different perspectives on what that means, but the reality still survives. Nevertheless, those different perspectives do not allow just anything; the eastern tribes know that there is a central sanctuary, and, however well intentioned they might be, they cannot build a second altar for sacrifice. However, with the altar properly understood as a sign of unity, the groups can once more be at peace with each other. Understanding and true faithfulness need to go together to enable the unity of God's people, because these are vital to realizing God's presence among us. It is this that Phinehas finally recognizes, and in verse 31 he speaks for an Israel that has now come to know that there has been no infidelity.[33] It is because of this that the western group can return satisfied.

b. Knowing God's presence (22:30–34)

Phineas and the leaders do not go back rejoicing because they have succeeded in negotiating their way through a difficult situation (indeed, this is in many ways an excellent example of how not to negotiate); instead they rejoice because they have discovered that in

---

[31] Hawk, *Joshua*, pp. 228–229.

[32] Eph. 4:4–6.

[33] This declaration picks up on the verb used with reference to Achan in vv. 16 and 20.

real unity, a unity not necessarily apparent in their perceptions but still present in the reality of their worship, they truly are the one people. The Jordan, however much it might seem to be a barrier, does not exclude those to whom God has given the opportunity to live on the east even though it is not part of the land originally promised. And when God is present among them, different perspectives on what it means to be God's people can be set to one side. War is not needed; instead of acting in violence towards the eastern tribes there is the opportunity to worship God. Whether east of the Jordan or west, those who are God's people are those who live in faithfulness to him. The physical boundary of the river is not to divide them. Instead, all can now see the altar in the terms proposed by Reuben and Gad, which is that it is a *witness*[34] *between* those on both sides of the river that Yahweh is God, and those who can affirm that are indeed God's people.

So how was God present among his people? He was present among them as they discovered that, in spite of their differing perceptions of what it meant in practice to be the people of God, their underlying purpose was the same. They were one in God, and when they took the time to discover what others meant by this they also discovered that Yahweh was truly present among them. Indeed, it was at the very point of discovering where their true unity lay that they also discovered the reality of God's presence among them.

This is therefore a vital text for us to discover afresh today. Although not divided by a river, Christians often find many ways to separate themselves from one another, and questions of how we define ourselves are frequently at the centre of such discussions. We live, for instance, in an age when people have many different perceptions about what it means to worship God, and if the arguments today are no longer about whether it is acceptable to use guitars in worship rather than the organ, they are usually about other points of practice that are confused with matters essential to the faith. The challenge for us is to come to terms with the fact that there are many ways of worshipping God appropriately and therefore to understand what we are all trying to do. There is no single way of worshipping God, though just as the eastern tribes' confession showed that they were authentic, we might today find something similar in the declaration 'Jesus is Lord'.[35] However, when we come together from the diversity of our backgrounds and confess our underlying unity in the one whom we worship, then also we shall discover the wonderful truth that God is in our midst.

[34] The exact sense of v. 34 is disputed – it is uncertain whether or not the altar is actually named *Witness* – but its function seems clear.
[35] Rom. 10:9.

Joshua 23:1–16
17. Parting words

When my wife and I purchased our own home we realized that it was important to receive proper legal advice. Although we had assumed that this would be about the intricacies of purchasing a property, including the vast range of documents detailing matters of title and the restrictions that applied to the particular house we were buying, we were still surprised when the solicitor asked us about our wills. We both already had wills but our solicitor helped us to see that the wills we had, although perfectly adequate before, no longer covered matters as well as they should now that we had a house. In short, adequate provision, both for each other and for our children, meant it was time to draft new wills. Of course, plenty can go wrong, and it has been said (no doubt by a particularly cynical lawyer) that where there's a will, there's a relative who wants to contest it; history is littered with disputed wills. Those familiar with the ruinous case at the centre of Charles Dickens' *Bleak House* (*Jarndyce v. Jarndyce*) may be aware that it was based, at least in part, on cases known to Dickens from his time, and problems with wills continue to keep lawyers busy today.

In Israel, though, the matter was somewhat simpler. Your estate went to your children with the simple provision that the eldest son received twice the share of the others, and there was also a series of provisions that outlined what would happen if there were difficulties with this.[1] There was thus no great need for the lawyers. However, there is one feature of the Old Testament that is somewhat more like our concept of the will, because our will is an expression of what we want to have happen after our death. In the Old Testament, this often takes the form of a speech issued by an elderly person to his family

[1] Our encounter in 17:3–4 with the daughters of Zelophehad, whose father had died without any sons, has already given one example of how this would be worked out. See also Num. 27:1–13 and 36 for the legal background.

or the clan structure, often looking back over what God has done in the past and exhorting certain behaviours in the future, though some form of blessings are also commonly given. It was the desire to obtain this blessing from Isaac, in what Isaac apparently thought would be his final words, that saw Jacob conniving with his mother Rebekah.[2] Later, Jacob would speak to his sons about their future,[3] while Moses' speeches in Deuteronomy are, in effect, an extended will given in the time leading up to his death.[4] Much later, we have both a set of 'last words'[5] and some instructions for Solomon from the aged David.[6] Of course, the fact that someone is old does not mean that his or her death is necessarily imminent; so although Samuel, in his extended speech, announced that he was old,[7] he appears to have remained alive for several years longer. Nevertheless, his charge to Israel then did constitute (in part at least) an expression of his will.

As we turn to this chapter, this is what we find Joshua doing. He is giving his parting words. However, where someone's final words might be given to his or her immediate family, that is not what Joshua is doing here. Rather, he addresses the people of Israel. Like Moses, Joshua is a national figure, and his parting words are addressed to the nation as a whole, though here (in words drawn almost entirely from Deuteronomy[8]) he is particularly focused on its leaders, those who have authority at different social levels.[9] Thus, where his first speech in these closing chapters was addressed to the eastern tribes,[10] exhorting them to faithfulness, his second and his third[11] are more national in focus.

There is a driving concern that runs through all that Joshua has to say. His final will and testament is that the uniqueness of Yahweh as Israel's God should be recognized, and that it should be recognized through the conduct of his people through history. This is essential because God has been faithful to all that he has said, both to his promises of blessing and to his warnings of judgment. Yahweh is unique and remains faithful, and that means that his people need to

[2] Gen. 27.
[3] Gen. 49.
[4] Deut. 34.
[5] 2 Sam. 23:1–7.
[6] 1 Kgs 2:1–9.
[7] 1 Sam. 12:2.
[8] Hawk, *Joshua*, p. 251, particularly stresses 7:1–5 and 11:16–28, but there are allusions to a wide range of passages in Deuteronomy, and the blessing/curse pattern through the chapter is also strongly reminiscent of Deut. 28.
[9] On the various forms of leadership, see esp. Philip S. Johnston, 'Civil Leadership in Deuteronomy', in David G. Firth and Philip S. Johnston (eds), *Interpreting Deuteronomy: Issues and Approaches* (Nottingham: Apollos, 2012), pp. 137–156.
[10] 22:1–8.
[11] 24:1–27.

show their faithfulness to him at all times. Remembering Yahweh's past acts of faithfulness thus serves both to encourage his people's continued faithfulness and to assure them that he will continue to be true to his word, even if that means having to discipline a people who rebel against him. Psalm 95, which reflects on the issue of rest which is of such importance for the book of Joshua, also makes this development, which is perhaps why the epistle to the Hebrews, which reflects on both Joshua and Psalm 95,[12] also makes a similar exhortation in its closing reflections.[13] Thus, although Joshua's words here are rooted in the Sinai covenant, they continue to shape the life of Christians today. And since his words here are addressed to leaders within Israel, they are particularly pertinent for leaders within the church today, reminding us of the responsibility we have not only to teach the importance of faithfulness but also to model it in our own lives.

1. A review of the past (23:1-5)

Although this is not an easy chapter to analyse[14] because of the way it keeps returning to key points, we can for convenience break it into three main sections. In the first, Joshua begins to establish the importance of faithfulness with a review of the past that points to God's absolute faithfulness in terms of his promises, while also pointing to what he will continue to do. Hints of this form were already evident in his speech to the eastern tribes[15] and will emerge again in his fullest speech in chapter 24. Here, however, he is speaking to the leaders whereas in the next chapter there will be a more obviously national focus, albeit one achieved through the leaders. Although on a larger scale, it is perhaps not unlike the fact that Jesus chose to work quite specifically with the twelve though he also had a wider ministry. One might also note that Jesus' upper room discourse and prayer[16] in anticipation of his own death follow a similar pattern to this, preparing the twelve, as the emerging leaders of the new Christian community, for the implications of his death (and resurrection) while encouraging them to continue trusting in God. Although to some extent the decision to work with the leaders on their own probably had a pragmatic basis, both Joshua and Jesus model the importance of providing teaching and encouragement for

[12] Heb. 4:1-10.
[13] Heb. 13:1-17.
[14] Nelson, *Joshua*, p. 255, observes that this 'homiletical style . . . does not lend itself to structural analysis'.
[15] 22:1-8.
[16] John 14 - 17.

those who will continue the work to which God calls his people as a whole. They recognize that there are some issues on which those who will take most responsibility will need additional teaching in order to be best equipped for the work. Of course, Jesus is able to emphasize the continued work of the Holy Spirit in enabling this,[17] something to which Joshua cannot point, but Joshua will be able to direct the leaders to be shaped by meditation on Scripture; and Word and Spirit should always go together.

But Joshua, as we also saw at 13:1, recognizes his age. He is now an old man, and several years have passed since Israel, under his leadership, first entered the land. We are not told how much later this is beyond the fact that it was *a long time afterwards* (1).[18] The repetition of the statement about his age clearly links this chapter to the land allocation, but the fact that it is now at a point when Yahweh has *given rest to Israel from all their surrounding enemies*[19] also provides a close link to the end of the land allocation in 21:43–44. So, as with 13:1, we are to read this speech as something Joshua urgently needed to share because of his old age, but also in the context of Yahweh having granted the promised rest, which in turn was also hinted at in 11:23. However, while old age in chapter 13 was a reason to proceed with the land allocation, Joshua's age did not then prevent him from carrying out this role himself; that he speaks here to the nation's leaders shows that his age is now such that he needs to hand over much of the leadership.

Joshua has been, without doubt, the dominant human figure in both the occupation of the land and its allocation. However, he does not want the attention to be thrust onto him. Instead, he insists – as all leaders of God's people must – that it was God who was the key figure in this. There are times when leaders will need to point to their own work, such as when Paul speaks to the Ephesian elders,[20] but in reality this is only so the work of God can be seen more clearly. Thus although Joshua acknowledges the implications of his advanced age, he here points to what Yahweh has done. Israel has certainly conquered the land, and Joshua himself has had it apportioned for the people; but who was the one who really won the victory? The answer is simple: it was Yahweh.

[17] E.g. John 14:15–31; 16:4–15.

[18] This could refer to the gap between when Israel entered the land, when Joshua began to allot the land or when rest was gained. Since there is a clear evocation of 13:1 here, it seems more likely that the *long time* is the period after the allocation began. However, the book does not appear overly concerned to situate this speech clearly in time and space since, unlike ch. 24, no location is given for it either, even if Shiloh is most likely.

[19] Cf. 2 Sam. 7:1 and 22:1, pointing to parallels between Joshua and David.

[20] Acts 20:17–38.

As we read this simple assertion it is clear that we are meant to reflect on the events described in chapters 3–11. There we saw how Yahweh had fought for Israel from the time he brought them across the Jordan.[21] He fought for them at Jericho with an extraordinary battle plan.[22] He did the same at Ai because he knew the best strategy.[23] He did the same against the southern kings in chapter 10, even raining down massive hailstones on the enemy. He did the same against the northern kings in chapter 11 as he worked through an obedient people. Again and again we see the simple truth outlined here by Joshua: Israel won their battles because Yahweh was the one who fought for them, and indeed he won battles that Israel on their own could not have won.

Of course, it could not be claimed that the process was completed because although Joshua had allotted the land that had been conquered, he knew that much of it remained to be truly occupied. Yahweh had indeed given the land, and it was Yahweh who had allotted it through Joshua in chapters 13–21, but as we have seen, a consistent theme in those chapters was that the allocation was often an act of faith. Israel therefore needed to be reminded of a simple truth: the one who would fight for them in the future, the one who was the guarantor of the completion of their rest, was none other than Yahweh himself. Yahweh could be trusted because he had promised that this would happen, and the principal reason for reviewing events up to this point was simply to make clear that Yahweh is faithful to his promises. God's promises are sure, and we can know they are sure because we can look back and see how they have been worked out in practice. It is this same certainty of being able to trust God's promises that is emphasized by the writer to the Hebrews, illustrating it through various texts from the Old Testament in order to encourage Christians to 'hold fast the confession of our hope without wavering, for he who promised is faithful'.[24] God's promises to us are sure, and they are a basic reason for us to continue in our discipleship.

2. A life for the present (23:6–13)

Because God's promises count for something, they must also affect the ways in which we conduct ourselves now. God's faithfulness to us means that we must be faithful to him in how we live. This is Joshua's starting point as he addresses Israel's leaders, though in a

[21] Josh. 3 – 4.
[22] Josh. 6.
[23] 8:1–29.
[24] Heb. 10:23.

sense he now applies to them the directives that Yahweh gave him at the beginning of the campaign to claim the land. Just as a race has a starting point, so also our faithfulness to God needs a starting point. And that starting point is our commitment to obey what has been revealed in the Scriptures. Israel would not go forward through military strategy but through obedience.[25] Unfortunately, NIV obscures the point by making verse 6 have two commands. ESV is clearer when it says, *be very strong to keep and to do all that is written in the Book of the Law of Moses.* Joshua's point is quite simply that his hearers (and, by implication, all who read these words) need to put all their effort into living out the requirements of the Torah. Although in the first instance this refers to the Pentateuch (or perhaps simply to the book of Deuteronomy) the principle has a wider application since his hearers could only access a small part of the Bible, whereas we can now read the whole of Scripture. However, it is not simply enough to know the content of the Bible – though various surveys have shown how biblical literacy in the West at least is declining.[26] Joshua himself had been directed to meditate on the Torah,[27] but also to be careful to put it into practice, and it is the importance of putting it into practice and not seeking ways of avoiding its implications that is central here. This indeed requires a proper knowledge of it, for unless we know the content of the Bible we will have little idea of what it means to obey it.

The dangers of failing to give our full effort to obey the demands of Scripture are illustrated in the metaphor of following a path. In essence, we all know that if we are journeying from point 'a' to point 'b', we need to stay on the right path – but as many of us know (even with the seemingly endless patience of a satnav), wrong turns are easy to take and these will stop us from reaching our goal. Joshua wants his people to experience the blessings of God fully, and that means staying on the path that he has set.

However, Joshua is also aware that there seem to be some alternative routes, perhaps signposted as 'scenic alternatives'. These 'alternatives', however attractive and reasonable they might seem, are the ways of sin. No doubt many of these could be mentioned, but the one that particularly concerns Joshua here is the risk that Israel might mingle with the Canaanites who are still in the land. This was not some form of xenophobia; rather, it was simple recognition of the fact that these were the nations that were under the

---

[25] Cf. Butler, *Joshua*, p. 255.
[26] See 'Knowledge of Bible "in Decline"', BBC News, 12 July 2009, http://news.bbc.co.uk/1/hi/england/wear/8146460.stm, for a report on the problem in Britain in 2009. Hubbard, *Joshua*, p. 539, points to similar issues in America.
[27] 1:8.

judgment of God, and to associate with them and to adopt their gods was to lose what was distinctive of Israel as the people who were to model God's presence by their very life. Joshua's speech recognized once again that, although all the land had been subdued and allotted, it had not yet been fully possessed and many of the peoples who were being expelled before Israel were still inhabiting it. Not all of them would pose a threat to Israel; those like Rahab who recognized who Yahweh was and effectively gave themselves to him were no threat at all. However, we have been reminded throughout the land allocation chapters of Canaanite groups who remained and who showed no sign of committing themselves to Yahweh.[28] The particular expression of the danger singled out here is intermarriage with the Canaanite groups which would lead the people to the worship of other gods, all forms of which are excluded here. This would become a particular problem after the exile,[29] when marriages with people from other groups caused the community to lose its distinctiveness and led to the existence of families in which the children could not understand God's teaching. Such a situation made it much easier to slip into the worship of other gods, or perhaps – equally likely today – the worship of none. Intermarriage in and of itself is not a problem – as we see in the case of Ruth's marriage to Boaz – while Matthew makes a special point of mentioning non-Israelite women in Jesus' genealogy.[30] What matters is faithfulness to God above all else and not moving into situations where this is put at risk.[31] This too is our responsibility – to be a people distinctive because of our commitment to God in Christ.

Instead, Joshua wants them to carry on with what they have begun, and not to give up now that there have been some worthwhile gains. God has been fighting for them, so they must continue to cling to him. The verb translated *cling* is used in Genesis 2:24 to describe the enduring relationship between a man and a woman in marriage, and its use here may intentionally echo that text. Rather than losing their distinctiveness through inappropriate marriages, the people of Israel are to continue in commitment to Yahweh, something that will affect them in all aspects of their life. The point is that a short-term commitment would not finalize the process of occupation. This could

[28] E.g. 15:63; 16:10; 17:12–13.

[29] Ezra 9 – 10; Neh. 13:23–31.

[30] Matt. 1:1–17 mentions Tamar and Ruth, while the inappropriateness of David's actions against Uriah in 2 Sam. 11 are hinted at in that Bathsheba is simply called 'the wife of Uriah'.

[31] Creach, *Joshua*, p. 118, observes that 'the problem of the book of Joshua is not ethnic purity but spiritual purity'. This is why such marriages are prohibited in Deut. 7:1–5. Paul gives this wider application in 2 Cor. 6:14–16.

not be like the effort students are sometimes tempted to put in when they do just enough to get through their exams. It had to be sustained. And just as the students who continue to keep their focus on their studies are the ones who truly learn, so also an Israel that kept faith was one that would know God's blessing. Likewise, believers and churches who hold fast to God and faithfulness to his Word are the ones who continue to experience his blessing.

The blessing here would be that Yahweh would continue to lead them to the point of full possession of the land. Up to this point Israel could look back and see that Yahweh had given them all that they had, that he had been faithful to his promise that no-one would be able to stand before them.[32] They could see how larger and seemingly more powerful foes had been put to flight, just as had been promised.[33] However, what emerges from this is not a sort of smug self-satisfaction that assumes that all we do must succeed because we are God's people;[34] rather, a people who have known God's blessing are required to *love* God, a summons which naturally echoes the great commandment of Deuteronomy 6:4–5 which Jesus indicates is the greatest commandment, albeit one that is to be joined with love for neighbour.[35] We might find it odd, though, that love is commanded. After all, is not love an emotional response? The answer, in part, lies in Ancient Near East treaties which routinely commanded subject peoples to 'love' the king who now controlled them, though this might be read rather cynically as warning them not to rebel and to pay their taxes instead. What this does establish, however, is that in Israel's world, commanding love was largely equivalent to commanding loyalty, and we would still recognize the latter as something that could be commanded today. However, we cannot leave this command solely in the treaty context, because the biblical command to love God also comes in a setting where we can see what it is that God has already done for us; that is, we see God's loyalty to his people in advance of their love for him, something that is distinct from these treaties. God has already worked for us, even before we had the opportunity to be loyal to him. Under these circumstances, seen most clearly of course in the work of Christ, loyalty can indeed be love, a heartfelt response to a God who has reached out to us. At the same time, however, this prevents us from seeing love purely as an emotional response, because love for God only makes sense when we as his people live for him and hold fast to him through all our lives, and not only when we gather and sing his praises in worship.

[32] 1:5.
[33] Lev. 26:8; Deut. 28:7.
[34] Mocked so sharply by Bob Dylan in his song 'With God on Our Side'.
[35] Matt. 22:34–40.

We might be glad to leave the passage at this point, because then we would have a happy ending. But Joshua does not do so. He knows full well that passages like Leviticus 26 and Deuteronomy 28 show that there is the potential for both blessing and curse, and that a people who do not love God, who do not show loyalty, stand under the curses laid out there. Faithful teaching here – indeed, a demonstration of Joshua's own commitment to Yahweh's Torah – means that the alternative also needs to be made clear. God has been faithful, but the process has not yet ended. Israel cannot assume that God will continue with them irrespective of their own faithlessness, just as the church cannot assume that blessing inevitably awaits it. Faithfulness to the promise of God's blessing demands that we also make clear the implications of not loving God above all else.

3. A warning for the future (23:14–16)

These are sombre words in which Joshua faces up to the implications of his own mortality, but they speak the truth to Israel, both in Joshua's own time and to later readers within Israel, as well as to us today. This is because the temptation to assimilate and worship other gods has always been strong – as was clear in the case of Solomon when his many marriages turned him away from following Yahweh.[36] An Israel – or a church today – that loses its distinctiveness loses its claim to be the people of God. Indeed, by transgressing covenant it instead places itself under the judgment of God, a judgment that in Israel's case would be carried out by the very people they were supposed to dispossess.[37] That is why Joshua's reference to the certainty of the fulfilment of God's promises here needs to be read with care. The statement by the narrator in 21:45 referred to the fulfilment of God's promises as a reason for continued hope, as indeed it is; but Joshua here takes that same theme and considers it from the other perspective. If God's promises of blessing are certain, his warnings of punishment for disobedience are every bit as certain. So when we claim today that all God's promises for us in Scripture are true we need to remember in full what that means, for there are promises of both weal and woe. For Israel, woe meant losing the land.

We need to remember that the faithfulness of God is a double-edged sword; for just as he has faithfully brought about every good word that he has spoken, so also he will bring about every disciplining word. God is consistent, and what he has promised he will do – both for blessing and for punishment.

[36] 1 Kgs 11:1–8.
[37] It is notable that 23:16 recalls 7:1, linking these observations with the story of Achan, which serves as an enduring reminder of the reality of the threat here.

We live, of course, in a context remarkably different from that of Israel. We might therefore imagine that these warnings do not speak directly to us. Yet the question is one that we must ask: to what extent do our lives show the distinctiveness of our Lord? How are we different from those around us? How are we the salt of the earth, the light of the world?[38]

This is not to suggest that we have to go and deliberately live in ways that are odd – but it does suggest that there is meant to be something about the way we relate to one another that is different from the ways of the world around us. That difference is to be measured by one simple test: to what extent do we place our loyalty and obedience to our Lord above all else that we do? We must ask this question because if that is not our priority, we have already started the process of assimilation. And a people who assimilate, a people who do not put their loyalty to Christ above all else, already stand under his judgment: 'You are the salt of the earth, but if salt has lost its taste, how shall its saltiness be restored? It is no longer good for anything except to be thrown out and trampled under people's feet.'[39]

This is the possibility held out before us in Joshua's last will and testament: to be distinctive, to point to Christ above all else, and like Joshua to know his faithfulness. And this is the threat held out before us: to know the other side of his faithfulness if we choose to depart from the way that Christ has set for us.

[38] Matt. 5:13–16.
[39] Matt. 5:13.

214

Joshua 24:1–33
18. Confessing faith anew

Anyone familiar with the genre of the television courtroom drama will recognize at least some of what is happening in this final chapter of Joshua. Normally, after all the events of the case have been presented, the lawyer stands up in court to make a closing speech to either the judge or, more commonly, the jury. In it, the lawyer sums up the evidence while appealing for a decision that goes in favour of his or her client. We, as viewers, are by this time convinced of the rightness of the lawyer's case, but will the court agree and act appropriately? This is not a bad analogy to what happens in this chapter. Like the barrister standing before the court, Joshua appeals on the basis of the evidence presented for Israel to make a decision to commit themselves to serve Yahweh absolutely. This is a decision that requires them to set aside all other commitments and recognize that Yahweh must have the absolute priority, because understanding God's faithfulness through history can lead only to such a commitment. However, as readers of the book of Joshua, like the viewers of the television programme, we are also privileged to have seen the story unfold, so that as Joshua appeals to his audience in Shechem, so also the book appeals to us to commit ourselves to God alone.

Of course, this analogy is not perfect, not least because what we have in this chapter is not a court case but an account of a covenant renewal ceremony within Israel and before Yahweh. This chapter is not the covenant itself, though it draws on many of the features which typified ancient covenant texts – not least of which is a recital of covenant history which explains why making this covenant is appropriate.[1] Even recognizing this, readers might find this chapter rather perplexing, especially because many of the themes addressed

---

[1] Delbert R. Hillers, *Covenant: The History of a Biblical Idea* (Baltimore: Johns Hopkins University Press, 1969), p. 47. For an accessible summary of the main features of ancient covenants, see Howard, *Joshua*, pp. 426–428.

THE MESSAGE OF JOSHUA

here have already been raised in the previous chapter, where Joshua also spoke to Israel's leadership. What is more, where the events of the previous chapter presumably took place at Shiloh, we are now at Shechem, roughly eight miles to the north. Since Shiloh was the site of the tabernacle,[2] it is perhaps unexpected that Shechem (which has not previously been significant in the book[3]) should be the site of this gathering, and indeed that it should be noted as having a sanctuary of Yahweh.[4] Why so much replication and this change of location?

We need to place this chapter in its immediate context as the last of the three successively longer speeches from Joshua with which the book of Joshua ends.[5] In each, worship is a crucial feature, though that is tied to the identity of the people of God. Chapter 22 has insisted that geographical boundaries cannot determine the people who can serve Yahweh. What matters is that their intent is to serve Yahweh. The overlap with chapter 23 is more substantial, but the primary issue there is *how* Yahweh is to be served – by remaining faithful to all that is written in Yahweh's Torah. The issue in chapter 24 is more *who* is to be served, and that is Yahweh alone.[6] Thus the people are challenged to appreciate that Yahweh is served only by those who worship him alone, and in the context of the book where unexpected people have continually been added to or excluded from God's people, it is this which ultimately defines them as God's people; Yahweh has chosen them and they have chosen Yahweh above all other gods.[7]

No clear reason is given for the move to Shechem, but it is not impossible that the site is chosen as a deliberate parallel to Genesis 12:6, the place where Yahweh first indicated to Abraham that Canaan was the land of promise – a promise which is now fulfilled[8] – and a place where Israel could reflect on the whole of their history with Yahweh.[9] Although Shechem is not the centre for Israel's worship, it is still appropriately considered a sanctuary here,[10] much as Gilgal

---

[2] 18:1.

[3] Apart from this chapter, it is mentioned only in 17:7; 20:7; and 21:21 as part of the land allocation, though the clan of Shechem is also noted in 17:2, while Mount Ebal, where the events of 8:30–35 occurred, is also nearby.

[4] 24:26.

[5] See introductory comments on Josh. 22.

[6] See Nelson, *Joshua*, p. 268.

[7] Hawk, *Joshua in 3-D*, p. 239.

[8] In Gen. 35:1–4 it is also the place where Jacob put aside foreign gods, creating another important parallel here.

[9] McConville and Williams, *Joshua*, p. 89.

[10] Butler, *Joshua*, p. 267, notes that Shechem as a cult centre was destroyed relatively early (Judg. 9), providing evidence that the tradition recorded in this chapter is quite ancient.

was,[11] as the place where the land promise was first made and where its reality is now fully claimed. History and location thus come together in defining the people of God as those who commit to serving him, and serving him alone.[12]

1. Reciting covenant history (24:1–13)

The appeal here begins, naturally enough, with the evidence. This, after all, is what is meant to convince any jury, which is what those gathered effectively are. And Joshua has a particularly strong case to make. As with the previous chapter, everyone is gathered to listen as Joshua speaks. In the previous chapter the emphasis was on the faithfulness of God and what that would mean. Now, however, the emphasis is on the need for Israel to remain faithful, though the reason for that lies in God's faithfulness. It is this which continues to provide the foundation for our own faithfulness today.

Joshua here provides a potted summary of the history of Israel. It is worth noting that Joshua's focus is not on the characters involved in this story, but rather on God. Joshua is not recounting events from Israel's history simply to help them remember key dates. This is history told with a purpose – that the people should recognize all that God has done for them. Moreover, Joshua here takes on a prophetic role, speaking as God's own mouthpiece. One key way in which Joshua achieves this is by blurring the generations involved, so that although he is well aware of the fact that the events he describes happened in the past, we often find him shifting between 'they' and 'you'. We see an example in verse 6, where God's actions in bringing the current generation's ancestors out of Egypt are described before Joshua then says, *and you came to the sea.* At one level, this is simply untrue: the people gathered at Shechem were not even born then. At a more profound level, however, it is fundamentally true, because they can be gathered there only because of what God has done, and through their ancestors they too were there in the crossing of the sea. This story of divine faithfulness with its blurring of generations is told through four periods in Israel's life.

a. The patriarchs (24:2–4)

Joshua first focuses on the patriarchs. Obviously in what is only a summary a great deal is left out because the emphasis is on how Yahweh was faithful to his people. Joshua's possibly surprising point

---

[11] 4:19–24.
[12] For a similar perspective in the New Testament, note Rom. 12:1–2 as Paul's appeal which emerges out of his detailed argument in the previous eleven chapters.

is that even though Abraham and his family were worshippers of other gods, Yahweh still chose to work with them. In other words, Yahweh did not call Abraham because he was somehow better than anyone else, as if he possessed some special virtue that made him worth calling; rather, he and his family were entirely typical of the culture of which they were a part. The Old Testament never tells us how it was that Abraham came to know Yahweh and so to worship him rather than other gods. It simply knows that God called him and that Abraham responded to that call.[13] This call was an act of pure grace on Yahweh's part, albeit grace that was ultimately part of his mission to restore all creation to himself. Davis notes that we often tend to read the stories of the Old Testament as if the virtues of these people meant that God had simply to finish off what they had started on the road to faith; but this is precisely what did not happen. God called Abraham and made him promises of land, descendants and a special relationship in which blessing was central. This was God's work alone, and we are meant to marvel at the wonders of his grace – the very same grace that has called each of us to him.[14]

What is more, God kept his promises to them. The God who called also promised, and he is faithful to his promises, even if the path that faithfulness takes might not be the one we would choose. Yet Abraham was not only promised land and a relationship with God, he was also promised descendants. Joshua emphasizes that this promise was fulfilled. The claim that Yahweh multiplied Abraham's 'seed' might seem odd if we think only of Isaac, but we should rather see Isaac as the beginning of that multiplication, a multiplication that continued through Esau and Jacob. The mysterious grace of God thus called a family who were anything but holy, and who, if we read their stories in Genesis 12 – 50, were particularly gifted in finding ways of putting those promises under threat by their sin; and yet he remained faithful, fulfilling his promises. How those promises were fulfilled was not straightforward. Joshua concentrates not on the delays each experienced in having children but rather on the land, since that was the promise of particular relevance for his hearers. Indeed, it is the promise of the land that is central to his whole exposition of Israel's story; but where the promise for Israel would take many generations, for Esau and his descendants the story was already complete in Genesis.[15] The longer period of fulfilment for Israel, however, turned out to be an extended way of seeing God's faithfulness.

[13] Gen. 12:1–9.
[14] Davis, *No Falling Words*, p. 189.
[15] Gen. 36:8.

b. The exodus (24:5–7)

The same is true in the account of the exodus. The people of Israel were afflicted by the Egyptians, but Yahweh was faithful to them, faithful to his promise. Having sent Moses and Aaron, and having struck Egypt with the plagues, God simply said, *I brought you out.* Those standing before Joshua had not come out in person, but even so they stood there because God had in reality brought them out. Israel could never confess anything else; they never had the power to do otherwise. In bringing Israel out of Egypt, Yahweh also heard Israel's cry and overthrew the Egyptian army at the Sea of Reeds.[16] More could be said – but the point is made. Yahweh is faithful to his people and has proved himself to be so. Beyond that, the point of the exodus was always that Israel should enter the land. It is easy to read of the exodus and see it as an end in itself, but as Joshua makes clear it had to be understood as part of a larger story of salvation. From the perspective of the New Testament, we can appreciate that this story of salvation is larger still, culminating in Jesus (though that too has a future element), but we need to begin here and see that the exodus was simply a beginning, one that came out of God's faithfulness to his promise.

c. In the trans-Jordan (24:8–10)

Passing over most of the period in the wilderness, Joshua then comes to when Israel was to the east of the Jordan. Mention of Sihon and Og's attacks on Israel[17] in conjunction with the exodus brings us back to Rahab's confession[18] and the motivation admitted by the Gibeonites[19] for wanting to make a covenant with Israel. The same events which had led them (in divergent ways!) to join Israel are now presented to those at Shechem as a reason for them to appreciate Yahweh's faithfulness. When Sihon and Og came against Israel, Yahweh was the one who won the battle. His faithfulness did not end at Sinai, and even though the generation who first came to the land failed to enter it because of unbelief, Yahweh's promise did not fail.

Joshua here takes the story a little further. When Balak attempted to battle with Israel by sending Balaam against Israel with the curse,[20] it was Yahweh who delivered the nation. True to his promise of

[16] Exod. 14:21–31.
[17] Num. 21:21–35.
[18] 2:10.
[19] 9:10.
[20] Num. 22 – 24.

blessing for Abraham's descendants,[21] Yahweh allowed no curse but instead Balaam *repeatedly blessed you*.[22] That Yahweh is faithful to his people is not simply an assertion, it is something proved by experience; and indeed when we read the story of Balaam we realize that Israel did not even know at the time they were being attacked. God was keeping his promise, and neither physical attack nor spiritual powers would stop him doing that.

d. The conquest (24:11–13)

Only now does Joshua reach the point where those gathered have been involved. Here he recognizes that it is all too easy to lose sight of what God has done in even the recent past. It is, after all, often easier to see what God has done in the distant past because of the perspective that time gives us, and indeed we often need to be careful in claiming too much today as a specific work of God. However, where we are able to draw directly on the promises of God as the framework for seeing what God is doing among us, it is then possible to have the perspective we need to do this. It is because Joshua knows the promises of God that he can put the experience of the current generation into the larger story of what God has been doing and so demonstrate that their experiences are a continuation of the story of God's faithfulness. Thus Joshua reminds the people of crossing the Jordan,[23] of the victory at Jericho[24] and of victories over the various Canaanite groups,[25] all of which are to be attributed to Yahweh's actions on Israel's behalf. More than that, Yahweh is said to have sent *the hornet* before Israel, which drove the land's inhabitants out. Exactly what this means is unclear, though it is consistent with Exodus 23:28. However, since there the 'hornet' is paralleled with 'terror' in the previous verse, we are perhaps to understand it as a metaphor which reflects the dread the Canaanite peoples would feel.[26] The result is that Israel can now celebrate the blessing of life in the land because

[21] Gen. 12:3.

[22] 24:10, HCSB.

[23] Josh. 3 – 4.

[24] Josh. 6. Nelson, *Joshua*, pp. 274–275, believes the idea that Jericho fought Israel is at odds with the earlier account which focuses only on what might be called the 'non-military' elements of the capture. But it is clear that even with the walls collapsed, Jericho did not immediately surrender. In any case, that Jericho was closed up for a siege is consistent with them fighting Israel, even if not in pitched battle.

[25] Josh. 10 – 12. The reference to *two kings* in v. 12 is unclear – normally this would be Sihon and Og, but they have been mentioned previously, and in any case Joshua is now describing events in the land. Perhaps we should understand them as Adoni-zedek and Jabin, the kings mentioned in 10:1 and 11:1.

[26] The vocabulary is different, but it is consistent with Rahab's testimony in 2:10–11.

Yahweh has shown himself faithful to his promise. It is this framework that continues to enable Christians today to interpret their experience and so recognize how God is working out his promises among us, challenging us to continued faithfulness in response.

2. Renewing covenant (24:14–28)

Having presented all the evidence, Joshua calls for a decision that represents a renewal of the covenant relationship that existed between Israel and Yahweh. It is important that we note this fact, because although it may seem like one, this is not, in the strictest sense, an evangelistic appeal. That would be an appeal to those who do not yet know God to come to him. Here, however, we have an appeal to those who are already God's covenant people to make their official status their lived reality. Joshua here recognizes an issue which would plague Israel through its life, and which has continued to plague the church through the ages. This is the problem of what we might call 'partial discipleship', in which people are prepared to claim the benefits of life in covenant with God but not live out its demands. Most pointedly, that here means removing all other gods from among the community. What God has always wanted is a people who are committed to him alone, who recognize no other allegiance. The obstacles to that have varied over time; there are perhaps few today tempted to serve the 'gods from across the river' – but issues such as wealth, comfort or family, which Jesus identified as problems after meeting the rich ruler,[27] continue to be barriers today. Joshua confronted Israel with the challenge to remove the safety net of these gods – which was in fact no safety net at all – just as Jesus challenges us to full discipleship today.

a. A first appeal (24:14–18)

We have in these verses a discussion between Joshua and the people in which he lays the choice before them. He challenges them to understand that because Yahweh is absolutely faithful to his people, so also he expects his people to be faithful to him. Israel cannot keep other gods and serve Yahweh, even though the traditional paganism was quite open to that possibility. Sincere worship cannot take place where other gods are present, as indeed is clear from the first commandment.[28] Yet Joshua recognizes that the community before him, for all they have experienced God's faithfulness, are not living out their side of covenant. They have experienced God's saving

[27] Mark 10:23–31.
[28] Exod. 20:3; cf. Deut. 6:10–15.

power, but they are not living as those who know that this means they need no other gods. Given that those standing before Joshua include those Canaanites who have declared their commitment to Yahweh, we might not be surprised that these gods are still present. However, Joshua makes clear that the problem is a deep-rooted one and that it is not just Canaanites who are concerned. The problem reaches back into Israel's past, to at least Egypt and probably back to the patriarchs. Idolatry in all its forms was remarkably difficult to remove because all other 'gods' seemed to offer something helpful or worthwhile, and many in Israel apparently clung tenaciously to these gods, even though they had experienced so much.

Joshua's own position is clear enough: he and his family will serve Yahweh. They have made their decision, and so must the nation. In a sense Joshua is not really offering a choice, for it is a choice between God and nothing. However, it is the peculiar temptation that we all experience that even nothing can seem good, and we invariably find it easier to trust what we can see and hold with our hands, even if it cannot make a real difference. Sometimes, of course, the modern idolatry of things such as money is based on the fact that they can make *some* difference, and this is why they continue to hold us in thrall. As I write this I am uncomfortably aware of many worthwhile ministries that have folded in recent years because of a lack of money. Often when this situation is reached we end up with numerous committees looking to save or raise funds, so that the necessary money seems to become the objective. This is not to criticize a proper attitude to stewardship, since that is always needed; but merely to observe that something which is good and helpful in one context can move from being a gift that God has given to becoming a goal in its own right. When that happens it has become a form of idolatry, and instead of being a good gift from God has become a snare for us. Instead, only total devotion to God is enough.

Given this challenge the people respond in what seems a wholly positive way. They confess that they cannot forsake Yahweh because they have seen what he has done. In effect, they agree with the reading of history that Joshua has presented. Joshua has declared that he and his family will serve Yahweh, and the people seem to make the same affirmation. But then something rather strange happens.

b. An appeal reframed (24:19–24)

It seems that Joshua has the response he desires. The people have affirmed that they will serve Yahweh. But with this response ringing in his ears, Joshua declares that Israel *cannot* actually serve Yahweh! No modern evangelist would do this. Why bring the people to the point of confession and then say, 'Sorry, but you can't do it'? Does Joshua sense some insincerity in their reply, perhaps because they have not yet come to the point of acknowledging that they have to throw away the other gods? This is possible but is not affirmed by the text. What is clear is that Joshua wants them to understand the demanding nature of following Yahweh alone. It is simply not acceptable to rejoice in the promises but not live in light of God's holiness. They must understand what it means to serve God, just as Christians today must appreciate the whole of God's nature. What Joshua emphasizes is that God is both holy and jealous. Both these attributes of God – holiness and jealousy – are usually expressed as a comfort to believers in the Old Testament. God is jealous for his people because he wants their absolute devotion,[29] something which is also true of his holiness.[30] Israel could not have Yahweh and other gods, just as we cannot have Jesus and the gods of our age! Choosing to follow is not just a matter of claiming the promises; it is also about living out the demands that God's grace now places upon us – which is precisely why Paul so often turns in his epistles from expounding the gospel as God's gracious gift to exploring the demands it places on us as we live out that gospel.[31] Claiming to serve God while continuing to live in a way contrary to this would bring the people under God's judgment, and Joshua will not permit this. However, his statement about Yahweh not forgiving must be understood as specific to this particular situation: it is the sin of claiming to serve God while not doing so that cannot be forgiven because it denies the very context from which forgiveness comes. Joshua's words thus express a proper pastoral relationship to a people who need to understand more fully the cost of discipleship, because, to paraphrase Bonhoeffer, cheap grace has always been the enemy of God's people.[32]

Only with this made clear is Joshua willing to hear anew the people's confession. Only then, when they are witnesses against themselves, can there be progress, as Joshua once again summons them to throw away their foreign gods. If Yahweh has proved faithful in history, then a half-hearted commitment is not acceptable. The significant change comes, therefore, when the people confess not only that they will serve Yahweh (i.e. worship him), but also that they will obey him. Only then is Joshua prepared to make the covenant with the people, because only then have they accepted that discipleship is

---

[29] Exod. 34:14.

[30] Lev. 19:2–3.

[31] Rom. 12 is a point where this is frequently noted, but a similar distinction is also seen between Gal. 1 – 4 and 5 – 6; Eph. 1 – 3 and 4 – 6; and Col. 1 – 2 and 3 – 4.

[32] Dietrich Bonhoeffer, *The Cost of Discipleship* (Complete edn, London: SCM Press, 1959), p. 1.

a whole-life commitment. It is this commitment, when worship and obedience go together, that truly defines what it means to be the people of God in every age.

c. A covenant ratified (24:25–28)

The verdict has been reached – the people must serve Yahweh alone – and there at the sanctuary at Shechem, near the place where the Torah had earlier been read,[33] a stone is placed under a tree to testify to what has taken place. The importance of the stone is symbolic. Like Ebenezer, the stone Samuel would later set up,[34] this stone will be a reminder to Israel of what they have done, of the commitment they have made. In particular, it will remind them that the gracious God who delivered them and fulfilled his promises is also the God who demands wholehearted obedience from them. So the stone is rather like a monument to what has happened, even if it is personified in the discussion. In this case, it also warns the nation of what it will mean if they forsake their promise.

This warning is not, however, restricted to the stone, as Joshua also writes the statutes and rules in the book of Yahweh's *torah*. Although this is clearly not part of the Pentateuch, or even our book of Joshua, reference to Yahweh's *torah* provides a bookend for Joshua as a whole since it began by reminding Joshua of the importance of shaping his whole life around it.[35] The reference here is more limited, with this text functioning to record a particular moment and set of events; but they are noted because a record needs to exist to provide a point of reference to which later generations can turn.[36] For most, the stone would be enough as the story would be told, but a written record was also important. And though the reference to *torah* here is limited, it serves as a reminder that the whole of God's people need this written word as a touchstone that reminds them of what it means to serve God.

3. Three funerals (24:29–33)[37]

After this, we have what might almost seem to be an anticlimax, with the record of the deaths of Joshua and Eleazar, the leaders of the

[33] 8:30–35.
[34] 1 Sam. 7:12.
[35] 1:7–8.
[36] Such documents were routinely part of ancient covenant ceremonies, so one would be expected here.
[37] LXX has a very different text here. See Butler, *Joshua*, p. 281, for the issues; in general the text represented in most English versions, which is based on MT, is to be accepted.

people to this time, and the burial of Joseph. However, it is not an anticlimax; it is rather the fitting conclusion to all that has happened in the book. The rest that the nation was awaiting has been achieved, and there is now time to remember the leaders who have brought them this far. God has given rest to his people. Joshua is therefore buried in the land Yahweh allotted him, as one who has thus received God's gift in full. And he dies with the title *servant of the LORD*, someone who has truly lived out what it means to live for Yahweh alone, the very thing the covenant ceremony has urged.

Before recording the burials of Joseph and Eleazar there is a warning that prepares us for the next stage in Israel's story. The people, we are told, served Yahweh all the days of Joshua's life and the days of the elders who outlived him. We might wonder if this is true; after all, the book has plenty of examples of Israel acting unfaithfully, not least the fact that this chapter presumes that they have carried other gods with them even as they have claimed the land. Actually, however, this verse is a key to understanding the whole book, because through it we see that events which might seem contrary to the law – such as the inclusion of Canaanites like Rahab – were in fact acts of faithfulness which recognized that Yahweh always had a larger purpose.[38] This verse is thus an affirmation of what has happened to date. However, because the people's faithfulness lasted only as long as the generation after Joshua, the people's own claim of faithfulness now stands as a witness against them. Always, there is a danger that our protestations of faith exceed the sincerity of our commitment, and that is why the challenge of this chapter needs to be heard again and again.

Nevertheless, we do not end with warning but with the burial of Joseph, fulfilling his own request to be buried in the land,[39] as well as that of Eleazar who, like Joshua, is buried in the land Yahweh had given him. Joseph contrasts with Eleazar in that he is buried as a member of a much earlier generation, one whose claim to the land where he was buried came through a commercial transaction[40] – albeit one which anticipated what Yahweh would ultimately do. While Joshua is not replaced, Eleazar's son Phinehas continues the priestly ministry. Thus, although there is a warning here, there is also a reminder of God's continuing and gracious provision for his people.

This is a powerful chapter because it calls us too to make a decision. It is not for us a call to make a decision for Christ in the sense of

---

[38] On this verse as a hermeneutical key to the whole book, see Rachel M. Billings, *'Israel Served the Lord.' The Book of Joshua as a Paradoxical Portrait of Faithful Israel* (Notre Dame: University of Notre Dame Press, 2013).

[39] Gen. 50:25.

[40] Gen. 33:19.

conversion, but a reminder that even those who know God, and who have experienced his blessing and faithfulness, need to take the time to stop and look back. We need to pause and consider once again what God has done for us, both personally and congregationally. The celebration of baptism and communion are times that are appropriate for this, though there are other occasions too. We need to hear the challenge that comes to us to *choose this day*: will we renew our commitment to Christ and the work of his church, and confess anew that we need to give him our undivided loyalty and service, recognizing that this is what defines the people of God? Or will we take the path of least resistance that is in the end no path at all? Choose this day! Indeed, we must.

The Bible Speaks Today: Old Testament series

The Message of Genesis 1 – 11
The dawn of creation
David Atkinson

The Message of Genesis 12 – 50
From Abraham to Joseph
Joyce G. Baldwin

The Message of Exodus
The days of our pilgrimage
Alec Motyer

The Message of Leviticus
Free to be holy
Derek Tidball

The Message of Numbers
Journey to the promised land
Raymond Brown

The Message of Deuteronomy
Not by bread alone
Raymond Brown

The Message of Joshua
Promise and people
David G. Firth

The Message of Judges
Grace abounding
Michael Wilcock

The Message of Ruth
The wings of refuge
David Atkinson

The Message of Samuel
Personalities, potential, politics and power
Mary J. Evans

The Message of Kings
God is present
John W. Olley

The Message of Chronicles
One church, one faith, one Lord
Michael Wilcock

The Message of Ezra and Haggai
Building for God
Robert Fyall

The Message of Nehemiah
God's servant in a time of change
Raymond Brown

The Message of Esther
God present but unseen
David G. Firth

The Message of Job
Suffering and grace
David Atkinson

The Message of Psalms 1 – 72
Songs for the people of God
Michael Wilcock

The Message of Psalms 73 – 150
Songs for the people of God
Michael Wilcock

The Message of Proverbs
Wisdom for life
David Atkinson

The Message of Ecclesiastes
A time to mourn, and a time to dance
Derek Kidner

The Message of the Song of Songs
The lyrics of love
Tom Gledhill

The Bible Speaks Today: New Testament series

The Message of the Sermon on the Mount (Matthew 5 – 7)
Christian counter-culture
John Stott

The Message of Matthew
The kingdom of heaven
Michael Green

The Message of Mark
The mystery of faith
Donald English

The Message of Luke
The Saviour of the world
Michael Wilcock

The Message of John
Here is your King!
Bruce Milne

The Message of Acts
To the ends of the earth
John Stott

The Message of Romans
God's good news for the world
John Stott

The Message of 1 Corinthians
Life in the local church
David Prior

The Message of 2 Corinthians
Power in weakness
Paul Barnett

The Message of Galatians
Only one way
John Stott

The Message of Ephesians
God's new society
John Stott

The Message of Philippians
Jesus our Joy
Alec Motyer

The Message of Colossians and Philemon
Fullness and freedom
Dick Lucas

The Message of Thessalonians
Preparing for the coming King
John Stott

The Message of 1 Timothy and Titus
The life of the local church
John Stott

The Message of 2 Timothy
Guard the gospel
John Stott

The Message of Hebrews
Christ above all
Raymond Brown

The Message of James
The tests of faith
Alec Motyer

The Message of 1 Peter
The way of the cross
Edmund Clowney

The Message of 2 Peter and Jude
The promise of his coming
Dick Lucas and Christopher Green

The Message of John's Letters
Living in the love of God
David Jackman

The Message of Revelation
I saw heaven opened
Michael Wilcock

The Bible Speaks Today: Bible Themes series

The Message of the Living God
His glory, his people, his world
Peter Lewis

The Message of the Resurrection
Christ is risen!
Paul Beasley-Murray

The Message of the Cross
Wisdom unsearchable, love indestructible
Derek Tidball

The Message of Salvation
By God's grace, for God's glory
Philip Graham Ryken

The Message of Creation
Encountering the Lord of the universe
David Wilkinson

The Message of Heaven and Hell
Grace and destiny
Bruce Milne

The Message of Mission
The glory of Christ in all time and space
Howard Peskett and Vinoth Ramachandra

The Message of Prayer
Approaching the throne of grace
Tim Chester

The Message of the Trinity
Life in God
Brian Edgar

The Message of Evil and Suffering
Light into darkness
Peter Hicks

The Message of the Holy Spirit
The Spirit of encounter
Keith Warrington

The Message of Holiness
Restoring God's masterpiece
Derek Tidball

The Message of Sonship
At home in God's household
Trevor Burke

The Message of the Word of God
The glory of God made known
Tim Meadowcroft

The Message of Women
Creation, grace and gender
Derek and Dianne Tidball

The Message of the Church
Assemble the people before me
Chris Green

The Message of the Person of Christ
The Word made flesh
Robert Letham